W9-AHG-765

# THE KEY TO
# Sustainable
# CITIES

## Meeting Human Needs,
## Transforming Community Systems

### GWENDOLYN HALLSMITH

NEW SOCIETY PUBLISHERS

**Cataloguing in Publication Data:**
A catalog record for this publication is available from the National Library of Canada.


**Copyright © 2003 by Gwendolyn Hallsmith.**
**All rights reserved.**

Cover design by Tom Daley.


Second printing January 2007.


Paperback ISBN 13: 978-0-86571-499-1
Paperback ISBN 10: 0-86571-499-1


Proceeds from the sale of this book will benefit Global Community Initiatives and the Institute for Sustainable Communities.


Inquiries regarding requests to reprint all or part of *The Key to Sustainable Cities* should be addressed to New Society Publishers at the address below.


To order directly from the publishers, please call toll-free (North America) 1-800-567-6772, or order online at www.newsociety.com

Any other inquiries can be directed by mail to:

New Society Publishers
P.O. Box 189, Gabriola Island, BC V0R 1X0, Canada
1-800-567-6772


New Society Publishers' mission is to publish books that contribute in fundamental ways to building an ecologically sustainable and just society, and to do so with the least possible impact on the environment, in a manner that models this vision. For further information, or to browse our full list of books and purchase securely, visit our website at: www.newsociety.com

NEW SOCIETY PUBLISHERS                         www.newsociety.com

# Dedication

This book is dedicated to
Dylan Jeremy Hallsmith,
Jessica Emily Huyghebaert, and
Kelsey Thomas Huyghebaert

# Contents

# *Acknowledgments*

WRITING A BOOK AND HAVING A CHILD are analogous experiences. First, there's the courtship. The ideas for the book flirt with you — in restaurants, at conferences, while you're talking to your colleagues about a project. Then things start to get more serious as they start to pester you for commitment. You draft the beginning of a book proposal, and put it down. You look for publishers who might be interested. Maybe you even talk to one or two about it in moments of courageous foolishness. What, me, write a whole book? I must be crazy. You take the step and send the book proposal off in the mail to a complete stranger. Then comes the engagement process: drafting the contract, finding partners who are willing to support the book. Once the agreements are in place, gestation begins. For a child, it's nine months. For a book, it can be a lot longer than that. It gets larger and larger quite slowly — painfully slowly at times. Then, after drafts and redrafts, copy edits, and cover designs, the book, your baby, is ready to emerge from dark obscurity and face the air, sounds, and lights of the real world.

Giving birth to this book was a lot less painful for me than real childbirth, thank goodness, and that's due to the support and encouragement that I had from many people who contributed to its success. I can't name everyone who has inspired me to get all of this down on paper, but I can at least give credit to several people who were significant in keeping the project on track.

A lot of the credit goes to my friends and colleagues at the Institute for Sustainable Communities (ISC), a group of unrestrained idealists who have successfully implemented their vision for a better world over the ten years that ISC has been in existence. Madeline Kunin, the former Governor of Vermont and founder of ISC, is a real role model for women everywhere who dare to dream. Peter Clavelle has served as the Chair of the Board of ISC for many years while also managing the awesome task of bringing the city of Burlington step by step closer to being the most sustainable city in the United States.

George Hamilton, the Executive Director of ISC, works hard to stay on the cutting edge of the sustainable development movement, and has grown ISC from a small group of like-minded Vermonters to a major international organization with offices and projects all over the world. Barbara Felitti, the Senior Vice President at ISC, brings out the best in the people she works with and encouraged me to write this book from the day I came up with the idea. Further thanks goes to Betty Weiss and Roger Clapp in the Community Action Program at ISC — they read the early drafts of the manuscript and made invaluable suggestions about how to improve it. I can't even think about ISC without including thanks to Paul and Deb Markowitz, Cindy Wyckoff, Keith Swann, Andrea Deri, Richard Czaplinski, Bill Ploog, David Boyer, Theodorina Lessidrenska, Andriy Demydenko, Volodymyr Tikkhi, Anna Phillips, Ada Bainova, Dafina Gercheva, Piotr Mancharski, Plamen Dimitrov, Besim Nebiu, Atanas Pascalev, Pavla Rakovska, Janos Zlinsky, Sofia Shatkivska, Roman Kokodyniak, Dan Thompson, Irina Belashova, Allison Mindel, Kevin McCollister, Susan Stitely, Diane Mackay, and all the other people affiliated with ISC whose ideas and hard work helped shape my understanding of sustainable development.

Another group of people who have been key in helping me understand systems thinking and sustainable development are all of the wonderful people associated with the Balaton Group: Dennis and Donella Meadows, Joan Davis, Niels Meyer, Amory and Hunter Lovins, John Peet, Aromar Revi, Vicki Robin, David Sattherwaite, Mathis Wackernagel, Betsy Taylor, Alan AtKisson, Lazlo Pinter, Manfred Max-Neef, Gillian Martin Mehers, David Korten, Hermann Knoflacher, Wim Hafkamp, Genady Golubev, Gerardo Bukowski, Bob Wilkinson, Robert Costanza, Bert de Vries, Jelel Ezzine, Faye Duchin, Hilary French, Askok Gadgil, Carlos Quesada-Mateo, Ferenc Toth, and so many others. The sessions we have along the shores of Lake Balaton are some of the most stimulating and enlightening that I've ever experienced.

While writing the book, it was also really important for me to be able to talk to people who forced me to defend what I was saying. For this process, I have to offer my deep appreciation to Dr. Steve Halls of the UNEP International Environmental Technology Center, who challenged my ideas about using sustainability as a meaningful conceptual tool for urban planning and helped me think through the relevance and importance of taking a systems approach to community development. I am also indebted to Michael Snyder, who worked with me on editing the book when the other demands on my life were overwhelming. His contributions to shaping the final draft were enormously helpful, both in terms of the editorial assistance he offered and the substantive comments he made.

Of course, the book couldn't have been done at all without the support and help of the staff at the New Society Publishers. The publisher, Chris Plant, and the editor, Judith Brand, were great to work with. They pushed me to keep at it when I needed to persevere and showed a level of understanding and flexibility that made my first effort at being an author a real pleasure. Another person who made a significant contribution to the process of making a real book out of all these words on paper was my friend Tom Daley, who stepped in and made a cover design that captures the spirit of sustainability I'm trying to convey. I am also thankful for Amos Baer, another helpful soul who was willing to struggle with the edits needed so that the project stayed on track, even though my life was trying to derail it.

Finally, I have to thank my family. My father and mother, Wesley and Joan Hall, and my sisters, Gaylynn Huyghebaert and Gretchen Bristol, are some of my best friends; their encouragement is always an important part of my life. My husband, George, and my son, Dylan, were also a big help. George is an excellent copy editor, in fact; I'd never be able to submit a manuscript with as few typographical errors if it weren't for his exacting review of my writing. And of course, Dylan is the whole motivation for the book to be written in the first place. The concern I have about creating sustainable communities has everything to do with making the world a place where he, his children, and his grandchildren will want to live.

# *Foreword*

S USTAINABILITY AND ITS COROLLARY, "sustainable development," can sound like overused buzzwords. Even worse, these words have been used by some organizations and governments to justify everything from nuclear power to genetically engineered foods, based on the rationalization that these activities are somehow sustainable. Yet, by acquiring a deeper understanding of the meaning of these terms, we can reclaim their enormous significance as concepts for improving our communities and the lives of our citizens.

In Burlington, Vermont, the city where I am mayor, an activist municipal government has worked in partnership with citizens, the private sector, and a network of municipally supported nonprofit organizations to pursue a strategy for sustainable development since the early 1980s — before the term sustainable development was invented. Through the 1980s and 1990s, this strategy involved generating new sources of public revenue, ensuring a publicly controlled waterfront, producing permanently affordable housing, stabilizing residential neighborhoods, reducing energy consumption and greenhouse gas emissions, requiring the recycling of solid waste, protecting the water quality of Lake Champlain, and removing barriers preventing women and minorities from enjoying the fruits of economic growth.

While our strategy and its policies long guided economic development efforts and city programs, we knew we needed to do more to develop a strong local economy, protect our environment, and build a more livable city. We became keenly aware of the need to establish a widespread understanding of how individual projects connect, to create a comprehensive vision for our future embraced by the entire community, and to develop an integrated approach to achieving that vision. To do this, we initiated the Burlington Legacy Project in 1999 to encourage our whole community to think systematically about our future and to bring all sectors of the community together to develop a vision for Burlington in the year 2030.

Our Legacy Project was the equivalent of the Local Agenda 21 planning process employed in communities around the world as a response to the first Earth Summit in Rio in 1992. Our approach focused on social, economic, and environmental conditions and needs. We engaged all sectors of our community with extensive outreach efforts, and a diverse group of key stakeholders steered the process. In addition, Burlington's full range of non-profit organizations, businesses, government agencies, and community groups participated in creating our vision, identifying priorities and goals, and defining local indicators.

In developing the Legacy Project, the City partnered with the Vermont-based Institute for Sustainable Communities (ISC). Incorporated in 1991, this independent, non-profit organization provides training, technical assistance, and financial support to communities around the world in its effort to promote environmental protection and economic and social well-being. Not incidentally, Gwendolyn Hallsmith, author of this book, served as the key ISC staff on our Legacy Project and contributed significantly to the project's success.

Through the Legacy Project, our community learned more about the potential of sustainable development. We began to look beyond pat solutions for narrowly defined problems and to define sustainability more comprehensively. Ultimately, we emerged from the planning process poised to talk less, to act more, and to ensure that our actions were based on better understandings of whole systems, rather than isolated parts.

Another important outcome of our Legacy Project was a detailed directory of the various strategies implemented by both the public and private sectors in Burlington over the past two decades. These strategies have played key roles in making Burlington one of the country's most livable cities. This directory, along with our Legacy Project Action Plan, can be found on-line at www.cedo.ci.burlington.vt.us/legacy/index.html.

This book offers conceptual tools fundamental to building sustainable communities, as well as a template for the building process itself. Gwendolyn Hallsmith explores the systems dynamics of social change and community development, developing the kind of comprehensive understanding that will help communities treat more than mere symptoms and achieve lasting results. She draws on her experience and

Burlington's experience with the Legacy Project to outline a way in which other cities can envision a more sustainable future and develop an integrated action plan to achieve it.

The upshot of all this is additional clarity about sustainability and its significance for the future of the Earth's cities. Much more than an overused catchword, sustainability becomes a visionary and practical tool, a concept that leads to meaningful action. For cities and towns, such action can mean a more cohesive vision for the future, a stronger sense of place, a shared understanding of community assets, more efficient use of resources, healthier ecosystems, more productive partnerships among community stakeholders, and public dialogue that is engaging, inclusive, and constructive.

As a mayor committed to building a sustainable city, I have gained much from other communities' best practices and lessons learned. I hope you find this book a valuable resource as you work to make your own community more sustainable.

PETER CLAVELLE
Mayor of the City of Burlington, Vermont
May 14, 2003

# Introduction

ALL OVER THE WORLD municipal governments are being asked to do more and more with fewer and fewer resources. National governments are delegating responsibilities to cities and towns, but not the budgets to match. The disconnect between the demands on city administrations and their capacity to provide services means that inequalities are being exacerbated, critical human needs go wanting, and the pressures of crime, poverty, illness, and the deterioration of public infrastructure continually add to the vicious cycle of underinvestment and impoverishment.

Yet even in the darkest times, there are people who are making a difference in their cities, creating oases of hope. They do it by combining a knack for public relations with a visionary program and the audacity to break out of old paradigms and try new things. Innovation can produce remarkable results. When Enrique Penalosa was the mayor of Bogota, Colombia, the city invested in pedestrian streets, libraries, and daycare centers in poor informal settlements creating jobs and raising the quality of life substantially for the neediest people in his city. He did this by diverting funds from the highway budgets, which he saw as supporting an inequitable transportation system, calling a proposal for an elevated highway "a monument to inequity."[1] Even in an environment of scarce resources, Vasily Tretetsky, as the mayor of Myrhorod, Ukraine, dedicated staff and funds to research and implement a World Health Organization Healthy Cities project, finding ways to help support the health and well-being of its citizens.

Unfortunately, innovative public entrepreneurs are the exception, not the rule. Unlike private companies who are always looking for new ways to beat the competition, municipal governments are often the last organizations to adopt innovative strategies for management or service delivery. There are a number of reasons for this. Public officials are under a great deal more scrutiny than private business owners, and mistakes can cost their reputations and careers. Taxpayers don't take kindly to the idea of elected and appointed officials using

1

their hard-earned tax dollars as venture capital for untested and risky ideas. Resources are always scarce, revenue streams can be uncertain, and when combined with the transience of elected office, it's hard to invest for the long term.

As a result, municipal officials find themselves mired in short-term problem solving, crisis management, and band-aid solutions. Those who have been in office long enough begin to notice that the problems they are struggling with today were once the solutions to different problems yesterday, but they don't have the tools or the resources to do anything about it. Most city officials would like nothing better than to get at the root causes of some of their most serious problems. They want to provide their citizens with safe neighborhoods, high-quality education systems, well-paid jobs, and a pleasant and healthy environment. But these goals often seem out of reach.

Officials might make progress in one area, but only at the expense of another important issue. They build affordable housing, and the environmental groups complain because it fills up open space that people in the neighborhood use for nature walks. A large manufacturing company decides to locate in town, providing hundreds of jobs, but the air emissions and wastewater discharges lower the quality of life in the area around the plant. In order to start an education program for children with serious illnesses like AIDS, recreational programs for other needy children are cut. Why isn't it possible to have good social services and a politically empowered citizenry and well-paid jobs and a healthy environment?

The idea that led to this book came to me one day in 1999 as I was wondering how to describe the multiplier effect to the Legacy Project Steering Committee in Burlington, Vermont. I thought back to my undergraduate years at the University of Colorado when I had a wonderful economics professor named Ruben Zubrow. Professor Zubrow would stand at the front of his enormous lecture hall and wave his arms in circles, yelling "Circular flow! Circular flow!" when he was describing how the economy worked. He'd illustrate economic circular flow every way he could, from the gold standard to the inner workings of a local economy.

The insight I had that day, in a moment that forever changed the way I think about communities, was that the entire community, not just the economy, works in cycles. All of our interactions — the purchase and consumption of goods and services, the ways we exercise political power, our social institutions and relationships — have cyclical characteristics. The ways in which the cycles of community life either strengthen or weaken themselves through time all impact the health and sustainability of the whole community system.

The Legacy Project was a joint initiative of Peter Clavelle, the Mayor of Burlington, and the Institute for Sustainable Communities (ISC) in Montpelier, Vermont. Mayor Clavelle had decided that he wanted Burlington to be the country's most sustainable city. The Arts & Entertainment Network had just rated Burlington as the most livable city in the United States, the economy was booming, and there was no better time to make the city as sustainable as possible. So the city officials and the Institute sent off a grant application to the U.S. Environmental Protection Agency and the 1992 Jane B. Cook Charitable Trust; and the Legacy Project was born, with some additional help from the Institute's Special Opportunities Fund.

At the outset, there were four goals for the project: (1) to develop a shared vision for the city; (2) to develop a consensus-based action plan to make the city more sustainable; (3) to engage the city's youth in a meaningful way; and (4) to document the best practices that Burlington had used so far in the collective pursuit of healthy economic development, environmental protection, and progressive social services.

Burlington was already engaged in a variety of initiatives that made it a leader — the city has a global warming task force, a renewable electric generation facility, an innovative approach to affordable housing development, a new multigenerational center in the North End, a bike path, and numerous other public projects. Private initiatives for sustainable development flourished around town as well. Gardener's Supply, located at the Intervale, an area of town that serves as an incubator for small farmers, built a demonstration project called the Living Machine for sewage treatment, as part of the community supported agriculture (CSA) gardens. Melinda Moulton and Lisa Steele, sustainable redevelopers of Main Street Landing Co., have been instrumental in helping the city redesign and redevelop its waterfront, which included the Lake Champlain Science Center, a non-profit educational center promoting the environmental health of the lake.

Despite all of these efforts, there was no sense of a shared vision for sustainability in Burlington. To complicate matters, Burlington suffered from public participation overload. New strategies were needed to entice people out of their warm homes on cold evenings to attend focus groups, hearings, meetings, and other events. The challenges were to explain the idea of sustainability to the public and to the Legacy Project Steering Committee, and to organize the planning process so it would involve youth and the wider community in developing a vision and an action plan that could serve as examples for other communities.

An assortment of focus groups were pulled together and asked to describe what they liked about the city, what they wanted to change, and what their ideas and visions were for the next thirty years. Neighborhood Planning Assemblies, businesses, environmentalists, school administrators, daycare providers, food shelf patrons, religious groups, service clubs, student government, students ... everywhere a group of people convened, the Legacy Project staff were there, asking them questions, filling out surveys, writing on flip charts, taking their comments.

What issues would the plan address? The project's first organizing principles were based on ISC's nine years of experience working in communities in central and eastern Europe, and Burlington's extensive history in progressive politics. The Steering Committee was encouraged to think about the Four Es of sustainability — Environment, Economy, Education, and Equity. As public input came in, however, more Es were added to the list: Entertainment, Eternity, Energy, Enforcement ... finally we had to settle on Etceteras to capture all of the miscellaneous comments.

I was struggling with the question of how to organize all the public input when, with a flash of inspiration, it all fell into place for me. The original four Es were on the right track, but they weren't everything — instead, they represented one aspect of each sector of a community's efforts to meet human needs. Our needs for material well-being depend on the environment's ability to provide food, clean water, clean air, and the resources we need for clothing, shelter, defense, etc. Our needs for economic well-being depend on the local economy and its capacity to provide jobs, investment, and income for the population. Our needs for freedom, conflict resolution, equity, and other forms of governance are met through institutions that are developed to respond to our real need for empowerment. The deep and very important needs we have for relationships with others, a sense of community, education, health care, and spiritual development are met in the social system.

Each of these community sectors, or systems, has its own cyclical dynamics, resources, and reproductive functions. In the environmental system, natural resources flow through the system, governed by natural laws and reproduced through natural and human cycles of construction, maintenance and demolition. In the economic system, money and labor are exchanged, invested, discounted, and generate profit. The banks, insurance companies, world trade organizations, and labor unions help insure the system's reproduction over time. In the governance system, power is the currency, and our interactions demonstrate how we use our personal power and how we collectively exercise power over other people. The social system, however, has a high level of influence over every other sector because it is where we form our values, where we define what we care about as a community and how we care for each other.

Each of these community systems serves us by meeting our needs for care, power, economic resources, and material well-being. What community systems do is actually more important than where they are or who is in them. So, one type of community system will meet our needs for potable water and sewer systems, roads, transportation, and housing, whereas another smaller community system within the same vicinity will meet our needs for spiritual development. Still another, often larger and more distant, will meet our needs for defense and safety.

For this reason, the word community is used here to connote a social structure that is relatively cohesive and meets the needs of its members. This book focuses on one of our more integrated forms of community — the municipality or local government. However, since local government does not always provide for the broad spectrum of our needs, the wider community that would be active in and around a particular locale also must be considered, along with the systems that have been developed on the regional, national, or international level.

## THE EVOLUTION OF COMMUNITY SYSTEMS

Ever since our earliest associations with family and clan, human beings have depended on a community for survival. We are, by our very nature, social beings. We organize ourselves in a wide variety of ways precisely because we cannot survive without being part of a community; the full range of our needs can only be met through cooperative community endeavors. While it is true that Western culture tends to promote a myth of rugged individualism, and people sometimes try to live their lives separated from society, they are the exceptions rather than the rule, and further examination of the ways in which they manage to survive would still link them inextricably with our socialization and communal production systems.

The first evidence of human communities has been dated at around 10,000 b.c. The advent of agriculture as the dominant means of sustenance marks an important watershed for community formation. In nomadic societies of hunters and gatherers, blood relations largely dictated the communal relationships. Clans, tribes, and other forms of community were the norm. With agriculture came a more integrated community; property ownership meant that communities had to be based more on proximity than on family ties. In both cases, the community's form related to how people were meeting their collective needs.

Civilizations rise and fall. The Mayans, with their sophisticated hieroglyphics and advanced intensive farming practices, began to form a relatively unified civilization in 2000 b.c., only to fall into decline and abandon most of their magnificent cities by a.d. 900. By a.d. 500 the Roman Empire had ceased to exist. In the wake of empires come periods of decentralization, often marked by increased regional warfare as smaller rulers compete with their neighbors to secure the material and social resources to meet the needs of their citizens. Yet even in the midst of this, communities continue to develop shared infrastructure for trade, education, worship, and decision making. Our real human needs bind us together in community through even the most violent and cataclysmic transitions.

Human needs are also the drivers of the dysfunctional and unsustainable community systems we have developed, contributing to the accelerating race toward global destruction. Our need for food and water, for example, has led us to develop community systems for agricultural production, water purification and distribution, and food distribution as well as access to a huge selection of restaurants, cafes, grocery stores, and other eateries. Our need to be healthy has led us to develop systems for physical and mental healthcare, along with exercise classes, sports centers, spas, and resorts that promote healthy lifestyles. We need to nurture our spiritual life, so we work together to create churches, synagogues, mosques, temples, monasteries, and programs for spiritual education, practice, and enrichment.

Four premises underpin the way in which this book speaks about community systems:

1. Over time, we have created community systems to meet our needs as human beings. Our cumulative needs are the drivers of the unsustainable activities that are moving us at an accelerating rate toward global destruction. We depend on communities to meet our needs — our community systems satisfy needs that we can't meet as individuals.

2. Communities exhibit all of the characteristics of a system (cyclical dynamics, stocks, flows, equilibrium, etc.); the insights offered by systems dynamics can help us understand persistent community problems. Systems analysis can also point to effective strategies for meeting our needs in new sustainable ways.

3. Community systems exist for all our needs, not just for material and economic needs. Our needs for care, spirituality, power, education, and other social development are filled or unfulfilled within community systems.

4. By looking at the community as a whole, we can see how the different systems interact with one another to erode or to enhance the community's capacity to meet its future needs. This is the core issue for sustainable development.

In its 1993 directive, the Catholic Church recognized the connection between human needs and community development: "There is an intrinsic connection between development, human need, and the stewardship of creation. For experience has taught us that development in response to human needs cannot misuse or overuse natural resources without serious consequences."[2] The church was partly right, but the misuse of resources in the fulfillment of our needs is not limited to natural resources. We can misuse and erode our other capacities — capacities for a community to care for its members, share power with the disenfranchised, and provide meaningful work for its citizens — as much as we can misuse natural resources.

The study of systems dynamics is fairly advanced and has been applied extensively to business applications, education, and ecological studies. Unfortunately, systems dynamics has not been used to comprehensively evaluate the sustainability of communities. Systems, by their very nature, are alive; they maintain themselves over time through the interaction of their component parts. They are dynamic — they move, they grow or shrink, they change. Understanding how these dynamics work within the community systems we have established to meet our needs gives us important information to use when we work with communities to make them more sustainable. Some of the systems we have developed have grown so complex or large that we do not recognize them for what they are. To see them more clearly, it is helpful to look at their evolution.

If you look at world history through the lens of human needs, it isn't hard to see need-fulfillment driving many of the innovations, upheavals, and developments human beings have initiated throughout our evolution. In the late 19th century, Karl Marx recognized this and theorized that our material needs drive the forces of material reproduction, which he saw as the primary driving force in history. By placing the primacy on our material and economic needs, however, Marx missed almost as much as he included. Beyond our need for food, clothing, and shelter we have a need for some level of power or control over our personal and community life as well health, education, spirituality (a very important factor that Marx discounted, to the world's detriment), and other social development.

Over time, the community systems have become more and more complex. To many people, they are invisible. If we live in a community with a public water supply, when we get up in the morning, we turn on our tap and expect water to come out. We don't think about the thousands of years of evolving water delivery systems that have brought water to our kitchen sink. We are not conscious of all the daily maintenance, testing, and decision making to keep it safe and available. We forget that even one hundred years ago indoor plumbing was a new and marvelous invention. Water is a basic human need — without it, we can only live a few days.

After taking a shower and making coffee, many people go to work. The structure of our economy, the exchange of labor for money, and all the taxes, insurance, and other benefits that come with our jobs are another complex community system that has evolved to meet our needs. We need to work. Throughout history human beings have been productive in one way or another. Still, many of us grumble about all the labor we perform, and certainly for millions of people around the world whose labor is exploited by the owners of powerful businesses, work is not a pleasure. Yet if given a choice, most people would opt to work instead of being idle. We need money, and people make money by working. But in addition to the money we earn from our labor, work also meets our need to feel like valuable members of the community.

Election day comes, and we go to vote. We take it for granted that we are now part of a national community that works together for shared defense, monetary exchange, justice, defense of our rights, welfare programs, social security, education, and food production. Even several hundred years ago, these functions would have been the responsibility of smaller, less ubiquitous forms of government. In Europe today, some countries are just now pulling these functions together into a federal form of government; until the past several years, they also had smaller, more regional governments responsible for the majority of these functions. Government, and the economic foundation that it provides through the monetary system, infrastructure, and defense, fills a wide variety of human needs, not the least of which is a level of power or control over our individual and collective destinies.

On certain days of the week, many people go to a local church, synagogue, temple, or mosque to worship with other members of a faith community. Here, there are constant reminders of the history of the faith, as scripture is read and discussed. Many theologies emphasize the collective and social nature of the spiritual experience itself. Yet the evolution of the community system for worship is invisible. We are not always aware of the deeper roots of the various forms of worship or why they have evolved into a community practice more than an individual practice (in most traditions). Most people are also not aware of the multitude of ways the faith community reproduces itself from generation to generation, such as the rituals and education courses that bring young people into the particular community of faith.

## OVERVIEW

The first part of the book characterizes our needs and demonstrates the cyclical nature of the systems used to satisfy them. Each system has actors and resources that move the circular flow in directions that either erode or enhance its capacity. Each of the four main subsystems of the community — the social, governance, economic, and environmental systems — has a set of needs that drive the system's development and behavior. These individual needs are described in Chapter 2.

After defining the needs and showing how community systems work to satisfy them, I will explore the link between the satisfaction of needs and community sustainability. This involves defining sustainable development, as well as exploring the concept of community system capacity. The capacity of different community systems is described, and the ways in which the systems work to either erode or enhance the community capacity are discussed in detail in Chapter 3.

To understand the various aspects and drivers of community systems, you must know something about the discipline of systems dynamics. Chapter 4 describes the current understanding of the ways in which systems work — feedback loops, reinforcing cycles, balancing cycles, equilibrium, emergent properties, and system archetypes that can be observed in common and familiar community systems.

Once we understand that needs are the underlying drivers of the unsustainable systems we have developed, we can change the way we look at the community development process. Rather than starting with the problems we are facing, it makes more sense to start with the ways in which our communities meet their needs. By doing a needs assessment, we can begin with a statement of all the positive aspects of our communities, our assets, and all the ways we meet our needs. This gives us the information we require to create a shared vision of what we want in the future, another important step in the community development process. If we start with our assets, the things we are proud of, it is easier to form a collective vision of how we can meet our needs with less impact. When we start with problems, often the vision is limited to having fewer problems, or solving an isolated problem; it does not necessarily encompass how we can satisfy our needs more effectively, or how we can live rich and meaningful lives. Chapter 5 outlines a process for defining a community vision. Chapter 6 uses the Earth Charter,[3] a global vision for a peaceful, just, and sustainable future, and the Melbourne Principles for Sustainable Cities[4] as two examples of comprehensive visions that cities can use to initiate the sustainable development planning process.

The vision for a more sustainable community will only be realized if the government and residents are capable of working together toward a common goal. Achieving social change is very difficult, so attention must be paid to the change process, the skills and tools that can be used to mobilize people toward new ways of seeing the world and behaving in it. The means that are used to pursue change must be congruent with the vision for the outcomes. The planning process must reflect mutual respect, whole systems understanding, peaceful resolution of conflict, and openness to new mindsets and paradigms. There are skills that can help people master these important elements of the change process. In Chapter 7, I explore the change process and the skills that are needed for it to be successful.

Once a vision is formed and the project group is functioning as a team, then it's possible to design strategies and action plans to realize the vision for a community. Here again, an assets-based approach, combined with a deeper understanding of how systems work, can help us develop successful strategies. Often, problem-based strategies only address the symptoms of a given situation. If the needs that caused the problems are the focus of the strategy and the lessons from systems dynamics can be used to meet the needs more effectively, we can avoid unintended consequences and succeed. Chapter 8 describes how we can take advantage of the lessons from systems dynamics to develop strategies for change. Chapter 9 discusses the leverage points that a systems understanding can help us identify. They are pivotal positions, in terms of other systems dynamics, where a small amount of effort can achieve big results.

Once the strategies have been identified, cities need to chart a course of action that will succeed. The action plan must identify the resources and actors that will work to achieve the vision. It also must incorporate implementation strategies that are consistent with the cyclical, whole system orientation, including management and decision support systems based on continuous feedback, life cycle design and accounting, and sustainable procurement systems. Chapter 10 describes how to develop and initiate an action plan using all of these insights.

Residents, government officials, the children in the schools — everyone involved in planning for a sustainable future needs to define specific indicators that can help determine if the goals are being met. One of the lessons of systems dynamics is that everything works cyclically, so revising our understanding of project development and implementation to close the loop and provide ongoing timely and accurate feedback is an important strategy for success. The ways in which we can plan for success in a project by establishing monitoring and evaluation systems are described in Chapter 11.

Factors can be identified and emulated that contribute to a community that cares for its members, that treats the environment as an integral part of humanity, and that provides people with opportunities to improve their lives, participate actively and effectively in the governance structures, and to be employed in work that enhances life instead of degrading it. All over the world, communities have been working on sustainable development strategies for many years; best practices for sustainable development have been identified by a number of different organizations. It is relatively easy to find information about new strategies that have worked to make communities healthier and more sustainable. Learning what is happening in other places is one powerful way to explore new approaches that can be used in any community. Putting these strategies to work by using the best information available on achieving effective change is part of the goal of this book. It is my sincere hope that the practitioners, citizens, and professionals who read it will have new insights about their own communities, much as I did the day a few years ago, when the spirit of Professor Zubrow made me see things in a new way.

## CHAPTER 1

# How Communities Meet Human Needs

CONGRESSMAN TIP O'NEIL, the former Speaker of the House, coined the saying, All politics is local. He told a story about a time he attended a local Town Meeting in Massachusetts as a newly elected member of Congress. The Town Moderator introduced him at the beginning of the meeting, with all the proper pomp and circumstance, and asked him to say a few words. O'Neil went up to the podium and explained to the audience that he was their representative in Washington, and if they had concerns about national issues, they should contact him. He talked about social security, defense spending, and other federal programs to clarify for people the kinds of issues he would address. After the meeting, an elderly woman came up to him and started complaining about the fact that trash wasn't collected on Tuesdays anymore. She wanted it to be collected on Thursdays. After listening to her story, O'Neil explained that he was responsible for national policy and that she needed to report her problems with local trash collection to the selectboard in town. "Well," she said, exasperated, "I didn't think I would have to start *that* high."

All politics *is* local, and so are all of the problems we have today with unsustainable development. All environmental problems are located somewhere — the effluent discharged from a factory, the emissions from a smokestack, the waste that is collected from people's homes. Social problems — crime, homelessness, drug addiction — all have a local face. When a factory closes, people suddenly find themselves without jobs, and they often look to other local businesses to fill the gap. The way local government manages all of the opportunities

13

people have for a voice in governmental decision making affects everything from local ordinances to national elections. All the actions people take on a local level aggregate to significantly impact the local, regional, and global environment.

The impetus for all these local actions is the real needs we have as human beings. The effluent that is discharged into the stream comes from a sewage treatment plant that was built so that our dangerous human waste wouldn't contaminate our streets, yards, and homes — unsatisfactory sanitation leads to epidemics of bubonic plague, cholera, and many other deadly diseases. The emissions from the smokestacks are from plants that produce the energy we need to light our homes at night, to power all the important health equipment at local hospitals, and to make mass production of goods and services possible. The waste we throw away is often a side effect of the process of feeding ourselves every day — our need for food is not going to go away, simply because satisfying the need strains the ability of the planet to provide adequate sustenance for the human population.

Our needs have driven the development of ever more complex community systems for thousands of years. We take these systems for granted now, most of them are invisible to everyone but the municipal departments and other institutions that are responsible for managing them. Yet there are significant differences between the ways in which the systems function on the local level. Some systems are enhancing the community's ability to meet its needs in the future, the core definition of sustainable development, and some are eroding this same capacity. To illustrate the systems at work in a community and to demonstrate how different two communities can be in terms of the full satisfaction of local human needs, let us consider the story of two towns on opposite sides of the planet — Randolph, Vermont, and Naryn, Kyrgyzstan.

Randolph and Naryn can be compared to each other, although their distance apart makes them, quite literally, polar opposites. Even though they are almost as far from each other as you can get on Earth, they are at approximately the same latitude and are about the same distance from their nearest major metropolitan centers. The climate in Naryn is quite arid, whereas Randolph gets a lot of annual rainfall, but both communities have hot summers and cold winters. Located in the mountains, they both depend on animal husbandry, agriculture reliant on grazing rather than cultivation, for their economic base. Both towns have been through hard times since the early 1990s: in Randolph a series of fires destroyed large parts of downtown, and in Naryn the breakup of the former Soviet Union led to many changes that have crippled the local economy. The resilience of the two communities, their ability to take the hardships in stride and forge a new future, even out of the ashes of a difficult past, is a poignant indicator of the factors necessary for real sustainable development to succeed.

## A TALE OF TWO CITIES

*It was the best of times, it was the worst of times, it was the age of wisdom, it was the age of foolishness, it was the epoch of belief, it was the epoch of incredulity, it was the season of Light, it was the season of Darkness, it was the spring of hope, it was the winter of despair, we had everything before us, we had nothing before us, we were all going direct to Heaven, we were all going direct the other way — in short, the period was so far like the present period, that some of its noisiest authorities insisted on its being received, for good or for evil, in the superlative degree of comparison only.* [1]

Charles Dickens

## Two main streets: One in Randolph, one in Naryn

Ten years ago, Randolph's mainstreet was overshadowed by the burned-out hulks of three-story brick buildings. Empty store windows stared out at the street, their forlorn For Rent signs peeling at the edges. The train raced through town at speeds close to 60 miles per hour, rattling windows and endangering pedestrians — one man was killed when he walked too close to the tracks. Today, the small commercial district's storefronts are full, a new park with a bandstand fills one of the burned building's lots, and trains now stop at a new station that serves passengers coming from as far away as Washington, DC.

Naryn today resembles Randolph of yesterday. The town office contains little that would identify it as an office to someone from the West: no computers, no filing cabinets, no fax machines, one antique phone sits on an empty desk. A few desks fill the rooms, and a meeting room has a large table and several chairs clustered around it. Photos of former communist leaders stare down at you with uncompromising frowns. These were serious men. Out on the street, the town leaders point with pride to a school that is under construction. The local people are building it with their own hands, their own materials. The bleak construction site tells the story — a few piles of chipped and broken cinder blocks lie exposed to the rain and snow; the weather-beaten skeleton says that this project will take a long time to complete. The main street feels like a scene from an old western — dusty, hot, waiting sleepily for something exciting to happen. Stores do not liven the streetscape with their window displays. It wasn't too long ago when a commercial enterprise like a convenience store was illegal. If you know where to go, what barred-up window to open, you can find a small kiosk that sells cigarettes, nylon stockings, soda, candy, fancy lighters, beer, and liquor. What little food is available for sale — most families grow all of their own food — is at an open-air market that is held one or two days a week.

## Two forms of communal life: Western civil society, post-Soviet isolation

Ten churches dot the landscape in Randolph, one for every 500 people in town. On Sundays, the churches are full to overflowing. Not everyone in Randolph belongs to a church, but those who don't, miss out on a big part of small-town Vermont life. The Rotary Club meets every Thursday for lunch; filled with local business people, teachers, public officials, and other professionals. Rotary (and other service clubs) is dedicated to helping the community; members regularly *volunteer* for projects. The club supports many charities and recently took on a sister-city project with a city in Ukraine, delivering three shipping containers of medical supplies and thousands of dollars of hearing aids to a local school for the deaf in Myrhorod. Two community choirs practice once a week during concert season. The local opera house offers a wide variety of entertainment, including a summer musical that is produced locally with volunteer actors from schools and colleges.

In Naryn, organized religion has been outlawed for the past 70 years, so there are no churches, temples, mosques, or other houses of worship. A vestige of local indigenous spirituality survived the Soviet Union — people believe the local shaman to be in contact with the spirit world. Forced to *volunteer* under the communist regime, people often resist getting involved in any organization that would label them politically or that would make demands on their time. The difficulty of scratching a living out of the thin soil makes for long hours spent on basic necessities. Guidebooks list a performing arts theater; but it has not had a budget to produce any programs since before Soviets fell. People do get together — in an elaborate local custom a sheep is roasted and shared, serving as a focal point for community life. There is so much vodka consumed during the sheep feast that many of the men cannot see or walk straight when it is over. If you avoid alcohol, you are not a real man. You must drink more, drink "to the bottom," offer another toast.

## Two economies:
## Rural American simplicity, Kyrgyz subsistence

The livable wage campaign in Randolph has raised awareness locally about the need for even small businesses to pay their employees a fair wage, with benefits when possible. The hospital, schools, and technical college employ the professionals in town. Several industries offer higher-paid manufacturing jobs, and the commercial district sells retail goods. It is possible to live in Randolph and never shop outside of town. The two types of industry that bring income into the community — very important from an economic development perspective — are the local farming and forestry operations, and the local manufacturers. Waterbury Plastics does injection molding; Vermont Castings forges wood stoves and other metal products.

In Naryn, people raise sheep and other livestock that can survive the high altitudes and arid climate. The sheep produce wool that is pounded into felt; some of Kyrgyzstan's highest quality felt comes from Naryn. The proximity to China provides work for some able-bodied men as security guards at the border crossing. Town officials *somehow* manage to live comfortably, even though their state salaries have been virtually non-existent for years now. A study done by the European Union discovered that the income levels were so low that people had long since given up paying local taxes and levies — what few of them there were — in cash, preferring instead to use a kind of barter system. Much of the local tax is paid in sheep. Most local industries have been closed; the demise of the Soviet Union interrupted supply and sales networks irreparably. Yet so many of the industries that were part of the former Soviet Union were outdated and under-capitalized that, even if they had stayed open, they would never have been competitive in the global marketplace.

## Two relationships with the local environment

Individuals own farms and forest resources in and around Randolph; they take responsibility for the land use and natural resource protection that is in place, with comparatively little regulation by local and state authorities. Agricultural runoff and erosion from forestry practices is a concern — but by comparison with other areas of the world, the private landowners in Vermont do a pretty good job. If a new development is proposed in Randolph, the applicant comes before the Development Review Board (DRB) for technical review and approval. The DRB interprets and enforces the regulations that were drafted by the planning commission and adopted by the Town Selectboard, after several public hearings and a lot of public input. If the town doesn't like the proposed zoning, which it didn't when new zoning was proposed in 1998, citizens can circulate a petition and repeal the law the Selectboard passed. The Town Meeting, which consists of all registered voters in town, has the ultimate legislative authority for local government in Vermont. The local Conservation Commission, charged with environmental protection education and advocacy, sets up a land conservation fund, establishes policy to manage town forests, and works to identify the important natural resources throughout the town.

In Naryn, the local authorities do not have much control at all over the environment, except insofar as they control a few of the landholdings. The main natural resource installation in the area is a hydroelectric facility on the Naryn River. Local officials would like to control the facility — it would be an important source of revenue — but the national policy (aided by the United States Agency of International Development) is in the process of *privatizing* the hydroelectric installations and selling them to the highest (foreign) bidder, effectively eliminating any local control over resource use. Private land ownership is still not widespread. Most of the land and buildings belong to the state, so there are few initiatives that people can take to manage resources more effectively. Even if the town had some ideas about using its natural resources more sustainably, 80 to 90 percent of the local budget comes from the national authorities with predetermined expectations about expenditures, so there is no room for creativity or flexibility.

In Randolph, on the other hand, the town discovered a good site for a landfill. They voted a bond issue to build it and took in trash from the Burlington area, the largest city in Vermont. The town made a $3 million profit on this venture, which has helped it pay for infrastructure improvements that were long overdue. The landfill, a state-of-the-art facility, helped solve a critical solid waste problem in Vermont at a time when there was not enough capacity to accommodate all its trash.

## Two governance systems

Town Meeting in Randolph, and throughout New England, is a rite of spring. Every year, the registered voters in town have a chance to vote on the town budget, elect officers, and pass laws and resolutions proposed by people or committees in town. Although the Town Meeting can be scheduled more than once a year, if necessary, it is usually the first Tuesday in March, as perennial as the crocuses peaking out through the melting snow. Direct democracy breeds a cadre of people that takes town business very seriously. Not everyone is interested enough to participate, but those who are serve on local committees and work hard to raise issues at the Town Meeting. The level of participation in higher levels of government is also enhanced by participation in Town Meetings — Vermont has a higher percentage of voter turnout than many other states during national elections (with a 63.7 percent turnout in the 2000 presidential elections, Vermont had the fifth highest in the nation).

The governance structures in the former Soviet Union have not changed as much as the media reports would have us believe. In many places, local officials are still appointed by the central government, and Naryn is no different. Local elections for mayors have been announced; the first ones took place in August of 2001. Most observers with any experience in Kyrgyzstan would agree that these elections would be tightly controlled (read: rigged) by the central government, as illustrated by this short article that appeared in the *Eurasia Digest* soon after the elections.

### Independent NGOS criticize Kyrgyz local elections
Tolekan Ismailova, who is president of the Coalitions of NGOs, said that the local elections held in Kyrgyzstan the previous day were unfair in that local government officials created privileged conditions for pro-government candidates, RFE/RL's Bishkek bureau reported. She accused the Central Election Commission of being unable to act

independently of the government. Some 1,900 candidates contested a total of 460 posts as heads of local councils; 194 local officials were elected, and runoffs will take place on 23 December in the remaining 266 constituencies. [2]

Even with locally elected mayors, the central government will still control all the local budgets, so real self-determination on the local level is still not a reality.

Contrast this to Randolph, where local revenues are raised by local property taxes, and expenditures are set and monitored by the community. The state and federal governments do contribute to the tax-supported services that are offered locally — education, welfare, roads, and community development — but these funds are consistently less than the funds raised by property taxes (although it is difficult to know exactly what the total value of this support is, since there is no local data on the level of support that the federal government makes to individuals who collect welfare and social security). There are citizens in Randolph who even fight against the grants and other support that comes in from higher levels of government, just out of a sense of raw Yankee independence and a desire for less government involvement in all areas of people's lives.

## FOUR COMMUNITY SYSTEMS

In Randolph and Naryn, we can see four main community systems at work, all meeting the citizens' needs with different levels of success. In Randolph, through the churches and other forms of worship, the health care system, the educational system, and the cultural and recreational systems, the community cares for social development. The government plays a role in this, as do several private organizations. Individuals interact with both government and private organizations to meet their needs in this area. In Naryn, social development occurs on the family and clan level, but there is much unmet need on the community level. Schools are almost non-existent. Community gatherings can reflect some of the glory of the cultural life in the past, but alcohol abuse is only one symptom of deeper problems and unmet needs.

The town, state, and federal governments provide for the needs that Randolph citizens have for public safety, for conflict resolution, and for a voice in shaping Randolph's future. The Town Meeting form of government gives every registered voter a voice in how the municipal government works; people are also able to serve on its many committees that discuss and make recommendations on town policies. In Naryn, there are few opportunities for citizens to help determine the community's future. Stagnation of community life is the inevitable result.

The employers in Randolph are all part of the local economic system. The town is home to several banks, which help the economy grow through the loans they offer new businesses and through the multiplier effect that the banking system creates throughout the economy. (The multiplier effect is the additional economic activity that is made possible through the dominant Western myth of money on deposit in the bank. People put their money in the bank, feeling confident that if they need it, it will be there for them. The money is not there, in fact — it's being loaned out to businesses and individuals so that the banks can pay their depositors interest on their deposits.)

In response to several fires that the town had in the early 1990s, Randolph set up a Community Development Corporation that plays a role in economic development and, more recently, in the provision of affordable housing. For people without jobs, the federal and state welfare systems are available, as well as unemployment insurance and social security payments. Unemployment in Naryn is staggering, although the degree to which its citizens can remain self-sufficient without formal employment (albeit with subsistence agriculture) is a bright spot on the otherwise dim horizon. There are no structures to encourage new enterprises. The adventurous entrepreneurs who venture over to China to buy goods to sell in Kyrgyzstan do so without any of the community supports they might have in the West, including low-interest loans, small business assistance, and business incubators with joint marketing and administrative support programs.

The people in both communities have many needs for material goods and services. The farming economy in Randolph is largely associated with the dairy industry; it ships milk to the regional milk processors for the metropolitan markets in Boston and New York. Large food distributors ship food to the grocery stores in Randolph; the groceries are part of a national chain. There is a local food co-op that specializes in organic food — its inventory comes from the Northeastern Cooperatives. In Naryn, people grow their own food and depend mostly on sheep. One resident of the area explained it this way: "Sheep are the most efficient food; they have already processed all the vegetable matter, so when we eat sheep, we get the benefit of meat and vegetables." It's an expedient premise, given the virtual non-existence of vegetables in the Kyrgyz diet during most of the year.

In Randolph, the village areas where the homes are more concentrated have public water supplies; the rest of the people get their water from private wells. Housing is largely bought and sold on the private market, although there are rental units, low-income housing, elderly housing, and cooperative housing available. In Naryn, much of the water supply is surface water. Well-drilling technology has not been used to take full advantage of groundwater resources in Kyrgyzstan. People are exposed to higher levels of surface water contamination. Nitrates in the water are a problem, due to the proximity of the sheep herds to the surface water. Data isn't available on the number of babies that suffer from blue baby syndrome (Methemoglobinemia) in Naryn, but in many parts of the former Soviet Union it is a serious problem. Much of the housing and land in Naryn is owned by the state. Repairs haven't been made in years, but there is little incentive for people to improve their homes. Yurts, made with the felt produced from the sheep's wool, are well-suited to the nomadic life that raising sheep requires. Many people still use these ancient forms of housing. Although the yurts are cozy, decorated with colorful felt blankets, they are essentially large tents with no sanitation, indoor plumbing, or central heat — unless you count the fireplace in the middle of the large single room.

In both communities — Randolph and Naryn — there is no one local system that is responsible for fulfilling the need for social development, the need for governance, the economic needs, and the material needs. Each local government provides many collective services to meet needs, but not everything. It is not useful to try and define the community by its organizational, physical, or economic boundaries because there are many parts of the community which serve different purposes, with different members. It is possible to define the community by what it does, however, which is to meet the needs of its people.

## SUPPLY AND DEMAND

Randolph is a good example of a fairly stable small city. Its population has remained about the same for the past century. As a result, its infrastructure is not strained by increasing population, and the community has been creative, devising new ways to meet its needs. The churches in Randolph team up to provide a food shelf and a thrift store for people who can't afford to pay retail prices. A free medical clinic gives people access to medical care. The community supports several low-income and elderly housing developments through low-interest loans and community development block grants. The recreational opportunities for young people continue to expand; the town has pulled together to develop a teen center and a skateboard park in recent years.

Naryn is an example of a city that is not meeting the needs of all its citizens, despite its small size and relatively stable population. Some of the problems it faces can be blamed on a lack of local funds that are dedicated to local government functions and services. Most of the city's revenue comes from the central government, as does the power to determine how it is spent. It is possible for the central government to decrease or completely eliminate funds for local projects without there being any dialogue or discussion with the people whose lives will be affected by the cuts. It is also possible for the central government to take control of the local facilities that might actually produce revenue, such as the hydropower facilities throughout the mountainous country, and spend the money or even sell the facilities without representation by the people in the area where the facility is located.

The legacy of the Soviet regime is tragic. It has left a people without many of the basic community and social skills they need to succeed in a democratic system; skills like group decision making, conflict resolution, problem solving, communication, and tolerance. These skills represent part of what constitutes the *capacity* that a community has to deal with meeting specific governance and social development needs. Yet for all the unmet needs, the problems in Naryn are more of supply (or capacity) than of demand. The needs haven't changed dramatically; there have not been large influxes of new population to the area. The people in Naryn are not all demanding new cars and washing machine — yet.

These stable cities are now the exception, however. All over the world, cities and towns are challenged with sudden and significant increases in population that tax their ability to meet the needs of residents. In his book *The Gaia Atlas of Cities: New Directions for Sustainable Urban Living* Herbert Girardet looks at urban trends worldwide.

A great migration is underway. Some 20 million people move to cities every year, a human transmigration unprecedented in history. From 1950 to 1990 the population of the world's cities went up from 200 million to over two billion, with three billion people expected by 2025. Today, there are 20 "megacities" of over 10 million people, and 19 out of the world's 25 largest cities are in developing countries. Worldwide, 60 cities have now grown to over four million people. [3]

Population is not the only factor that can disrupt a community's ability to meet local needs, but it does tend to influence the demand side of the equation. Another factor that can increase demand is a changing perception of our needs. When every family *needs* an SUV, three television sets, five stereo systems, three skimobiles, a boat, and other unnecessary consumer goods, demand increases even if the basic needs do not.

On the supply side, environmental conditions can change. Water that had been available can dry up, as is the case in the Aral Sea region that is downstream from Naryn. Political conditions can change. A community that was managing its own affairs fairly successfully can be overrun by an outside force that takes power and resources away from local residents. Economic conditions can also change. In Naryn, the Kyrgyz government was almost ready to decentralize power in 1998 until the Russian rouble crashed and lost its value, forcing the economies in the dependent countries into involuntary hardship.

Supply and demand: the resources that meet the needs and the needs themselves. In economics, the circular flow of money through the economic cycle has led to theories of the multiplier effect and a more sophisticated understanding of how the economy works. A similar understanding of the flows of other resources through the community system can help us understand the sustainability of the system as a whole — on the social, political, economic, and environmental levels.

The *demands* that a community places on community systems come in the form of *actions* taken to meet needs. The reason for this distinction is that there may be needs, which exist, and yet there are no actions taken — this is certainly the case where totalitarian governments are in place.

On the other side of the sustainability equation, the *supply* of resources that a community has to meet needs — its *capacity* in a particular area — is influenced by the regeneration rate. In a forest, this would be the rate at which the trees grow to replace trees that are harvested. In a housing market, it would be the rate at which new housing units are created. In governance, the ways in which a political system recreates itself — how much success a political party has recruiting new members, for example — would be akin to a regeneration rate. In the social development sphere, how the community's care systems, which provide spiritual, cultural, recreational, health, and educational services create those programs and services, supply the capacity a community has to meet these needs.

Figure 1.1 illustrates how this supply and demand, the *actions taken* to meet needs and the community's *capacity* to meet them, affect each other. This expresses the idea of sustainability in its simplest form. In order to meet our needs today without denying future generations the ability to meet theirs, we have to be mindful of how we enhance or erode the capacities we have to meet all the different needs.

Figure 1.1 The Sustainability Cycle

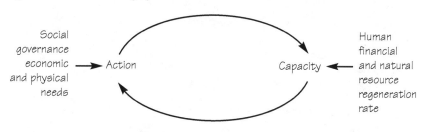

Of course, all of the capacities a community has for meeting our needs are interrelated. If a community experiences a hardship (such as drought or a flood, or other natural disaster) that adversely impacts its ability to grow food and other agricultural products, the overall capacity the community has to meet its needs in all areas will be reduced if the production of agricultural resources is one of the community's main sources of revenue. Conversely, if a community's education system consistently strives to offer the best education available, then the citizens in that community are more likely to have success in other areas, enhancing the social, economic and political capacity of the whole community.

## CONCLUSION

Of all the people who were writing about the definition of community, Martin Buber came the closest to the conception described here, where a community is defined by the ways it meets the needs of its members. He wrote that community "is the commonness of need and only from this commonness of spirit. Commonness of trouble and only from this commonness of salvation...It is only truly a community of faith when it is a community of work." [4]

We all have common needs: We need to be cared for, to have relationships with others, and to feel as if we belong. We need to have some voice, some control over our lives and the life of our community. We need protection from people who would hurt us. If we have a conflict with someone, we need a way to resolve the conflict. We need equity, to feel that we are being treated fairly by our society. We need to work. We need water, air, food, shelter, transportation, energy, clothing, and a clean and safe environment.

The systems we have set up over time to meet these needs often work at cross-purposes with our continued survival as a species. If we learn to diagnose their cycles and internal processes, the hope is that we can find the leverage points that will make them more sustainable. Our continued existence depends on it.

## CHAPTER 2

# Perceiving the Community as a Whole System

CONNECTEDNESS IS ONE DEFINING PRINCIPLE of any community; to perceive a community accurately, it is important to see it as more than the sum of its parts. You cannot separate the sidewalks and roads of a community from its children or its values, its recreation from its businesses, its government from its potholes. Interconnected systems of relationships weave human values throughout all activities, events, regulations, and economics. The community is a whole system with many subsystems nested within it. The perceived connectedness of everything reveals that changing one part affects all the parts, and that their collective effect can produce results that are unexpected when you only look at one part. The whole community moves in rhythm like a dance; it's as fascinating as a drama, and it is truly a celebration of life!

### COMMUNITY ACTORS AND THE FOUR COMMUNITY NEEDS

Who is the whole community and what constitutes a community need?

The whole community is just that — whole: all of its elements and actors, all of its parts function together to provide life-giving and life-sustaining support. The whole is more than just the sum of its parts. The whole includes the quality of support resulting from the interplay of all its parts. The quality of support shows up as the friendship and safety citizens provide for each other. The opportunity for, and acknowledgement of, participation and the reward that comes from sharing one's expertise and talent all enhance the quality of life for people in the community. The root of all of these community benefits is often buried so deep in history that we don't perceive it anymore. The whole community is a collection of systems people have established over the years to meet our needs as human beings. Human beings live in communities because we are fundamentally social creatures; we cannot live whole human lives in isolation from each other.

A need is defined here as the lack of something required to live whole human lives. We tend to think of needs as only being related to basic material sustenance, things like food, clothing, and shelter, but our needs as human beings go far beyond that. We do need to maintain our physical beings with material goods and services, but we also have needs that are related to our status as members of a community. We need to work — not only to earn income but to participate in the community. We need to have a voice in the decisions that are made, and we need a level of social well-being that comes from being cared for and caring for others in return.

We can distinguish three main community actors as part of the system: (1) individuals/households, (2) organizations, including businesses and non-profit organizations, and (3) the governing bodies. All of these community actors respond to community needs, and they can all be seen playing their parts in the recreational system of the community. These three community actors play key roles in systems established to meet our needs. Examining one facet of community life in depth can reveal the web of relationships and interactions among the different actors.

In the recreational system, for example, we know recreational activities created by communities satisfy needs for leisure, play, and socializing. Citizens from all parts of the community participate in recreational activities, creating opportunities for informal connections, increasing and enriching the flow of relationships, and providing that spark of fun we all enjoy. Many municipalities have large recreation departments, with a staff and a budget, to manage activities and facilities. When the community meets the recreational needs of its citizens, it also creates employment, bringing capital into the community while providing a much needed and wanted service.

Community needs can be identified as: (1) physical, (2) economic, (3) governance, and (4) social. If we meet community needs for recreation, communities will have a higher level of social well-being, so we include recreation in the category of a social need. The purpose here is to cultivate the ability to perceive the community as a whole and analyze its parts only out of the necessity to show that they function as part of the big picture.

There is an old saying, "If you want to know another person, walk a mile in their shoes." Let's imagine we can examine the recreational system through the eyes of the three main community actors: individuals/households, organizations, and government. We now have at least three different points from which to view the system. For example, individuals and households participate in recreational programs and use the facilities. Organizations — the scouts, the Rotary Club, various social clubs — the businesses that sponsor programs, and stores that sell sneakers and skis all offer their viewpoints. We may also look through the eyes of various levels of government. The local government probably maintains some public parks; it might have a community center with a swimming pool and fitness programs. The state government also manages a park system, and the federal government provides funds for a variety of recreational activities and for the purchase of more parks and facilities. Each level plays a role and has a particular viewpoint.

How do the different community actors interact with each other, how are these viewpoints expressed and responded to, and, how does this activity contribute to the sustainability of the community as a system? Let's look at a relatively new recreational activity — skateboarding — as an example.

## A COMMUNITY CONNECTEDNESS STORY

Kids love to skateboard. Sidewalks and handicapped access ramps are perfect for skateboarding, from the kids' perspective. In Randolph, the downtown sidewalks were particularly good for skateboarding because the town is built on a slope, the sidewalks making a natural hill for the skateboarders. The town had gone to some trouble to put in new sidewalks, ramps, and other pedestrian amenities, and the facilities were in perfect shape for the sport. The skateboarders were having a great time. Part of the joy of the sport is the showiness of it — so being right downtown with a ready-made audience met their needs perfectly.

All was not well, however. Elderly pedestrians didn't like risking life and limb when they walked out of a store only to find themselves in the middle of a skateboard stunt ramp. Store owners complained. To make matters worse, skateboard wheels often left grooves in new and expensive sidewalks, so the town was faced with damage to its brand new infrastructure improvement project.

The Selectboard, faced with citizen and business complaints and the threat of costly damage to town property, took action. They quickly passed an ordinance banning skateboards on all sidewalks in town. The penalty for infractions would be a ticket, much like a traffic violation ticket.

The skateboarders, with the help of a few sympathetic adults, did not stand still for this infringement on their rights to enjoy public amenities. They organized and petitioned to change the law. After all, if the town's concern was the downtown area, why ban skateboarding on all sidewalks in town? Furthermore, if the town wanted to support their interest in this type of recreation, then perhaps construction of a skateboard park would be one way to do it.

After several meetings with the young skateboarders, the Selectboard voted to amend the law so that only the downtown sidewalks would be off-limits. Since that time, the town has also built a skateboard park, which has been very popular since it opened in 1998.

In this example, we have illustrations of many different needs and all the community actors. It begins with the need for recreation. Some young people want to skateboard — it's their way of relaxing, rejuvenating; it's fun. We all need to take time to play, to enjoy life, especially the children. So, these *individuals* take action to meet their need for recreation by turning the downtown into their playground. This action comes into conflict with the individuals and business organizations in town. Older people need to feel safe on the sidewalks. If they don't feel safe, they don't shop downtown, and so the business owners lose customers. These *individuals* and a few *organizations* (businesses) contact the local *government* to fix the problem. The local government, in turn, takes action to constrain the activities of the kids who were meeting their needs in a way that was annoying and a safety hazard for others. The original action has now gone full circle — individual action provoked an organizational reaction, which in turn helped initiate a government action that regulated individual action. All the community actors were involved in the situation in their own particular way.

Figure 2.1 Cyclical Community Interactions

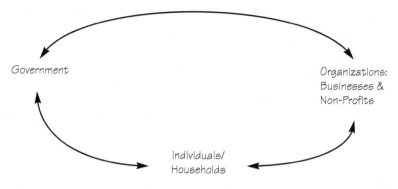

Government

Organizations:
Businesses &
Non-Profits

Individuals/
Households

There are several examples in this story of different community needs driving the system. The need for recreation is a social need. Community social needs relate to how we care for ourselves and for each other, and they express what we value about our lives. Community social needs also include the need for safety; we want to feel safe on the streets. Other community social needs are peace, health care, lifelong learning, meaningful relationships, a sense of belonging, self-expression, self-esteem, beauty and spiritual life.

The skateboard story also speaks to community economic needs — losing customers due to annoyance and the possibility of injury from the skateboarders was a threat to the economic security of business owners. Businesses fulfill many of the community economic needs, providing employment and income for citizens. The community government fulfilled their obligation to individuals, organizations, and businesses by providing reliable, safe pedestrian infrastructure. They wanted to protect their new investment in sidewalks.

Once the ordinance was passed, other community needs and interests emerged. The young people organized themselves to protest what they perceived as an unnecessarily harsh reaction to their legitimate recreational pursuits. The community need not being met here was the skateboarders' sense of access to public amenities and self-determination, permission to freely interact with the environment. They also needed to know they were being treated fairly in comparison with other people who live in the community; they expressed a need for equity. When conflict arises between the interests of people and organizations, we want to know that the dispute can be resolved fairly through conflict resolution procedures. Policies devised by the community government address the ways in which power and information are used to coordinate services and to fulfill community needs.

## THE ACTORS IN THE SYSTEM

Looking deeper into the community system, we will explore three community actors and the four major categories of community needs as described above. Three community actors are: (1) individuals/ households, (2) organizations, and (3) government. Four major categories of community needs are: (1) physical well-being, (2) economic security, (3) governance, and (4) social well-being.

As community actors, individuals and household units participate in congregations in churches, as voters at the polls, customers in the stores, and clients of professionals. They are hikers, swimmers, campers, artists, audiences, children, teachers, the elderly, the homeless, and the unemployed. All of the roles and responsibilities of community actors and their audiences are seen in live performances on stage in the business and play of living in a community.

Organizations, as community actors, form when groups of people work together to take action in any area they wish to explore or improve. When they perceive a need, groups of people organize non-profit organizations, businesses, clubs, associations, churches, synagogues, mosques, temples, environmental groups, human rights' groups, dance troupes, circuses, etc.

Government is distinguished from organizations, due in part to the orderly delegation of power conferred to it by the collective wish of all the individuals and organizations who desire to be represented in the decision-making process. Local, regional, state, and national government all play their specific roles in helping communities meet their needs.

The three community actors — individuals/households, organizations, and government — connect and interact in many kinds of exchanges. These transactions form a fulfillment cycle within each system's own needs and requirements for satisfaction. For example, as in the skateboarding example, individuals make demands on the system to meet their needs, and organizations and governments respond to those demands. Organizations also make demands on the government or on individuals. The government, in its turn, often makes demands on both organizations and individuals. The cycle of demand and response by the actors, the ways in which the transactions build on each other, create the internal dynamics, the giving and receiving of different need satisfiers. These cyclical dynamics will enhance or erode the community's capacity to meet its needs in the future.

## THE NEEDS AS THE GOALS OF THE SYSTEM

The extraordinary power of needs to attract or demand satisfaction deserves a deeper look. Our definition of need is a lack of something required to live whole human lives. Manfred Max-Neef, Abraham Maslow, and Jurgen Habermas are three contemporary philosophers who published theoretical works on human needs. Manfred Max-Neef suggested there are nine basic human needs: subsistence, protection and security, affection, understanding, participation, leisure, creation, identity/meaning, and freedom.[1] Abraham Maslow developed a hierarchy of needs which included physiological needs as well as needs for safety, love, esteem, and self-actualization.[2] Jurgen Habermas described three main interests, or needs: the technical interest, which reflects a need to have some control over the environment; the hermeneutical interest, reflecting a need to communicate, interpret, and be understood; and, the emancipatory interest, which reflects the need for freedom.[3] Community needs fit the descriptive categories as the philosophers defined them, but their common bond is a focus on *a lack of something required for each of us to live whole human lives.*

For our lives and our community to be whole, how do we sense what requires improvement? How do we collect accurate data for making decisions? When do we go beyond complaining about problems as our main source of direction?

When a needs assessment is done for the system that is our community, the main subjects are the people in the community. When their stories are gathered, along with their viewpoints, four broad categories of community needs emerge: physical well-being, economic security, governance, and social well-being. These also correspond with the needs that have been proposed by Maslow, Max-Neef, and Habermas. If we apply systems thinking to each community need in detail, we would find them intimately and dynamically interconnected. They are choreographed with all of the others in a dance of mutuality, mutually beneficial or mutually detrimental for all. If one system is improved or meets needs more effectively, all the other community actors benefit. For example, if the school system is doing a better job preparing young people for civic responsibilities and employment, this will have an effect on the lives of their parents, on the amount of juvenile crime the police department handles, and on the businesses in town. Change one thing and, in response, the system changes. If a community system is not working, other areas will also suffer some impact. These community needs are immediately useful for developing our ability to perceive the community as a whole and for demonstrating the concept of the community as a system created to meet the needs of its inhabitants and the sustainability of the natural environment.

The working definition of sustainability begins with a focus on human needs. One of the first statements about sustainability was from the Brundtland Commission — the World Commission on Environment and Development established by the Secretary General of the United Nations in 1983. Members of the Commission traveled throughout the world interviewing people to find out what they thought about environmental problems and came back with findings that showed how environmental concerns were interdependent with concerns about the economy, health care, population pressure, and social issues. They defined sustainable development as "development that meets the needs of the present without compromising the ability of future generations to meet their own needs."[4]

The Natural Step, a science and systems based approach to planning for sustainability, identifies human needs as a key factor in achieving sustainable development, stating that resources must be used fairly and efficiently in order to meet human needs globally.[5] The Natural Step inspired Manfred Max-Neef to define the nine human needs listed above, but to date there has been no systematic approach developed to identify, connect, and compare the needs to the gaps in need satisfaction on any level.

The Bruntland Commission assumed that meeting material needs is the primary goal for sustainable development, but in fact this cannot be achieved in isolation from all the levels of need satisfaction. This is reflected in the Natural Step's further clarification of the importance of meeting human needs efficiently.

> If the total resource throughput of the global human population continues to increase, it will be increasingly difficult to meet basic human needs as human-driven processes

intended to fulfill human needs and wants are systematically degrading the collective capacity of the Earth's
ecosystems to meet these demands. This means using all of
our resources efficiently, fairly and responsibly so that the
needs of all people on whom we have an impact, and the
future needs of people who are not yet born, stand the best
chance of being met.[6]

Basic human needs — the low ones on Maslow's hierarchy of
needs — are those that fill our material needs. Maslow refers to our
physiological needs, Max-Neef refers to sustenance, but they are both
talking about the same thing — what we need for physical well-being.
Material needs place demands on the environment, so it's no surprise
that they are focal points of sustainability planning. Examining the
mechanisms through which these needs are satisfied, however, demonstrates their interdependence on our needs for economic security, for
self-determination and equity, and for social well-being. All of these
facets of community needs work together in the community system.
Changing our ability to meet basic physical and material needs equitably cannot be done in isolation from other important community
needs. Perceiving the whole community as a dynamic system requires
us to examine its parts in relation to their effect on the system, to
show how change in one part affects all others.

## PHYSICAL NEEDS AND THE ENVIRONMENT

Physical well-being begins with a clean and safe environment. This
covers a lot of ground, so we might for a moment imagine our community from above — it helps to picture the whole community when
trying to imagine its total physical well-being. If the air is clean, and
the water is clear, if the trees and plants are healthy and green, if the
transportation system is efficient and quiet, if the houses and buildings
are safe, and if the waste of the community is managed well, all of
these systems are important to the overall health of the community
and the individuals in it.

Visiting countries in Central and Eastern Europe after the changes
took place that allowed contact with the West, I was shocked by some
of the degraded environmental conditions there. In 1993 I visited one
city in Bulgaria where the copper smelter had poured so much arsenic
into the environment that all the smaller insect life — including the

bees — had died, leaving agriculture in crisis. I remember the initial shock of meeting people in town; their skin color had changed to a pallid grey. I stood out because I had healthy-looking pink skin.

It would appear to be common sense that if we don't live in a clean and safe environment, our health is compromised. We can't morally or ethically send our waste down the river or into the air to the next community; but we have, and often we still do. Humans have demonstrated an ability to adapt to and live in deplorable conditions. But even basic subsistence does not equate with well-being. The need for sustenance, for food, clothing, and shelter, is closely interwoven with the need for economic security. Yet the resources that meet our physical needs are different and flow in different cycles than money, investment, and labor, so for the discussion in this book, they are kept separate.

Our physical needs require us to interact with Earth in a constant and demanding way. We would not survive for one minute outside Earth's atmosphere; air — preferably clean air — is one of our critical physical needs. We would only survive a few days without water, another life sustaining resource that Earth provides. All of the energy we have and use is another gift from our planet — the food we eat, the warmth against the winter cold, the lights in the dark, the productive energy for our creativity and manufacturing processes.

We need housing. Even when humans were at the beginning of their evolutionary path, they constructed shelter from the elements or lived in naturally occurring shelters. Earth provides us with a wide variety of materials to make adequate housing.

Transportation is another derivative need — resulting from our needs for food, clothing, shelter, and our need for social contact. Yet so many of our unsustainable practices are linked to transportation; it deserves to be addressed on its own.

We need food, clothing, hardware, blankets, and a wide variety of goods and services to meet our needs for sustenance, creativity, and meaningful work. The productive capacity of the community, derived from the natural resources that are available, is very important for our ability to live whole human lives.

We need to communicate with other people. Telephones, telegraphs, electronic communication, fax machines, cable networks, TVs, radios, smoke signals, letters, newspapers, carrier pigeons, words, grunts, moans, books, and magazines are all forms of communication that are rooted in the material world, despite the intersubjective nature of the communication itself.

Finally, waste is a fact of life. The sustainability of all our systems is largely dependent on our continued ability to manage, reuse, recycle, reduce, transform, and dispose of waste. This includes trash, sewage, compost, tires, white goods, cars, metals, cardboard, plastics, wastewater, and emissions.

## THE NEED FOR ECONOMIC SECURITY

Economic security includes our need for an income and employment. We perceive it to be closely tied to our physical well-being and our freedom to have and to do things. There was a time in human history when needs were met without money, through barter, and through crafting one's own things. Most of us now believe it is not possible to live without money. Our need for work is related to our need for money, which is why it is included in the economic needs.

Work also fills an array of social needs, from meaningful productive activity to self-expression and self-esteem. Maslow talks about our need for self-esteem, which is often found through our work. For Max-Neef, the need to work is linked to one's need to participate and serve. For those people who are unable to work or don't make enough money, the U.S. government offers limited subsistence in the form of welfare, unemployment subsidies, and Medicaid. These also are elements of economic security. As our global system changes, what we really need to achieve economic security is an economy that enables people to pursue their creativity and natural productivity in directions that can be sustained by the natural world. Our current reliance on national government programs for economic security in a global economy will be an historic relic before the end of the next millennium.

## SOCIAL WELL-BEING

Social well-being includes our needs for peace and safety, valued relationships, recreation, lifelong learning, health care, child care, a sense of community, self-expression, aesthetic enjoyment, and a spiritual life. Community systems that have evolved to meet these needs have an important element in common: they are all linked to the ways we care for one another and to the way we form and express values. What we might call the caring social system provides the collective expression of affection. When we get sick, or injured, we need a way to get care. To prepare for such a possibility we created an elaborate, insurance-controlled, profit-motivated, healthcare system. In the United States, the caring function of health care may have been upstaged by economic factors, for example, in the efficient delivery of an expensive service. But it's not called health *care* for nothing. We need care, not just medicine, when we are sick.

Being healthy, that is, living in such a way to promote well-being, is a holistic, proactive approach to health care that requires living in harmony with the world. Recapturing that element of the health care system is an important challenge. Health care is largely about care — care for our families, care for our bodies, care for our communities.

Probably the most important function of our social system is *lifelong learning*. We educate our children because we care about them and we want them to function and succeed. Our need for education has increased, as more complex conceptual skills are required to live in today's world. People need to learn an enormous amount of complex information in order to function effectively in the world. Education is not the same as information — information is power. Sharing information with people, part of education, is a function of caring rather than power.

Although *childcare* could be considered a subcategory of education, there is an important distinction to be made. Education has the goal of sharing values, information, skills, life skills, and thinking habits with others. Beyond this, there is a need for nurturing, for caring for the physical, psychological, and social needs of children. Children who are too young to be in an educational system often need care while parents work. Older children need care and activities after school hours, if parents are still at work.

Another critical element of our social system is the *spiritual life* of a community. Ever since the dawn of consciousness, we have sought to make sense of our existence, to connect with a transcendent reality that is greater than we are as individuals. The need for practices, values, beliefs, and social activities that address this fundamental sense of connection and self-transcendence is an historical fact, whatever our particular faith, belief system, or values. Our spiritual needs include the needs to develop a philosophy of life, to find meaning in what can sometimes seem like a senseless world, to find ways to withstand tragedy and loss, to forgive others and come to reconciliation, and to belong to a community that shares our values and moral code. Not everyone can be a mystic or live within a religious system of rituals, symbols, and celebrations, but everyone does have some basic spiritual needs. Ignoring them can produce excesses or dysfunctions in other areas.

We need to have a *sense of community*, a sense of belonging. This corresponds with Max-Neef's need to participate/serve, and Maslow's need for belonging and esteem. People seek to meet this need in a variety of ways — the fact that the social systems we have established are not fulfilling our need for a sense of community is probably why participation in *intentional* communities around the world has increased so dramatically in the last 30 to 40 years. Intentional communities have many names. In the 1960s, they were communes; now, they are co-housing communities, ecovillages, Camphill Communities, or other instances where a group of people has decided to build and live in a community that is formed around a common purpose.

No man is an island, and while some people go through life as loners, very few will deny that, as human beings, we need *meaningful relationships* with others. Maslow calls this need a need for love, for connectedness with others. Max-Neef talks about the need to be surrounded by family and friends to share emotion.

Maslow describes a need for safety; for Max-Neef, this is a need for protection and security. Without *safety*, we can't meet our other needs. The need for safety is a basic, fundamental need; on the community or national level, it is a need for peace, for national security, for law and order. This need, writ large, drives many unsustainable systems that exist in our world today — nuclear weapons being one of the worst examples.

The ways in which we pursue arts and culture are twofold — *self-expression and beauty*. We have a need to express ourselves — this is partly described by Maslow as the need for self-actualization and by Max-Neef as the need for creativity. The inadequate attention given to the arts in the United States is probably linked closely with our tendency to over-consume. After all, when you buy that new dress or new car, aren't you just trying to make a statement about who you are? Max-Neef's need for identity could also be included here. In addition to our need for self-expression we find the need for beauty, the need to enjoy the pleasures derived from our five senses. The need for self-expression can complement the need for beauty to drive the creation of art and music, drama, dance, architecture, gardens, landscapes, good food, literature, and spiritual ritual in which we realize our full human potential.

In addition to all the ways in which we care for others in the community, we also need to care for ourselves. *Self-esteem* is important, and increasingly education programs have recognized this and have sought to find ways to help youth reinforce their self-esteem. The mission of the National Association for Self-Esteem (NASE) is "to fully integrate self-esteem into the fabric of American society so that every individual, no matter what their age or background, experiences personal worth and happiness." NASE believes self-esteem is "the experience of being capable of meeting life's challenges and being worthy of happiness."[7]

## GOVERNANCE

Our governance needs include self-determination, conflict resolution, equity, and access. The community systems established to meet these needs all relate to the way we use power and the way we share power and information with one another.

Max-Neef refers to the need for *self-determination* as freedom. Self-determination is part of Maslow's need for self-actualization. Self-determination means having the personal power necessary to make choices that help determine the path of one's life. It is also a fundamental need, one that drives many unsustainable practices — America's love affair with the automobile is only one example.

As individuals and as communities, we need *conflict resolution* systems. The first non-kin political systems emerged in the Nile River Valley as a response to the need to resolve conflict over water rights. Since then, we have developed a wide variety of systems to resolve conflict. A standing army used to be an important conflict resolution mechanism. Today, court systems, mediation services, and the legislative process are a few ways that our communities meet this need.

*Equity* is an interesting concept to characterize as a need, especially as a need that is related to the way we use power. Equity is often considered more a characteristic of the economic sphere. Yet even though economic equity is one way in which this need expresses itself, our ability to gain economic equity is directly related to the power we have. There are also other equity issues that are not related to economics. Do we have a need for equity? The first time you find that someone in your position is paid more than you for the same work, you recognize the need for equity. All of the rights movements through time — voting rights, women's rights, rights for people with disabilities — are powerful expressions of our need for equity.

*Access*, an aspect of how we use power, is hard to categorize completely on its own. It is a close companion of self-determination; if we have adequate self-determination, it may indicate that we have access to the facilities, institutions, systems, etc. that we need to meet our needs. Yet access is slightly different from self-determination, in that it describes the ways in which the systems themselves are structured, rather than the motivation and autonomy that individuals might have.

Figure 2.2 illustrates the cycles of need, demand, and satisfaction within a community as it responds to actions taken by the different community actors. The flow of need satisfiers, which are defined as various forms of social well-being, governance, economic security, and material goods and services, goes through and between the different community actors with each transaction. These flows, and the capacity of the community to continue to provide the different need satisfiers, can be enhanced or eroded by actions taken by each community actor.

Figure 2.2 The Whole Community System

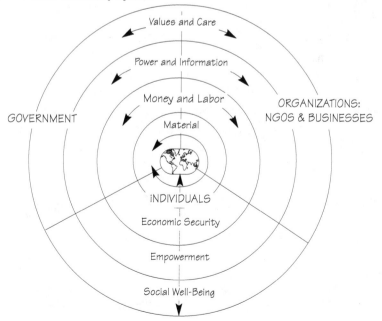

Within each category of need, the flow of interactions defines the corresponding subsystemic capacities. In the social system, the interactions consist of the caring relationships we form in a community and the values that shape our worldview. In the governance system, the interactions determine how we use power and information to exert influence on our world. In the economic system, money flows through the community, and labor is exchanged for money. In the physical, or environmental system, the flow is made up of materials — including air, water, buildings, infrastructure, plants, animals, soil. The capacities within each of these systems can be enhanced or eroded by the collective effect of the different interactions.

The subsystems also are interdependent. Our values play an important role in helping form the power structures and legal systems we establish to manage community affairs. These in turn play a formative role for the economic systems we develop, which in turn have an enormous impact on the environment.

It is possible to track the cyclical interactions to demonstrate how the flow works. In the social system, for example, the government establishes the legal and regulatory framework for health care and provides subsidies for people who can't afford to pay themselves. The organizations, businesses, hospitals, and doctors in turn work to actually provide the healthcare, and the individuals use the systems to address their healthcare needs.

The needs are the primary drivers of the systems, the flows of transactions between the different community actors. It is also true that the systems themselves can drive the transactions, once the pattern is established. Quite often, unfortunately, an unsustainable pattern of behavior will be well-established and will perpetuate itself because of an unhealthy systemic inclination to maintain the particular pattern. So, transactions can continue to occur that aren't meeting any particular need in a meaningful way. Nonetheless, understanding the needs themselves gives communities powerful tools to diagnose problems and pursue strategies that meet the needs in a new way.

The integrated system, which includes the same basic components as the community system cycle is described in Figure 2.3.

There is a strong linkage between improving social networks and community improvements on many levels. Crime studies in the United States have demonstrated, for example, that it is possible to predict the level of crime in a neighborhood by merely quantifying

Figure 2.3 Community Systems Dynamics

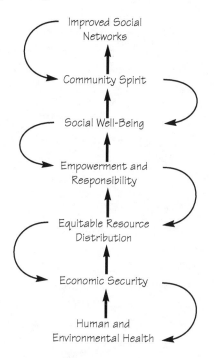

the social interactions of its residents. Improved social networks tend to reinforce a sense of community, which in turn improves the level of social well-being. This in turn builds trust — a critical component for any level of power-sharing within a community.

More trust means that higher levels of empowerment and responsibility will be possible, as community members work together successfully on a variety of tasks. As power is shared and responsibility is taken for local issues, the groundwork is laid for a more equitable distribution of resources, since power is a key factor in how resources are distributed. With a higher level of equity, there will also be a higher level of overall economic security, as the gap between the rich and the poor is reduced. Only then can there be some hope for improved human and environmental health, since most of the environmental problems can be directly linked to over consumption of resources that result from a lack of economic security.

As human and environmental health improves, the process has a reinforcing effect through the community system. Higher levels of health can lead to greater security, which can reinforce the equitable distribution of resources, the levels of empowerment and responsibility, social well-being, and a sense of community. It all works together to produce a sustainable outcome, but if the higher levels of need are ignored, and we continue with the inequitable and socially fragmented system we have in place today, we will not be able to achieve economic and environmental sustainability.

## VICIOUS CYCLES

Of course, the opposite effect — where the system is progressively eroded by actions within it — is also possible; in fact, it's all too common. The following is a story about how these systems can work in reverse.

The Selectboard in Randolph was frustrated. Its members worked as hard as they could to keep up with the road repair work, but it was endless, and the roads seemed to be getting worse every year. The potholes on Main Street made it almost impassable in the spring. The Beanville Road, home to most of the town's major industry, was full of holes, making it hard for trucks to get to the different industries.

Like most public servants, the Selectboard members (the five elected officials who served as the town council) were particularly sensitive to complaints. If they got complaints about a road, they would try to give it some attention, i.e., the squeaky wheel gets the grease. As a result, the roads in the worst shape got all the attention, and the roads that were only in moderately poor condition were ignored. To fix the worst roads cost a lot of money, and as a result, the budget for road repair grew larger and larger, with less and less to show for it.

What the Selectboard didn't realize was that they were inadvertently caught in a vicious cycle. By ignoring the roads in need of moderate maintenance, their entire road infrastructure was deteriorating rapidly. When they focused on the worst roads in response to citizen complaints, they spent people's hard-earned tax dollars less and less effectively. This is because it costs much more to rebuild roads that are badly deteriorated than it does to maintain good roads, by a factor of ten in many cases. So, as long as the town was spending most of its budget rebuilding the worst roads, it was neglecting the investment needed to keep the good roads from deteriorating to the point where they needed reconstruction. Sealing cracks every year, putting another coat of asphalt down to extend the life of the road, none of these things were being done.

Figure 2.4 A Vicious Cycle: Road Deterioration

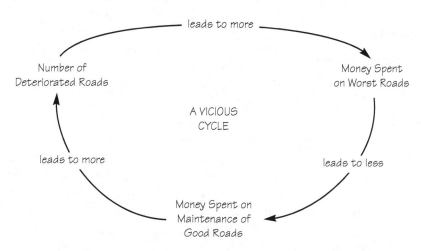

Vicious cycles are common in government. Anyone who has worked for any level of government knows the painful disillusionment of having yesterday's solution become today's problem. Whether it is a social program designed to alleviate poverty that creates a new class of people dependent on the welfare system, or a trash disposal system that suddenly becomes a significant source of groundwater contamination, government's isolated solutions never seem to get things right.

While it is impossible to anticipate every possible contingency when officials are developing solutions to serious problems, it is possible to bring a more holistic view of the community to the table to see the community as a whole system, rather than seeing an agglomeration of different isolated problems to solve. Problematic side effects can be minimized when we understand the whole system and how past actions on our part prejudice the possibility for future actions.

Randolph's road repair is a simple example of this. The Randolph Selectboard needed a way to consider the entire road system when they decided where to spend limited repair dollars. As long as the issues were being presented to them as a complaint here, another one there, they saw a partial, fragmented view of the system. Fortunately, the state highway department had developed pavement management software, so all the road repair data could be entered into a database and considered as a whole.

Using the pavement management software, the Selectboard was able to understand the effects their decisions had on all of the roads, rather than just the roads people complained about. If they continued to spend all of their limited dollars on the worst roads, the others would suffer. By taking the whole road system into consideration, the vicious cycle could be turned around. They shifted the money in the maintenance budget so it was dedicated to roads that were only in need of moderate repair and moved the worst roads into the capital budget, fixing them as capital funds allowed over a longer period of time.

This was not just a simple accounting exercise. If people are complaining about a road being impassable, it's not easy to tell them that they will have to wait four years for the road to come up on the capital improvement schedule. The whole community needed to be involved in the capital budget process, so there was some level of consensus about the priorities for spending. There needs to be a level of trust, mutuality, and respect for participatory decision-making processes to work, but the long-term success of decisions and policies that are made in the context of this trust and respect is worth the effort.

## SOCIAL CAPITAL

Social scientists have coined the term social capital to describe the measurable elements of a healthy civil society — high levels of trust and interaction with other community members; a sense of belonging; participation in public life; connections with family, friends, and neighbors; tolerance of diversity; and active community networks. The term has been used by some to set it on equal footing with financial, natural, and human capital.

Social capital is of interest to decision makers and social scientists because there is ample evidence that increased social capital leads to increased productivity with respect to a community's action and collaborative efforts to solve common problems. Cities where social capital exists are better at responding to challenges and keeping the community on track. The World Bank has even begun to evaluate funding development projects based on the existing social networks in an area; they are taking it quite seriously.[8]

All social networks are not necessarily created equal when it comes to strengthening community bonds and making collective action more possible and effective, however. The Ku Klux Klan was certainly something akin to a social club, but it had a corrosive effect on community life. In evaluating how a community works together, it is important to distinguish between inclusive and exclusive social networks.

Yet for all the value that the discussion of social capital has for pubic policy and for understanding how to make our democracy work more effectively, the term itself implies an inverted sense of priority. Social capital is called *capital* and considered useful because it helps democracy work more effectively and because it helps make economic growth more successful. Yet the social life we have — the relationships, the sense of community, the cultural fabric — all this responds to the needs we have on the deepest level. All of the other community systems should be working to enhance these parts of our lives, not vice versa. If our economy is eroding the social fabric of our communities, our economy should change. If modern democracy, with its emphasis on sound bites, political consultants, and mass media is undermining the degree to which local communities can participate in a meaningful way so that their values are reflected in the decisions that are made, the system should change.

Our community social life is the essence of human existence. Without it, our lives are dry, meaningless, and without value. It is through our associations with each other that we meet all our needs, from the basic material needs to our need for connection with a transcendent reality. Rather than looking to these social networks as servants of economic growth and representative democracy, our economic system and democratic system should be refined to enhance our abilities to form meaningful communities on a variety of different levels.

## CHAPTER 3

# Community Capacity and Sustainability

COMMUNITY CAPACITY: It's one of the most important elements of sustainable development because a community's capacity to satisfy its needs is critical for current and future development. A community that can satisfy the needs of all its members will be a community where people can live whole and healthy lives. All of the needs that were described in Chapter 2 are satisfied only when the community has the capacity to satisfy them. People are able to eat because the community systems they set up are able to provide them with food. People are able to work for a living because the economic system has the capacity to provide them with jobs. People participate in governance and decision making when the established systems enable participation. People are educated and grow into whole human beings because the community systems nurture them and provide them with opportunities to fulfill their potential.

Community capacity has several characteristics. The capacities of each system — social, governance, economic, and material — are all made up of particular elements that satisfy particular needs. For simplicity, the word asset will be used to describe these individual need satisfiers. For example, the need for water has a corresponding set of water assets — the reservoirs, the distribution system, and the annual rainfall in a particular place. The need for education has the schools, colleges, and educational programs in the community as assets that help meet that need. Assets are not all physical infrastructure — the need for self-expression might find one of its corresponding assets in a local ensemble that brings musicians together on a regular basis.

Community assets are the facilities, services, relationships, programs, natural resources, and people that help the community meet its needs. The aggregation of these assets is the key to the overall community capacity. Like all systems, the whole is always greater than the sum of its parts. If a community has assets in one system and not others, the whole system might be impoverished, or there might be a synergistic effect that compensates for particular shortcomings.

Each asset in turn also has several characteristics. There is the critical mass — the aggregate amount of the asset required to satisfy the demand. If a community has a demand for one million gallons of water per day, but the reservoir and rainfall only provide half a million, then the critical mass of the asset isn't there to satisfy the need. There is also the distributive quality of the asset — the ability the system has to distribute the asset equitably. A community is impoverished if only a very few people are able to satisfy their needs. The ability of the asset to regenerate itself is also important. If a forest is harvested more quickly than the trees can grow, this will erode the ability of the forest to be an asset that satisfies the need for wood in the future. Also, the interaction that the asset has with the larger regional, national, and global community is an important factor. Very often, the assets that are available at the local level are dependent on some form of action at another level.

It is possible to identify the assets within each community and to evaluate the community's capacity for satisfying all of its needs. To do this, it is also important to look at the interactions between the different need satisfaction systems, because they have an effect on the capacity and the sustainability of the community as a whole. Within each system it is possible to track the transactions that occur and identify the cycle of interactions that define whether or not the system is being eroded or enhanced by the actions that are being taken to meet the community's needs.

## ECONOMIC CAPACITY

To illustrate the process of identifying assets and evaluating capacity, we examine a familiar and well-studied example of a cyclical interaction within a community that meets our need for income and work — the local economic system. The actors in the system are the individuals/households, the organizations, and the government. Individuals earn income by working. They often deposit their money

## A New England Capacity Building Story

A large, well-endowed foundation decided that it wanted to work in rural communities to explore ways in which they could be made more environmentally sound, economically viable, and have more effective civic societies. They provided a grant to six rural communities in Maine, New Hampshire, and Vermont, in the hopes that the grant might improve the lives of people in the area by helping them implement sustainable community strategies. The large foundation formed a partnership with three small community foundations in each state to do the work, and each state took a different approach to the project. New Hampshire focused on organization building, Vermont on mentoring/nurturing, and Maine on capacity building, especially of emerging leaders.[1] The Maine foundation was primarily concerned with civic capacity, so they encouraged and trained leaders, recruited and involved volunteers, created and used networks, and developed new partnerships for the projects they proposed. The goal was to develop trusted relationships, credibility, and, therefore, a level of legitimacy within the communities they served.

When an evaluation of the finished project was completed, the evaluators said that their most surprising finding was that "...the approach of capacity building seems to be the most successful strategy for delivering community results ... it turns out to be the essence of both process and products." As one practitioner commented, "You can't have economic development until you have community development. Community development means building trust."[2]

in the bank, which in turn loans it to businesses to help them expand, to people who buy houses or make other large purchases. Businesses produce goods and services; they hire employees; they pay taxes. The government uses the taxes to provide infrastructure as well as educational programs that train new workers. Government also regulates the economic activity through land use regulation, permits for activities, laws that set the constraints and boundaries for certain practices, etc.

This cycle of transactions, known to economists as the *circular flow*, can produce a synergistic effect as the money flows through the system. Typically, a description of the cycle starts with goods that are either manufactured or cultivated for export. When products are sold outside of the local community, they have the effect of bringing income into the community that wasn't there before. When this income is invested in bank accounts or equities, it allows businesses to have access to more capital for their work. When it is spent on goods and services, the businesses earn income from the purchases. More business activity translates into more income for owners and employees, which means that when income is generated in a community through the creation of new products and either invested or spent on consumption, it can translate into still more income. Thus, the capacity for a community to produce the income, production, and employment that people need can increase through local consumption and investment. It can also increase through the development of more goods and services that bring income into the community. The development of new goods and services, in turn, depends on the resource base that is available and its sustainable yield. The resources that are required to produce goods and services need to be carefully managed, so that the economic activity that depends on them won't erode their capacity to be available not only for human use, but also for the critical ecosystem needs.

There are five key variables for sustainable economic development:

- the degree of trust, cooperation, and leadership in the community, so that collective action toward an improved local economy is possible;
- the equitable distribution of economic resources;
- the new products and services that are created or that have value added to them (like processing food or making lumber into furniture) within the community;
- the income in the community that is spent and invested locally; and
- the ways in which the products and services are manufactured, cultivated, or otherwise created. This has to be sustainable and environmentally sound or the resource base that the product or service depends on will erode, making it less possible in the future to produce that same product or service.

The capacities that relate to these variables demonstrate the inter-related nature of all the different system capacities. There needs to be a level of relationship, trust, and goodwill — the factors of social well-being. There also must be a measure of equity, which is a function of governance. The environmental/material sector also must be healthy — the natural resource base that is available for new products and for ecosystem functions is a key variable. The ability of the local community to add value to either natural or human resources is somewhat dependent on education but also on the availability of investment and production capacity. The institutional capacity in the community to direct investment and consumption so that it is sustainable is another important factor related to governance. The community has to be able to make collective decisions about the ways it wants to move forward.

## ENVIRONMENTAL CAPACITY

For environmental goods and services, the capacity to meet the demands that are made has been described as the *carrying capacity*, the sustainable level at which a particular natural or physical resource can be used. So, if the recharge rate for a particular aquifer from rainfall and infiltration was two million gallons per day, and people using that water were drawing three million gallons per day out of the water table, then depletion and ecological problems would result. They would be overshooting the carrying capacity of the water source. This is happening in many parts of the world — one example of this is the Ogallala aquifer in the Great Plains of the United States. The aquifer provides water for roughly one-fifth of the irrigated agricultural land in the United States. Current calculations of the water withdrawals show that the aquifer is declining at a rate of 1,082,631 acre-feet per year. The North Plains Groundwater Conservation District estimates that about 3/16 of an inch, or 84,720 acre-feet per year, is recharged into the aquifer. Like any balance sheet, if income is a lot less than the expenditures, bankruptcy is the inevitable result.[3]

The carrying capacity of a given physical resource is related to several key variables. The *stock* of the resource is important; in some natural resources, such as fossil fuels, this is the only variable, because the time it would take to naturally regenerate the fossil fuels is so long. The *regeneration rate* of the resource is also important; in the case of a forest, this might reflect the growth rate of the trees, combined with factors such as the variability of weather, natural death rate, etc. The *migration*, or inflow and outflow of the resource under normal circumstances is a third vital factor; for the fisheries off New England, this is reflected in the migration patterns of the different target species, such as cod and flounder.

If the carrying capacity of a particular community were evaluated, then the stocks, regeneration rates, death rates, migration rates, and other variables for the different resources would be taken into account first and then compared to the demand that was made on these resources by both human and natural communities. When this is done for water systems, the result is known as a water balance for the community. Agricultural systems typically describe this balance in terms of sustainable yields.

Communities in the developed world often far exceed the local carrying capacity. Mathis Wackernagel, the Sustainability Program Director at an organization called Redefining Progress, developed a tool to measure the impact of our consumption patterns on the rest of the world — the tool he called the ecological footprint for an individual or a community.[4] This measures the amount of land that is required to produce the resources that a person or community needs to sustain their lifestyle. Much work has been done to measure ecological footprints, both of actual and ideal situations, and in 1998, the United Nations determined that if you divided the world's population by the biospheric resources available, then the sustainable ecological footprint for each person on the planet would be approximately two hectares, or about five acres.[5]

Contrast this to the ecological footprint of the average American, estimated at 24 acres, the average Canadian at 21.8 acres, and the average Swiss at just over 10.2 acres.[6] Now, it's true that each of these countries has its own biocapacity that is slightly higher than the global average. In the U.S., the biocapacity is estimated at 13 acres, which leaves a deficit of 11 acres per person. In Switzerland, the biocapacity is estimated at 4.5 acres per person, leaving a deficit of 5.7 acres. By contrast, in Canada, the biocapacity is estimated at 35.2 acres, leaving a surplus of 13.4 acres.[7] In the developed world, we have a long way to go to live within the carrying capacity of the planet — the developed world is already straining the limits of this equation.

The systems transactions that erode or enhance the carrying capacity of a community are the exchanges of material goods and services among the different actors — the individuals/households, organizations, and government. If our exchange of goods and services exceeds the natural world's ability to provide them, and to stay healthy with rich and whole biodiversity and ecosystems, then the community system is inherently unsustainable. We can show through calculations that the developed world is taxing the global ecosystem beyond its sustainable yield right now. One urgent task of people interested in a healthy future for the planet is to work in their communities in the developed world to reduce their global impact.

## GOVERNANCE CAPACITY

How is it that some cultures promote overconsumption, where others have so much less than they need for a reasonable lifestyle? This speaks to an unmet global need for equity with respect to resource distribution. The capacity human beings have to share power over resources has long been the subject matter for political scientists, yet there are lessons for sustainability that everyone needs to understand.

How do our governance systems work? What are the transactions that take place in the cycle of relationships that produces the circular flow? How do these transactions contribute to or detract from the capacity of the governance system to function sustainably? The cycle of transactions and resultant capacity is easy to see when we are discussing the economic or ecological capacity of a community. Natural resources like water and food are exchanged in a cycle that determines the carrying capacity of a community. In the economic system, money and labor are the transactions that determine the economic capacity of a community. Transactions of power in the governance system are a little harder to measure because they are not as tangible as money or natural resources. But they are just as real.

Let's look at the governance system. What are some of the power transactions?

1. In a democracy, people vote for the government and give it legitimacy. This effectively conveys power to the government, in a similar way as paying money to someone conveys wealth. People also pay taxes. They abide by laws (or they don't). They receive their professional licenses and other permission to conduct their business. They write letters to their representatives to try and influence legislation. They join

organizations or work for businesses that also try to influence the way government works.

2. Businesses and organizations are regulated by the government and contribute to its success. They support candidates with contributions — in the United States, efforts are being made to restrict the funds that can be raised from corporations for candidates. By funding campaigns, businesses offer power to the government. Businesses and non-profit organizations are also contracted to do work for the government; they lobby legislators, regulators, and executives; they pay taxes. All of these are power transactions.

3. The government issues laws and regulations. It funds infrastructure projects, education, health, welfare, defense, and economic development initiatives. Government shares power by involving citizens and organizations in decision making. It provides courts for conflict resolution. It serves as police. If governmental officials are corrupt, they take bribes and play favorites, or keep all the decision-making power to themselves. All of these activities represent the exercise of power.

What are signs that a community's capacity for meeting people's needs for power are adequate, or that they are inadequate? It helps to go back to the specific needs themselves. We need power for self-determination, for equity, for conflict resolution, and for access. If people do not feel as if they are in control of their own lives, free to make their own choices, how does this express itself in terms of an unmet need? This has been the case in many countries in the world over time — in the former communist countries, the party could control the school you attended, the profession you chose. The result was a disempowered population, who, when the walls came down, had to learn how to make decisions and how to take personal initiative all over again. The monopolization of decision making by the government eroded the capacity of the community as a whole to make decisions, which led to serious consequences when the changes occurred. Some of the younger people in these countries have been good at developing new skills and capacities themselves and are thriving in the brave new world. Others have slipped into a life of depression, poverty, and dead ends.

## The Governance Cycle at Work

An example of the governance cycle:

Citizen A has a conflict with Citizen B over the boundaries on their properties. They engage a law firm and end up going to court. The court makes a decision that resolves the conflict.

If the conflict resolution capacity in the community was being enhanced by this series of transactions, it might look like this:

Citizen A engages a law firm to sue Citizen B. Citizen B hires a law firm for defense. The two firms review the case, recognize that it's a minor matter, and sit the two parties down for a mediation session. The court then is only asked to put its stamp on the final outcome, to make it legal for the change in the deed.

If the capacity of the governance system to resolve conflict was being eroded, it might look like this:

Citizen A hires a law firm. Citizen B hires a law firm. The two firms, interested in winning at all costs (and making some hefty fees in the process), take the maximum adversarial approach. They take up an enormous amount of the court's time, and the citizens' money, filing arguments and counterarguments, etc. The citizens' needs aren't being met — a small disagreement has turned into a major battle; relationships are strained; a lot of money is being spent. The court's needs aren't being met — they have other more important cases to consider. This is capacity erosion, not enhancement.

If non-violent communication and conflict resolution systems are inadequate, there might be a greater level of physical violence or crime. People are more likely to take the law into their own hands if they have no faith in the judicial system. The law may lose credibility; it may be hard to enforce it if people don't believe they can win in court. Again, this is the common situation in many countries of the world where the judicial system is not separate from the political system and the courts are subject to direction from the people or parties in power. To build a sustainable community, it is important to look at the ways in which conflict is resolved and to build capacity for everyone in the community to do this themselves. Even in places where the rule of law is well-established and the courts function well, people have become so dependent on the formal system to resolve their conflict that it is over-burdened and backlogged.

A lack of equity in social and political systems can have stark and horrific results. One way this is most painfully evident is in the continued slave trade around the world. A British organization called Anti-Slavery International now estimates that there are 27 million people who have been forced into slavery, most of whom are women and children.[8] Reports come in from Pakistan, Sudan, Brazil, Mauritania, and The United Arab Emirates. People are forced to work for no wages, forced into the sex trade, working as child domestics and being subjected to physical and sexual abuse; the list of stories is long and heartbreaking.

A lack of equity has effects on society that fall short of widespread slavery and exploitation, although the fundamental orientation that underpins slavery also contributes to other inequitable structures. The roots of inequity are historic; the violence that has led to the oppression people suffer from today is hidden in the power structures that we take for granted. The situation of African-Americans in the United States is one example. The violent enslavement of hundreds of thousands of Africans by the colonists happened centuries ago, yet the echoes of that violence linger today in the prisons, in the inner city slums, and in the dramatic difference between US white and black populations on average in terms of life expectancy, educational achievement, health, and family stability.

Severe inequities are not limited to the United States. The violent oppression of Roma people in Europe has led to a permanent underclass in many countries. Gypsies, vagabonds; there are many names for them. Their persecution began in earnest in the 15th and 16th centuries, when they were said to be enemies of the Christian people. For a long time, it was not illegal to kill a gypsy in some countries in Europe because they were considered less than human. They were taken for slaves in Bulgaria, Hungary, Romania, and the Balkan states, burned at the stake in Austria, or hanged in Germany. During the holocaust, the Roma were rounded up along with the Jews, put to death by the thousands in the death camps; their culture was destroyed. Roma children still beg on the streets of Skopje, Sofia, Bucharest, and other European cities.

Everyone who experiences inequity, from the woman in a 21$^{st}$ century office who earns a fraction of the salary that her male counterpart does, to races of people who are struggling to overcome the legacy of a past full of violence and oppression, knows that equity is a basic human need. The need for equity drives all of the civil rights, human rights, and children's rights movements around the world. It was the basis for Gandhi's liberation of India, of the Europeans' emigration to the New World, for the socialist movements and revolutions of the past, and the liberation movements that continue today in a variety of forms.

In fact, the cycle of transactions that comes with any movement toward more equity can be traced through the three main community actors, to show how the system can either build capacity in this area or erode capacity. Individuals have a need for equity, and if they exist in a community where inequity is severe enough to cause dysfunction, they band together in organizations that put pressure on the government to change the rules. The government can respond by repressing these movements — this is almost always the first reaction — or it can respond by increasing the degree to which power is shared among people equitably. By sharing power, governments and communities increase the capacity for people to meet their needs for equity, self-determination and conflict resolution, and to access the empowering strength of a community. By concentrating power in fewer and fewer hands, the capacity to meet these needs is reduced, and the governance system as a whole in a community will be less and less sustainable.

## SOCIAL CAPACITY

The other critical capacity that a community has is the way it fills the social needs of its members. Our need for social development is reflected in the assets of our education and healthcare systems, the artistic and cultural life of a community, the spiritual practices, the recreational activities; all of the ways in which we care for each other and express our values. The capacity of the social system might be called the *caring capacity* of the community, the aggregate ability of the community to care for its members and to reflect levels of care toward the natural world and the greater global community. The transactions that occur in this sector are sometimes even harder to define than those in the governance sector. Every time a neighbor makes contact with someone else, or a community group volunteers at a nursing home, or someone goes out of their way to befriend someone who is in need of social support, these actions contribute to the overall caring capacity present in the community.

What is it that makes one community a warm and friendly place to live, with good schools, good health services, and neighborhoods where you really feel like you know your neighbors, or makes another community merely a place on a map, where people are disconnected from the city and from each other? Research has shown that communities where there are high levels of volunteerism and many opportunities for people to have contact with non-family members outside of work or school are also more resilient and can pursue projects that require collective action more successfully.

Robert Putnam's account of the decline of social capital in America, in *Bowling Alone: The Collapse and Revival of American Community*,[9] identifies changes in work, family structure, age, suburban life, television, computers, and women's roles as contributing to the reduced social contact we have in the 21st century. Many of these variables boil down to one very simple ingredient needed for social development: time. Caring for other people takes time. Belonging to clubs, associations, fraternities, churches, reading groups, planning commissions, all takes time. In most of the developed world, but especially in the United States, we have less time for leisure activities than ever before, despite all of our efforts to create time-saving conveniences. Of all the industrialized countries, only Japan scores higher than the U.S. for hours worked per year per person, and most other countries have much more paid vacation than we do.

But work isn't everything. The average American spends seven hours per day watching television. Seven hours! That's almost as long as many people spend at work, earning a living. As a culture, we are giving up more and more of the time we have to be with friends and family and using it to entertain ourselves. What need is being filled by this activity? When people's habits start to spiral out of control in an unhealthy direction, it can often mean that our real needs are being filled in ways that reinforce the habitual behavior, without actually satisfying the need in the best way possible.

The television allows people to feel as if they are relating with others vicariously. Watching people relate to each other on television evokes many of the same emotions as really relating to other people. People who watch a lot of television often feel like they have a real relationship with the characters on the screen. The needs we have for relationships with other people, for a sense of belonging, for a sense of community, are all being artificially met through television: a powerful proxy that erodes our capacity to have real relationships. social skills decline when they are not practiced. The violent confrontations that are epidemic on TV serve as false and dangerous models for real life.

The American propensity for over consumption is another indicator of a social need that is being filled in an unhealthy way. What we consume is one way we have of expressing ourselves to others. The new dress, the car, the boat, all of these speak to the ways in which we define ourselves and convey who we are to other people. Before the consumer culture took over, people did this in other ways — through music, art, and their work, when that was fulfilling. Today, our need for self-expression gets filled not by being creative but by consuming things. We buy things to replace unmet needs for creativity, for security, for spirituality, for all the social assets that community life used to provide before the modern era allowed people to substitute TV and video for real social contact.

We are spending our time on activities that erode our capacity to care for each other, rather than enhance it. The more time we spend shopping and watching television, the less time we have to join the kinds of organizations and associations that really might give us the feeling that we belong to a community. Once these organizations start to disappear because of a lack of interest, which is happening already according to Putnam, then the capacity the community has to care for its members also declines.

This trend can be seen as a negative cycle — where the overall capacity of the community is being eroded by the cycle of transactions people initiate to meet their needs. Individuals have needs for relationships with other people, and if they satisfy these needs by watching television, then the capacity for action that meets these needs will decline within the community's organizations and government. If this declines, then these organizations are less able to meet the future needs of individuals, which will reinforce the disengagement and lack of involvement — a vicious cycle.

Figure 3.3 A Vicious Social Cycle

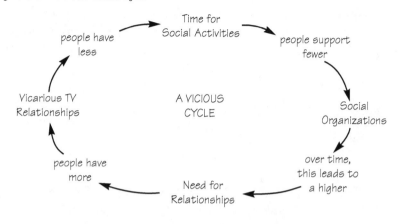

## NEEDS, CYCLES, AND SYSTEMS

The fact that the needs satisfaction processes work in a cyclical fashion supports the premise that communities are fundamentally *systems* that are designed to meet our needs. As systems, they have particular characteristics that we can use to describe and evaluate. While systems dynamics typically relate to material or economic resources that are relatively easy to quantify, the community systems that meet our needs for power and for social development also exhibit the characteristics of a system, even though they might be less conducive to quantifiable measurements.

Communities have capacities for meeting human needs, and the continuous, cyclical processes that satisfy these needs can either erode or enhance this capacity over time. If the community capacity is being enhanced, then it will be easier to meet the same needs for future community members. If it is being eroded, then this will be more difficult.

These positive or negative cycles within systems that meet particular needs also have an impact on the way other needs are met. If a community has strong, cohesive neighborhoods, a good education system, active civic clubs and religious organizations, a vibrant cultural life, and recreational facilities and programs, wouldn't the probability be much higher that people will be active in the governance system as well? If more people are actively involved in governance, wouldn't the decisions tend toward being more equitable? Wouldn't this in turn reinforce the degree to which people are empowered to meet their material and economic needs? Likewise, if the environment in a community is healthy, wouldn't it be more possible to meet material and economic needs, which in turn would also reinforce the democratic process and the degree to which people will feel able to participate in the social life of a community? Figure 2.3 (page 43) illustrates this interrelated dynamic, where social well-being affects all the different community systems, and environmental integrity is both the result and the impetus for even higher levels of community health.

It is vital to understand that for communities to realize their goals of being environmentally healthy, economically sound, socially cohesive, and democratic, *all* of these systems have to be addressed in tandem. They are all linked, and if one set of needs is satisfied without thinking of its impacts on all the other systems, then the result could erode the community's other capacities over the long run.

## USING CRITERIA TO ENHANCE CAPACITY

The following criteria can be used to help communities think through all of the inter-sector ramifications of the activities they propose to address their needs. If people try to answer these questions when activities are proposed and develop strategies to enhance the capacity in all of these areas with each step forward, they will minimize the likelihood of inadvertently eroding capacity in another area. To use the criteria, any activity proposed would have to demonstrate how it:

- creates or supports systems in a community that care for people in some way
- strengthens civic participation in decisions that affect the community
- distributes benefits and burdens equitably
- increases the value and vitality of human and natural systems — locally and wherever the activity has an impact
- conserves and renews human, natural, and financial resources

The main lesson learned from introducing sustainability criteria to a municipal decision-making process is that community capacity is built through participation, through the development of shared values, and through the reinforcement of relationships of trust, mutual care, and concern throughout the community. As people are empowered, as they develop a new respect for each other, the ability to engage in collective action will improve, to everyone's benefit.

For example, a municipality might be considering the development of a new industrial park to strengthen the local employment and tax base. In this hypothetical case, the criteria for reviewing the development's impact on the environment are already in place through the local zoning and land use regulations, so there is already a lot of information available on how the environmental impacts of the industrial park will be mitigated. This level of review would ensure that local capacity would not be degraded. Using the criteria above, however, the developer would have to show how they will improve the local environment.

To meet the first criterion, the municipality could consider whether the daycare and eldercare facilities available need to be supported or expanded with the industrial park. To meet the second criterion, public forums could be held to get the entire community involved in deliberating the decision and in reviewing both the need for the park and its impacts. If there are negative impacts from the park, are there ways for the whole community to share those impacts, rather than dumping them on the low-income area in town; this would address the third criterion. To meet the fourth and fifth criteria, the park might be built to make products that also have a close relationship to the resources available locally — are there raw materials that are being shipped out of town without further processing? Are there local needs for goods and services that aren't being met? How do the production facilities plan to obtain trained labor for their facilities? Where do the by-products of the facilities go for disposal — are there any local uses for things that the new park might consider waste? Finally, what are the steps that the industry in the park has taken to conserve resources — is it energy efficient, does it use recycled resources? There are several possible answers to these questions.

Environmental protection and resource conservation can produce good jobs — many of the activities that are necessary to mitigate environmental problems are labor-intensive. By exploring ways that the creation of new jobs can support the environmental, governance, and social systems that are already in place, communities can find sustainable solutions to many of the issues they are facing.

## CONCLUSION

Community capacity reflects how effectively a community has developed assets that meet its members' social, governance, economic, and material needs. Community assets, in turn, are eroded or enhanced by the cycle of interactions that define the ways in which the community uses them. The cycle of interactions forms a system that exhibits all of the characteristics of systems dynamics, which is described in the next chapter in more detail. It is important to take all of the different sectors of the community into consideration when strategies are proposed for changes or improvements, so that action in one area won't inadvertently lead to deterioration in another. Creating a sustainable community means working towards wholeness, where all of the members' different needs are met.

CHAPTER 4

# Systems Thinking for Communities

SYSTEMS THINKING HAS ITS ROOTS IN SYSTEMS DYNAMICS, a process invented in 1956 at MIT by Jay Forrester who was looking for a better way to test new ideas about social systems. By building computer models that simulated how all the elements of social systems interacted with each other, Forrester challenged the dominant analytical methodology where social problems were identified in isolation, and solutions were crafted for specific, narrowly focused objectives. He recognized the need to understand the relationships between disparate elements of the larger social system and found that the connections and relationships are more important than the elements themselves. Systems thinking works by expanding the view of social and environmental issues to include the relationships between different problems and to look for cyclical patterns of behavior over time. By recognizing the cyclical processes at work within systems, we can better evaluate whether they are tending to be *sustainable*, where the local capacity to meet future needs is being enhanced, or *unsustainable*, where the local capacity to meet future needs is eroding.

This chapter introduces the language of systems thinking and systems dynamics as it relates specifically to community systems. The conceptual tools of systems theory are invaluable for understanding the ways in which any particular community system is enhancing or eroding its local capacity to meet its future needs. Community members want to understand what must change when problems get worse or when, despite their best efforts, the problems don't go away. Systems thinking represents a far more effective way to think about complex issues.

- Systems are *alive*

  Community systems exhibit characteristics of living beings: They are alive! Being alive means evolving and growing, having a sense of identity, and developing goals and the capacity for autonomous action. This includes having living parts and an ability to grow or create the system's own processes. A community is capable of regeneration, and a community maintains its existence over time through mutual interactions with and among its members.

- Systems are *dynamic*

  Systems change. Over time systems exhibit patterns of behavior. They may form internal processes that keep the system from fully interacting with all of the elements in the environment, a characteristic of closed systems. Closed systems are like machines, created to stay in balance, with amazing capacities to resist change. Open systems, on the other hand, have the capacity to flex and respond to changes in the environment by assimilating new elements or by absorbing such changes in a way that keeps their systems operational. The process of staying in balance, achieving equilibrium so that the internal and external forces at work on a system are absorbed without disruption and dysfunction, is called *homeostasis*.

- Systems are *extraordinary*

  A system always becomes greater than the sum of its parts. One of the best ways to illustrate this is to think of an airplane. If each of its parts were somehow placed at 30,000 feet, the parts would fall to earth immediately. When all the parts are working together, however, the airplane can fly. This characteristic of systems, all the parts working together to do things that the individual parts cannot, is called *emergence*.

## THE LANGUAGE OF SYSTEMS

One of the objectives of describing systems is to discern patterns of behavior, their underlying causes, and the forces at work to keep the system in a state of change, or in a state of equilibrium. Language and mapping processes developed by systems thinkers can visually and graphically illustrate the different components of a community system working dynamically together. Some important concepts of systems thinking one can use to understand and describe even simple systems are links, feedback loops, stocks, flows, and archetypes. These concepts, the language of systems, are described in more detail in the following sections.

## Cause, Effect, and Feedback Loops

The logic of cause and effect is one of the fundamental relationships described by the language of systems. When one element in a system influences another element, an arrow is drawn that links the elements in a cause-effect relationship. This arrow, or link, is known as feedback.

Figure 4.1 Simple Causality

In maps or drawings of these cause-effect relationships, elements form intricate webs of causes and effects, influencing other elements in the system. The study of systems dynamics has discovered, over many years of research, that cause and effect do not necessarily form a linear process but can often be a cyclical process. This means that for every element extending influence in a system, the cycle will eventually return to the original cause.

Figure 4.2 Cyclical Causality

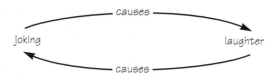

This has led people involved in systems thinking and systems dynamics to rethink cause and effect completely, calling it, more accurately, *causeffect*. The illustration above demonstrates the most basic type of system, a closed loop system. In other words, the feedback in the system forms a closed loop, so that the original cause becomes the effect.

The loop we describe in a system is a loop of feedback — a change or a signal that has an effect on other parts of the system. For example, if I push a domino over within a circle of dominoes stacked next to each other, the causeffect, or feedback, of one element falling on another will eventually cycle around the loop of dominos to strike the original domino. The result is a *feedback* loop where every element is both the cause of effects in other elements and is affected *by* other elements.

## Feedback in the Same and Opposite Directions

It is important to recognize that feedback in a system doesn't always take the same form as the original influence. If an influence on a system causes another part of the system to change in the same direction, then this is illustrated with a + sign. For example, if an increase in A causes an increase in B, then this would be drawn as a + feedback loop, as shown in Figure 4.3:

Figure 4.3 Positive Feedback

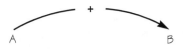

So, if point A represented the first domino and B represented the second domino, then the push given to the first domino would cause the second domino to fall over in the same direction. This is known as a *positive feedback loop*.

If the change that is occurring in the system goes in the *opposite* direction as a result of a specific action, then this is drawn as a 0 sign. For example, if I sit on one side of a teeter-totter, then the other side will rise *up* while my side goes *down*. This is known as a *negative feedback loop*. Newton was the first to capture this aspect of systems dynamics when he posited his third principle of motion, which said that "for every action there is an equal and opposite reaction."[1]

Figure 4.4 Negative Feedback

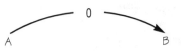

Feedback loops are the simplest ways to illustrate the dynamics of a system. This chapter will focus on causal diagrams that use feedback loops. When describing complex systems, if you only use causal loop diagrams, the diagrams won't be completely accurate, although it will still serve as a good way to convey the main dynamics at work.

## Stocks and Flows

Two other key components of systems that are represented in the feedback loops are stocks and flows. The simplest illustration of a stock is to think of filling a bathtub with water. As the inflow fills the bathtub, the water in it can be described as the bathtub's *stock* of water. At any time, the bathtub will have more or less water in it depending on what flows in and what flows out. The inflow into the bathtub is the water through the faucet, and the outflow is the water through the drain.

This can be illustrated with arrows, valves, and boxes in systems diagrams. Figure 4.5 illustrates this example.

Figure 4.5 Bathtub Stocks and Flows

As the stock of water in the bathtub increases, your interest in keeping the faucet on will decrease, if you are trying to fill the tub for a bath. The negative feedback loop between the water *stock* in the bathtub and the water *flow* through the faucet in this instance is illustrated in Figure 4.6.

Figure 4.6 Bathtub Feedback Loop

The feedback loops pictured in Figures 4.5 and 4.6 illustrate the relationships between stocks and flows. If we were to develop a computer simulation model of community systems, developing accurate estimates of stock levels and flow rates would be important. For our purposes, however, we will focus on what are known as causal loop diagrams, which don't encompass detailed information about stocks and flows. Mapping the elements of a system in more general causal loop diagrams gives policy makers the broad idea about how systems work, and the causal loop diagrams are simple and easy for a layperson to understand.

## Reinforcing Feedback Loops

The most simple pattern in systems is the *reinforcing feedback loop* where each action reinforces the movement of the system in the same direction. So, if the system is changing in a positive direction, reinforcing feedback will amplify its change in a positive direction. If it is changing in a negative direction, reinforcing feedback will amplify its change in a negative direction. Reinforcing feedback loops that occur in the world often behave as exponential functions over time, such as compound interest or population growth. If a phenomenon is observed to be expanding at an increasing rate, you can be reasonably sure that a reinforcing feedback loop would describe it. Population growth for any species in an ecological setting where there are no natural predators is a good example of this. Figure 4.7 illustrates the reinforcing feedback loop for population growth.

Figure 4.7 The Reinforcing Population Loop

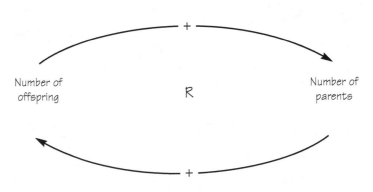

Number of
offspring

R

Number of
parents

Graphed over time, the reinforcing feedback loop is an exponential function as shown in Figure 4.8.

Figure 4.8 Population: Exponential Growth Curve

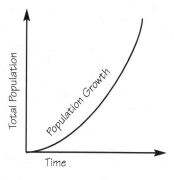

## Reverse Reinforcement

Something may happen to make a positive reinforcing loop turn into its opposite, a negative reinforcing loop. For example, if an organization's members perceive it to be doing well, then the goodwill and high morale that comes from that perception can make them perform even better. But if something happens that changes their perception to a negative one, then low morale can cause the members to perform worse and worse, in a negative reinforcing cycle. Figure 4.9 shows how this reversal of fortune might look over time.

Figure 4.9 Reverse Reinforcement

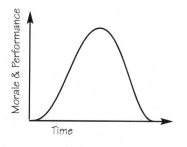

## Balancing Loops

The second type of simple systems pattern is a *balancing loop*. A balancing loop seeks equilibrium so that the action within the system will work to bring the system to either its original or its target condition.

If there is an increase in A that increases B, then the increase in B will cause A to decrease. It is depicted in Figure 4.10.

Figure 4.10 Balancing Feedback Loop

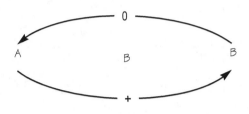

One example of a simple balancing loop is the way our bodies regulate internal temperature. If we get too hot, we perspire to cool off. If we get too cold, we try to warm up. The effect of this balancing process over time is illustrated in Figure 4.11.

Figure 4.11 Balancing Feedback Curve

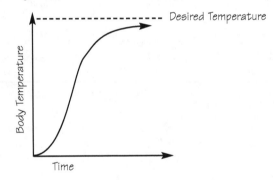

## Delay

Systems are harder to understand as they get more complex because the effects within a system don't always happen immediately; they are often delayed. A delay in a causal relationship can invite actions to be taken that are counterproductive or that overshoot the mark. Delays in the system are shown in Figure 4.12.

Figure 4.12 Feedback Delay

 OR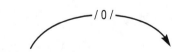

Delays that occur in the time between a specific action and its consequences are common in our everyday world. People who are trying to lose weight are very familiar with the delay between the time they eat something and the time that they aren't hungry anymore. In a community system, the delay between the time new building permits are issued and the impact the new houses have on the school population, or other public infrastructure, can be significant. Many communities grow so fast that the demands on new roads and schools quickly exceed the capacity for which they were designed. As we learn how systems work, the patterns discussed above will be easier to recognize. In fact, these patterns are so common in systems they are called *archetypes*, after the Jungian idea that a unitary pattern of reality lies at the foundation of all matter and psyche.[2]

## SYSTEM ARCHETYPES

System archetypes are patterns of energy, or process structures, that recur in many systems. For example, archetypes appear in systems dynamics as feedback loops, reinforcing loops, balancing loops, reverse reinforcement loops, and delays. People who have studied systems dynamics for many years have identified a set of archetypes that are repeated in a wide variety of systems. Archetypes have become useful in identifying the common dynamics of systems and developing strategies to overcome dysfunctional patterns of behavior.

Archetypes usually consist of combinations of reinforcing loops and balancing loops. These basic building blocks of systems combine in a variety of ways to produce common patterns of behavior that are applicable to many types of human and natural systems. Archetypes offer insight into the ways in which we can work with complex issues to identify points in the system where we can act. This chapter further discusses examples of archetypes in relation to particular issues that many communities face, including what are known as the "shifting the burden" and the "limits to growth" archetypes, as well as some simple reinforcing cycles.

## Traffic Congestion and Sprawl

A common issue in many municipalities where we can easily see an archetype working is that of growth and sprawl. One of the leading indicators of sprawl is increased traffic congestion, caused by people living far from where they work and shop. The typical response to this issue, widening the roads, deals only with the symptoms of sprawl. By addressing only the symptoms, the proposed solution can make the underlying problem worse. How does this happen? The situation is illustrated by the *shifting the burden* archetype shown in Figure 4.13. As illustrated, the symptomatic solution (building new roads) causes the inadvertent side effect of increasing the development potential, which in turn serves to worsen the underlying issue (a lack of growth control). Attention to the symptomatic solution causes a delay in the implementation of the real solution (growth management), *and* because increasing the development potential makes growth management more difficult, the original solution to the problem ends up making things worse.

Figure 4.13 Shifting the Burden: Traffic and Sprawl

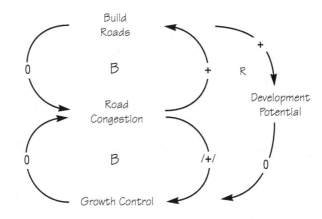

To follow the diagram through its causal loops, start with the identified problem — road congestion. The strategy to build more roads is an attempt to have *less* road congestion by building *more* roads, in effect creating a balancing feedback loop — *more* roads, *less* road congestion. Unfortunately, *more* roads lead to the unanticipated side effect of *more* development potential, which leads to *less* growth control, as long as the development potential remains unchecked by regulations. *Less* growth control means *more* road congestion. So, the dominant feedback loop in the system is a reinforcing loop — *more* road congestion leading back around to *more* road congestion. The delay feedback loop between road congestion and growth control reflects the delay that implementing the symptomatic solution (more roads) causes for the real solution (growth control).

## Reinforcing Feedback Loops in Education

One of the simplest system archetypes is the reinforcing feedback loop in which every action produces another action that moves the system in the same direction. So, a situation can either get worse and worse, or better and better, depending on the circumstances. When a system is getting worse and worse, it's known as a *vicious cycle*. When it's getting better and better, it's known as a *virtuous cycle*.

Figures 4.14 and 4.15 show reinforcing cycles at work, which in turn create conditions that are likely either to support the continuation of a high quality education system or to erode an educational system that already suffers from inadequacies. In the second diagram, the variables are the same as in the first, but the reinforcing elements of the system are moving the system toward an end result that is the opposite of the first example. This shows how a cyclical pattern of interactions can either erode or enhance our ability to meet needs in the future, the hallmark of sustainability.

Figure 4.14 The Virtuous Cycle: Intelligence Pays

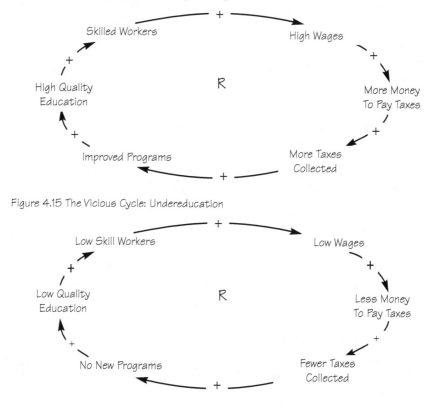

Figure 4.15 The Vicious Cycle: Undereducation

## Economic Cycles: The Multiplier Effect

Another reinforcing cycle found in many communities is related to the economic multiplier effect. The more the wages, profits, and sales from a firm stay in the community, the more possibilities there are for increased economic development in the community. If, on the other hand, the wages, profits, and sales are shipped out of a community to distant owners, there is less local capital available for new enterprises.

As shown in Figure 4.16, the sales, profit, and higher management salaries from locally owned companies stay in the community. The local financial institutions are therefore able to make more loans to other businesses, which in turn leads to more economic activity. The fact that there is more money in the local economy also makes it easier for the businesses to sell products locally.

In every community there are many types of business ownership including locally owned, and national or regional chains. Systems analysis by community leaders when considering which they might want to attract will reveal the options that will sustain or improve the quality of life for the community and will help them make better decisions.

Figure 4.16 High Local Multiplier

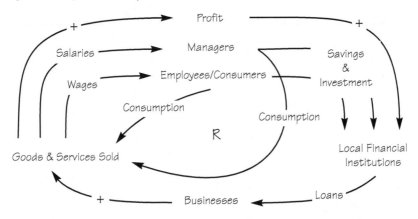

Figure 4.17 illustrates the causal loop where the salaries and profits from many of the businesses do not stay in the community. The dominant archetype is still a reinforcing loop, but the overall multiplier effect will be lower. The important concept to understand is that the local economy does work as a system and, as a reinforcing system, it can experience continuous improvement over time but, like any

reinforcing cycle, if things start to get worse, it is likely that the local economy will get worse and worse instead of better and better. Both scenarios demonstrate a reinforcing loop, but the benefit to the community from companies that don't recycle their economic resources locally are much less than from those companies, typically locally owned and operated, that do.

Figure 4.17 Low Local Multiplier

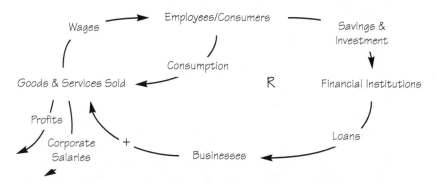

## Balancing Cycles: Growth and Development Goals

A very simple archetype is the balancing cycle in which action produces another action in the opposite direction. Short-term increases or decreases in the system may occur, but over time balancing cycles tend to achieve equilibrium.

A city's attitude toward new growth is an example of a balancing cycle at work. As the impacts of growth increase, the support for new development decreases. As support decreases, the impacts of growth also decrease, as a result of the increased difficulty of obtaining permits, due to local opposition.

Another systems archetype, *limits to growth*, illustrates the importance of growth management. In this case, the natural resource base

Figure 4.18 Growth Support Cycle

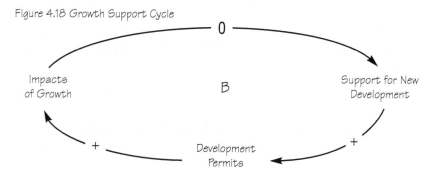

eventually produces a slowing effect on the economy, which otherwise tends to grow at an increasing rate, for all the reasons described in the section on the local multiplier effect.

It is helpful to look at both sides of the feedback loop in order to understand the limits to growth archetype. On the reinforcing cycle

Figure 4.19 Limits to Growth and the Economic Cycle

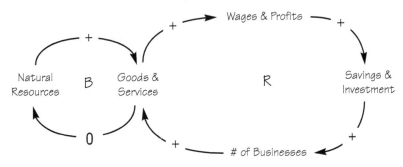

side (R), *more* goods and services sold means *more* wages and profits, which in turn means *more* savings and investment. This makes *more* money available for business loans, which can in turn produce *more* goods and services. On the balancing cycle side (B), the *more* goods and services that are made, the *fewer* resources are available. The *fewer* resources that are available, the *fewer* goods and services can be made. The B side of the archetype exerts a limiting effect on the R side. Over time, this limiting function can look a lot like the business cycle as shown in Figure 4.20.

The closer that an economic system is in sync with the renewal rate of the natural resource base, the more sustainable it is, and the

Figure 4.20 Limits to Growth Curve

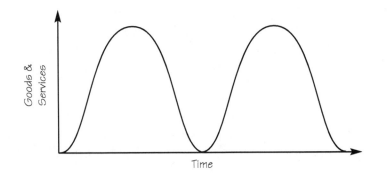

cyclical trend, shown in Figure 4.20, will have lower peaks and shallower valleys.

## Governance Cycles

The processes that drive the governance in a community also behave like a dynamic system. Figure 4.21 and 4.22 illustrate how governance cycles can exhibit the characteristics of a reinforcing feedback loop, both in a positive and a negative direction.

Decisions, after all, require effort and work. They are a product of deliberation, information gathering, information processing, and judgment. In Figure 4.21, a few people monopolize the decision-making

Figure 4.21 A Vicious Governance Cycle

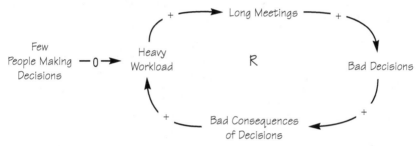

process, and the heavy workload that results causes bad decisions to be made, which increases the workload — a vicious cycle. Experience shows that if it is structured correctly, a system that encourages more people to be involved can be a better decision-making process, as shown in Figure 4.22.

Figure 4.22 A Virtuous Governance Cycle

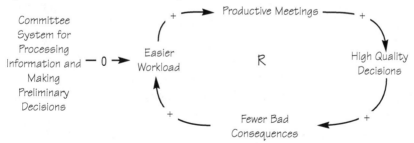

## EQUILIBRIUM AND ENTROPY

Healthy systems exhibit dynamics that enhance the capacity of the system to continue to meet its future needs. In nature, there are several examples of this type of system: the water transpiration– precipita-tion–percolation cycle is one in which the waters of the planet continually replenish the land areas with clean water. The atmo-spheric system, where plants use by-products like $CO_2$ to produce food and then exhale oxygen, is another cyclical process that con-tributes to global health. These two cycles, in their natural states, can be compared to the body's circulation system — the blood in our system flows cyclically, with processes and organs in place that con-tinually purify it and keep it ready for use by our muscles, brains, and other body parts. The processes for human and animal metabolism, internal combustion, and infrastructure operation and maintenance can be seen as analogous to the digestive system — waste is produced that is not particularly useful, and this waste requires assimilative capacity in the biosphere to ensure that it is not harmful.

The biosphere is full of cyclical systems at work. In addition to the water, air, and metabolic systems described above, there is the rock cycle, which slowly cycles rock through dissolution, metabolism through the plants in the ocean, forming limestone and continuing to recycle through subduction, which produces more rock that comes to the surface in volcanoes and the process of orogeny, mountain forma-tion. Volcanoes pump $CO_2$ into the atmosphere while the life in the oceans remove carbon from the air and water to produce their shells and other life forms.

Nature is not a perpetual motion machine. In addition to the pro-cesses that work to enhance future capacity, or to at least maintain a state of equilibrium, or homeostasis, there are also processes at work that reduce the productivity and vitality of the living systems. The sec-ond law of thermodynamics describes the tendency of all matter toward entropy — where in closed systems, disorder increases and matter will change in ways that make it increasingly useless for humans. As much as we might recycle bottles and cans, or change the by-products of some manufacturing processes into the raw materials for others, there are some by-products that would require more energy than they produce to reuse them: ash, rust, dust, and the dissi-pated heat in the oceans and atmosphere, to name a few.

Earth is an amazing life system, very complex and miraculously designed to support the life on the planet. It's not surprising, there-fore, that the systems that humanity has developed over the millennia to meet our needs also mimic the cyclical, homeostatic, entropic, complex, and chaotic systems of Earth.

Understanding equilibrium within a closed system is relevant to the study of human social systems, especially for people with an interest in changing them, because one of the defining characteristics of this type of system is that it is very resistant to change. Efforts to change the way it works, without a more complete understanding of all the different dynamics, can have unanticipated side effects, including the worst case scenario where efforts to improve something actually results in making the problem worse. The literature on systems thinking is full of such examples. It's as if Murphy's Law were the governing principle for social change. Here are a few examples of unanticipated consequences:

1. In the early 1990s, President Clinton became concerned about the increasing numbers of refugees attempting to sail from Cuba to Florida. He increased the number of U.S. Coast Guard patrols and moved them closer to Cuba, hoping to scare off would-be sailors with their presence. Few Cubans owned craft large and stable enough to sail the 90 miles to freedom, but they knew that the patrol boats would intercept them and take them to Florida where they would be placed in a refugee camp for disposition. As a result, the numbers of attempts increased from a few hundred to several thousand.

2. In England, the outbreak of mad cow disease during the mid-1990s led many farmers to sell their livestock before the cows demonstrated symptoms. In the cattle food production business, cattle parts are often ground up, dried, and added to livestock feed for protein. Unfortunately, the disease was passed on in the cattle protein, spreading widely to previously uninfected cattle.

3. A community mental health center had been losing staff due to low morale and experienced lower billable contact hours with clients. In an effort to reorganize, the administrators empowered the treatment staff and involved them in administrative decision making. As a result, they had even less time for clients, staff/administration conflict increased, and more staff left due to the unexpected pressures of seeing the larger picture of the problem.

4. The high costs of maintaining welfare recipients led the State of Wisconsin to revise its service policy, now known as the Welfare to Work or Wisconsin Works project, started in 1997. It was hugely successful, initially, with a client load of 100,000 families in 1987 reduced to 9,000! Yet the hidden costs began to emerge. Mothers who were unwilling, or unable, to work lost their benefits. Many were evicted, and slum landlords lost their tenants and incomes, daycare centers lost their customers, and homeless shelters ran out of beds. Some of the disenfranchised turned to crime, such as stealing, selling drugs, and prostitution — contracting diseases or ending up in jail. The children of these unfortunate women were most often sent to grandmothers for care. This in turn resulted in excessive financial strain on older single women on a fixed income, requiring transfers of money for their added support.[3]

## EMERGENCE, COHERENCE, CHAOS, AND COMPLEXITY

This chapter has shown that systems are extraordinary precisely because the whole is always greater than the sum of its parts, and the whole forms a coherent entity that can exhibit behavior that is very different from the parts would lead you to expect. These two characteristics — emergence and coherence — make systems difficult to pin down. There are other reasons that systems defy definitions that would capture them in reductionist logic and analysis. Wholes are the units of systems, not parts. Any attempt to break them down into parts with nice, neat, linear cause-and-effect relationships will be doomed to be ultimately inaccurate as long as it doesn't capture the emergent, coherent, complex, and chaotic characteristics of real systems. The old science of prediction and control is eclipsed by these properties of systems — dynamic behavior can be extremely sensitive. Very small changes in the conditions of the system can lead to dramatically different results, in much the same way as a minor change in a ship's bearing at the beginning of a journey can lead it to uncharted waters. We require new ways of acting, new ways of knowing, and more intuitive ways of sensing the dynamics in a given situation so that action taken is fully cognizant of the cyclical and potentially chaotic behavior that changes or deliberate strategies might elicit.

## DIRECTING INTENTIONAL CHANGE
## IN COMPLEX SYSTEMS

Changing a complex system, or managing innovation in the context of a complex system, requires an orientation toward the system as a whole, rather than an analytical approach that tries to solve individual problems. Incomplete understanding of the system's dynamic nature can often result in the innovation having the exact opposite effect than what was intended and in the creation of new problems, even as the old one was solved. The *problem* just changes form as the *solution* is passed along as the next problem. In this way, as long as we cling to the problem solving model, we will never run out of problems and the need for solutions.

Scientists studying the natural world have gained insights into the behavior of complex biological systems; insights that offer clues of how our complex human social systems might change. For example, when complex systems are about to undergo phase transitions, or sudden shifts in system properties, small external signals can dramatically change the system as a whole. Phase changes are critical moments in a system's life, and while this is happening, they teeter on the edge of chaos, held together only by self-organizing dynamics that differ greatly from the more regular oscillations of a more stable state. Further research into systems dynamics has indicated that for complex human systems, this critical state of being on the edge of chaos is perhaps a relatively normal condition.

## THE SELF-ORGANIZING PROPERTY

Perhaps one of the most pertinent attributes that complex human systems share with complex natural systems is their self-organizing property. Human systems did not emerge as a result of carefully planned design and implementation. On the contrary, they emerged out of chaos, and even though some level of intentional organization did have a role to play in the formation of many institutions, spontaneity was still an important element. Another important characteristic of self-organization is what the systems scientists call *attractors*, the focal points that create and maintain stable patterns within the system. The system adapts to its circumstances in ways that were unplanned and often apparently unconscious. The self-organizing property of systems simply must play a role in the change process.

For example, there are patterns of organizational behavior that illustrate the ways in which chaos and complexity can spontaneously evolve into some semblance of order. Municipal governments are often faced with chaotic experiences: a natural disaster that incapacitates a large percentage of the emergency response personnel and facilities; conflict that escalates into violence and man-made disasters that require a complex network of services and facilities to help stabilize the affected people. Without the leadership (attractors) of people who rise to the occasion and the almost intuitive, almost tribal cohesiveness of others involved, most of these situations would devolve into more chaos and more hardship. Yet for the most part, the stories you hear after it's all over are those of heroism, of teamwork, and of people who were energized and uplifted by the ways in which others sacrificed their own interests for those of complete strangers. When emergence occurs — when teamwork pays off, when people work together to do something they can't do as individuals — it is often an invigorating experience. People transcend their individuality to a higher form of being, and when they're in the midst of it, they love it.

## SOME LESSONS FOR COMMUNITIES FROM SYSTEMS THINKING

In this chapter, several points have been made about how community systems work, and the lessons that communities can take from the discipline of systems dynamics. Systems exhibit patterns of behavior that provide us with clues about where intervention might be effective. The cyclical and homeostatic nature of systems can cause escalating effects and make systems resistant to change.

But the most important insight is that in community systems, the whole is greater than the sum of its parts. The critical lesson learned from an understanding of systems dynamics is that isolated problem solving likely leads to unintended consequences. Yet isolated problem solving has been the dominant practice for public policy and even for some sustainable development methodologies. Based on a more complete understanding of the whole community system, new approaches integrating the policies and activities being considered for implementation are more likely to succeed.

Three other lessons learned for better understanding of intentional change in complex systems are:

1. Order will emerge in an evolutionary, self-organizing manner; it cannot be imposed through hierarchical control or by external force.

2. It is possible to increase the possibilities for positive change by maximizing the freedom of the actors within the system.

3. Pursuing multiple goals and having the freedom to make mistakes are important elements of the change process in complex systems.

These lessons have important implications for community level strategies to promote sustainable development and will be explored in the chapters that follow.

## CHAPTER 5

# Celebrating Assets and Creating a Vision

If you are looking at community systems with an eye toward making them more sustainable, where do you begin? In the last chapter, we explored the difficulty of directing intentional change in complex systems, and we said that it's important to try and understand the system as a whole, rather than to focus on specific problems and propose isolated solutions. A community's existing policies and processes, the habits people adopt, and the tendency for complex systems to resist change make it difficult to take action. To learn from the lessons of system dynamics, it is important to create an environment where spontaneous change is possible, where the whole system undergoes a metamorphosis, a phase change, and operates at a higher level, a new kind of normal.

This sounds good on paper, but it is a lot harder to achieve in the real world. Some of what is required can be planned, and some of the success will depend on variables that are hard to manipulate using the central planning, command and control models that government planners know and love. It is important to involve as many people as possible, which in itself can add an element of uncertainty. If their opinions and needs are taken seriously, the outcome will be impossible to predict at the outset, so it's also important to go into the process with an open mind and an empty agenda, at least in terms of specific policy and program outcomes.

So, where do you begin? One starting place is to involve all the community leadership in learning how systems work. The training can give the leaders new insights about how their community systems

86

function. As people learn system thinking, they will be applying it to their community and to their everyday life. Their perceptions will change; they will never be able to return to seeing things in isolation. With new conceptual tools, the leaders can perceive the information they receive about issues in the community in a new way. The new information and new perception will be essential for planning and in making decisions.

Of course, this might not be possible. You may be outside the city administration and unable to encourage them to go through a new training program. There are still ways in which you can take the lessons of system dynamics and put them to work in your community, to help everyone form a vision that can galvanize sustainable change. One step to take is to figure out a way to get the community to celebrate the good things that are happening, to be a little more self-conscious of your community assets.

To do this, take a look at all the ways in which your community meets the real human needs you have. Find examples of things that stand out as real positive contributions to the community. Maybe you have a downtown that has a lot of locally owned businesses, if so, celebrate homegrown entrepreneurs. Do you have farms that provide food for the local population? Celebrate homegrown produce. The local schools and colleges probably have some success stories that they would like to share. Celebrate the learning the community does together. Conduct a survey of all the people in town, to find out what makes your part of the world feel like home. What parts of your community would they like to pass on to their children and grandchildren? Celebrate the results of the survey. If you start the process of making your community more sustainable by emphasizing the positive, rather than focusing on what can be defined as problems, you'll attract people to the effort and you'll build a base of information about the community that can help identify strategies for improvement.

Once the community celebrates the assets they have, and communicates what they have learned to others, the next challenge will be to articulate a shared community vision. With the whole community involved, the visioning process will motivate people to work together to accomplish their shared goals. People are generally much more willing to support the ideas and initiatives they have helped create.

## LEARNING AS COMMUNITY

In the first three chapters, we discussed the community systems we have that have evolved over time to meet our needs as human beings. For the purposes of understanding how communities can change to be more sustainable, the community is defined as a system that is in place to meet our needs. At the level of municipal action planning, the first step in trying to develop a framework for effective sustainable development is to try to understand how all the needs in the community are met. This approach — as contrasted to the types of community planning that focus on solving problems — starts the community development process with an evaluation of all of its assets, rather than beginning with its problems.

If a doctor was going to evaluate a patient to see if there were things he could recommend to make the patient live longer, the doctor would start by doing an assessment of the patient's health, the vital signs, and the habits and practices used to meet such needs as food and support systems. That is a fundamentally different orientation than focusing on a symptom or trying to cure a disease. When communities focus on assets, rather than problems, new creative possibilities emerge for fulfilling community needs.

A community is for all the people. It is a challenge to any leader to invite all citizens to participate and then to listen to them. Often they are filled with complaints and anger about something that didn't work. Before the visioning process begins, there must be an opportunity to clear the air of the negativity and resentments. It's important to bring negative reactions, old complaints, etc. to the light rather than letting them fester — or the process could be undermined from the start. People must be heard and they must know they have been heard. Many complaints are simply an expressed need for someone to care; if complaints are ignored or suppressed, it can cause needless pain, anger, and alienation. Caring for others is one of the key functions of the community system, so responding to these calls for care with empathetic, reflective listening is an important way to overcome the negative experiences people have had in the past.

Another challenge for introducing positive change into complex systems is to engage all the actors in the building of trust. We build trust by being true to our word, by giving the best service we are able to at the time, and by believing and trusting that everyone else is doing the best they can. The building of trust takes time and contact and experience. We know trust can be broken in a second when violated, so it is important to take the time necessary to foster trust in any planning process.

Free and empowered people self-organize into new kinds of order. Engaging a diverse and representative group of people in the community change process at an early stage is very important. Some communities choose to have stakeholder groups, or steering committees, where people from all the different sectors in a community are represented. Communities often start the process with a survey or an information session where the public can share their viewpoints. It is important in the trust building process to demonstrate these processes are real and meaningful for those involved, not just window-dressing on another, less inclusive, process that takes place behind the scenes. When an equitably structured stakeholder group has formed and this group has generated a list of community assets, the community development process has begun.

## THE ASSET INVENTORY

The purpose of doing an asset inventory is to create a more comprehensive list of all the community assets, the ways in which the community currently meets its needs. This list would begin with the needs described in the broad categories defined in Chapter 2: social life, governance, economic development, and the natural and built environment. Within each of these categories, communities will all have a specific list of needs which include but are not limited to the list in Figure 5.1.

For education, as an example, the stakeholder group would identify all the community's educational institutions, and the particular educational need they were addressing. A list of community educational assets would identify the best experiences in adult education, pre-school education, driver education, religious education, along with the public and private schools and colleges serving the needs of the community. From the educational asset inventory that is created, some communities might choose to produce a directory, so that its citizens could be more aware of all the local opportunities.

Members of the stakeholder committee might not know all the ways in which community needs are being met. This could indicate a need to expand the committee or to invite additional people to speak

Figure 5.1 Human Needs

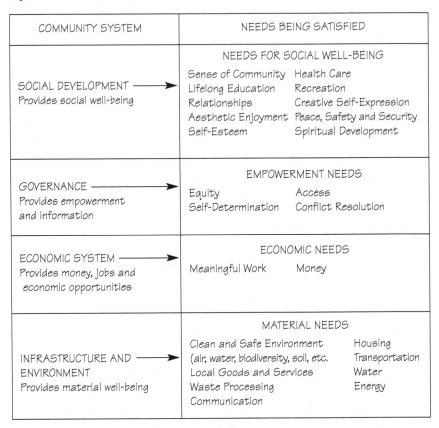

| COMMUNITY SYSTEM | NEEDS BEING SATISFIED |
|---|---|
| SOCIAL DEVELOPMENT ———▶ Provides social well-being | NEEDS FOR SOCIAL WELL-BEING<br><br>Sense of Community   Health Care<br>Lifelong Education    Recreation<br>Relationships         Creative Self-Expression<br>Aesthetic Enjoyment   Peace, Safety and Security<br>Self-Esteem           Spiritual Development |
| GOVERNANCE ———▶ Provides empowerment and information | EMPOWERMENT NEEDS<br><br>Equity              Access<br>Self-Determination   Conflict Resolution |
| ECONOMIC SYSTEM ———▶ Provides money, jobs and economic opportunities | ECONOMIC NEEDS<br><br>Meaningful Work     Money |
| INFRASTRUCTURE AND ———▶ ENVIRONMENT Provides material well-being | MATERIAL NEEDS<br><br>Clean and Safe Environment        Housing<br>(air, water, biodiversity, soil, etc.   Transportation<br>Local Goods and Services          Water<br>Waste Processing                  Energy<br>Communication |

on specific subjects. For example, the committee may not know how certain types of community waste are disposed of or how food the community needs is purchased and distributed. The process of mapping how all the needs are met can be fascinating — the stakeholder committee and involved community members will certainly learn a lot in the process.

How dependent are communities on other countries or regions to satisfy local needs? Perhaps the community meets its need for water by pumping it from another region and it probably meets its need for food by bringing in produce from all over the world. The community asset inventory will quickly reveal how interdependent it is with the rest of the world. If the community chooses to be more self-reliant, the asset inventory will offer insights on how this might be accomplished.

When one employer provides most of the jobs, we know what happens when that employer leaves town. A diversified employment base may provide a more economically secure community. How can this be accomplished? In much the same manner, a diversified base of decision makers in the community also makes it more stable, in contrast to places where a small group of people makes all the decisions. How do citizens get involved with local decision making? Why do citizens get involved with local decision making? Why do they not? What percentage of the population participates in some kind of regular recreational or spiritual activities? What opportunities are available for people locally for this? How open are these opportunities to all the members of the community?

Ideally, needs should be mapped in reference to the community's capacities to meet them. The original system diagram describing this relationship was shown in Figure 1.1, and is repeated below. Using the mapping processes of systems thinking to determine the sustainability of a given system, several pieces of information are needed, including the stock (how much there is) of the needs satisfier (water, for example), the inflow or outflow of the needs satisfier from the system, and the regeneration rate, or capability, of producing more of whatever satisfies the need. This information makes it a little easier to start evaluating the systems in reference to the community's ability to meet the present needs without compromising the ability of future generations to meet their needs.

Figure 1.1 The Sustainability Cycle

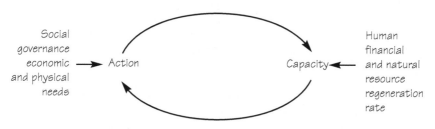

## THE SUSTAINABILITY OF THE SYSTEM

When the assessment of the ways in which a community meets its needs is complete, it is helpful to do an evaluation of how sustainable the community systems are. Obviously, conducting an assessment of the capacity available within the needs satisfaction systems — where it can be measured — is one way to do this. How much water is available in the water supply systems the city has access to? What is the capacity of the wastewater treatment systems? How much food is grown using local resources compared to the overall demand of food within the community? In several systems, however, the information describing the capacity might not be either available or measurable. An alternative method for evaluating the sustainability of the community systems can begin by ranking assets by the level of impact they have. When the community maps the system's components and discovers they can meet their needs with less impact, they may shift some of their behavior from high impact to low impact, and this will help move the community in the direction of sustainable living.

An activity would have high impact if it

1. Produces waste that is not recycled into something else.
2. Draws resources (like water or food) from other regions to provide for the needs of an urban area.
3. Uses nonrenewable resources, such as fossil fuels.
4. Uses renewable resources at a rate that is higher than the natural regeneration rate (paper, wood, water).
5. Produces pollutants at a rate higher than the environment has the capacity to assimilate them (acid rain, river dumping, factory effluent, etc.).
6. Works through institutions that erode the capacity of the community to care for its members.
7. Relies on power structures where the people affected by decisions aren't involved in making them (any non-representative government decision-making process, for example).
8. Causes unnecessary conflict.
9. Produces benefits and burdens that are not shared equitably by all the people involved.

After a comprehensive list of assets, needs, and need satisfiers is made and ranked by their sustainability and impact, it is helpful to identify gaps where needs aren't being met adequately, or at all. For example, mapping the systems visually will help people see the ebbs and flows of materials, money, information, power, and caring. The mapping will make it easier to identify gaps that will be important elements in developing a vision for the community, the next step in the process.

Once the community members have the big picture and can see all of the different ways that needs are met, along with the assessment of the system's sustainability and gaps, it is possible to view it as a whole system and to look for ways in which the different sectors either reinforce the activity of the other sectors or work at cross-purposes. To truly discern a system as a whole, it is critical to see and understand the interrelationships among subsystems. A system will meet many needs but it may sub-optimize other subsystems. For example, does the local economic system encourage construction of expensive homes and sub-optimize lower-income housing developments? Do the local jobs encourage resource extraction by not paying a livable wage, causing people to take shortcuts to produce a short-term profit to make ends meet — like clear-cutting forests?

When the community understands the system as a whole, it will be possible to find areas of synergy — where more than one need can be met using a single strategy. For example, if a city wants to encourage volunteer associations, establishing a cooperative food purchasing system might both enhance the social opportunities available and lower the cost of food. When people pool resources, work together, and pay wholesale prices for produce and other foods, they build relationships and networks that weren't there before.

## THE VISION QUEST

In the absence of a vision, a community is likely to muddle along with business as usual, not satisfied with the way things are, with no clear plan that takes them to another reality. A visioning process can be inspirational and liberating for a community. The value of a vision emerges when the community creates a common understanding of its direction and goals. This shared sense of a desirable future will help encourage, motivate, and coordinate actions that create transformational change. A shared vision, held by community leaders and communicated continually to the community is a powerful leverage point for changing or evolving a system. Dysfunctional systems have tacit, unspoken, and sometimes unconscious ideas that drive them; if they were brought to light, most people would want to do things differently. A vision is a conscious attempt to bring people together for a common purpose, to make the values and principles that drive the system conscious ones that reflect the hopes and dreams of the people involved. The power of a group of people guided by the same vision is very strong. It is a double-edged sword, however, and can be destructive. Many horrific dictators throughout history have been visionaries, albeit evil ones. In this writing, we aspire to the positive application of vision, a vision for the good of all people, now and in the future. To state a positive future that includes the types of conditions that we want for our grandchildren is a powerful alternative path and antidote to the profit-at-all-costs, consumption-driven ideas that serve as the unconscious vision promoted by many of the dominant forces in Western society today.

How is it possible to get a whole community to articulate a shared vision? This is a huge task, and one that is rarely successful. There are many reasons why the intense effort to articulate and communicate a vision fails. It fails because the steering committee doesn't really get it. They often are managers, not communicators, or leaders. The vision statement doesn't vibrate in their very bones; they don't walk the talk; they don't live it; they don't *hold the vision* as a vision but only as words on paper. When the leadership *gets it* they all resonate energetically with possibility, with the excitement and the adventure of it. The vision can be in front of every person in some way — on the wall, on the local TV station, in the mail, on milk cartons. The whole community needs to embrace it in some way for it to serve its purpose.

The message must be simple, so anybody can understand and get excited about it. It is important to recognize that to be compelling a vision must touch people and speak to their hearts. It must reflect shared values, preserve and enhance the things people care about, and change whatever might be changed for the better. A vision is a positive forecast of the way we want the world to be, an affirmation of our values and hopes. To consciously communicate a vision that engages the collective heart of a community taps into the deepest wells of energy and motivation we have. Our collective passion is infinitely more powerful than the forces of fear and divisiveness that keep us trapped in old paradigms.

The future oriented aspect of the visioning process brings our imaginations to bear on the direction we want the community to take. In addition to bringing our minds and hearts and actions to the process, creativity, the arts, other types of expressive, inspirational activities can further engage the community and motivate real change.

Real change means changes in behavior, in the way we think and act. Most change efforts fail because whatever the process used, whether it be strategic planning or another change process, *behavior does not change.* When visioning processes do work, they have motivated people to conceive new ventures and, new activities, and to create unexpected opportunities that would not have happened if it weren't for the collective creativity put to work on visioning.

## COMMUNITY VISIONS IN ACTION

### Burlington, Vermont

In Burlington, Vermont, the community took a participatory approach to a shared vision for the city. For several months, the members of the stakeholder group sponsored focus groups and hearings and passed out thousands of postcard-sized surveys which asked the members of the community three questions:

1. What do you value about Burlington? What do you want to make sure stays the same for your grandchildren's generation?
2. What do you think needs to change?
3. What ideas do you have for improving things in Burlington?

All of the responses were compiled, and the steering committee used the results to form a vision statement for the community. The vision for the city was simple, and it reflected the hopes and dreams of a wide cross-section of the city's population. Here's the way the citizens of Burlington wrote their vision:

> Economy: In the year 2030, Burlington is a vibrant and growing urban center with a diverse mix of businesses and transportation alternatives. Citizens have access to livable wage job opportunities to meet their basic needs.

> Neighborhoods: Development has enhanced the quality of life in all neighborhoods and residents feel safe and free from crime, while enjoying opportunities to work together for community goals. Affordable housing is available for all citizens.

> Governance: The city has a diverse and responsive government, where all citizens, young or old, participate freely and voice their opinions.

Youth and Life Skills: Burlington is committed to providing people from birth through the golden years with quality opportunities to acquire the education, social, and job skills critical to being successful members of our community.

Environment: The city's environment and natural attributes are preserved, with water and air quality improving and increasing investments in resource conservation and renewable energy sources.[1]

## The City of Balaclava, Crimea

In the city of Balaclava, Crimea, leaders used the visioning process to create a radically new direction for the community. Balaclava is famous as the locus for the "Charge of the Light Brigade," a poem by Tennyson describing an ill-fated attack by British troops on Russian forces. They were told to charge up the wrong hill, which resulted in a massive defeat for the British — hundreds of soldiers killed. Well, the city has been charging up the wrong hill ever since, depending on the defense industry as its primary source of income. Yet over the past ten years, the city has captured something a little closer to the image of a Light Brigade — a newfound pride in the city, captured by this quote from a member of the city administration: "They say Balaclava is not a city, rather it is a state of the soul." A local NGO described it this way: "People just love their city so much. If we were able to unite this love, it would be a great thing."[2] The city is already on their way to doing this. The District Council has decided that it wants to remove military forces and the naval shipyard from the bay and make the city an ecotourism destination. This is their new vision.

## The City of Geneva, New York

"The City of Geneva, New York, will be a great place to live, work and invest; with a commitment to positive, open communication and community pride; and a model community boasting vibrant residential neighborhoods and downtown, and a strong economic environment."[3]

## Flagler Beach, Florida

"Flagler Beach, Florida, is a diverse coastal community committed to enhancing our quality of life by: preserving our environment as a community asset, maintaining our old Florida heritage and small town charm. Providing a safe, healthy, and clean environment. Supporting the development of local business to provide services to residents. Promoting and supporting ecotourism through our natural resources. Providing opportunities for education, culture, and recreation."[4]

## Independence, Missouri

"The pride we feel as a community will make Independence, Missouri, a centerpiece for the metropolitan area. The city of Independence will be a community that provides an exceptional quality of life for residents through a healthy economy that provides jobs and livelihoods for citizens, with well-planned, safe and secure neighborhoods; and through excellence in the delivery of public services. The city of Independence will be a community that takes pride in its history, by maintaining its unique heritage for future residents and for visitors from throughout the world. The city of Independence will meet the needs of its citizens through fostering citizen participation and involvement in local government; through the establishment of clear policy guidelines; and through a responsive, well-trained, professional City Staff."[5]

### CONCLUSION

The vision statement should reflect how a community meets its needs to care for others, to empower its citizens, to have stable incomes, and to maintain a healthy and safe environment. Drawing from survey results, the vision will speak to what people in the community care about and what they want preserved for future generations. Once the vision is a part of the consciousness of its citizenry, the co-creation of strategy and implementation plans will emerge spontaneously, as the system self-organizes around its new direction. The task then will be to facilitate and coordinate all the energy generated and released.

Vision statements can be simple, like Burlington's, or detailed and comprehensive, like an extraordinary document called The Earth Charter, which is discussed in the next chapter. The statement can signal a substantial change in direction for a city, as with Balaclava, or in the case of The Earth Charter, it signals a substantial change in direction for the world. Whether a vision is simple or complex, it is important to have one to create constancy of purpose and to guide the actions and strategies to be developed. A vision needs to be compelling. A vision works like a road map — if you don't know where you're going, it's hard to get there.

Whole systems have emergent characteristics that transcend their independent parts. The cities we design and live in can be ravenous monsters that devour everything in their path leaving a trail of waste and destruction, requiring centuries to mend. Or, cities can be thoughtful global citizens that respect their neighbors, reach out in compassion to others not so fortunate, and enhance global security. For the latter to be possible, values and principles can guide our practice in much the same way as thoughtful, careful individuals might follow certain ethical guidelines. A vision for the future of your village, town, or city is the place where these values and principles can be articulated.

## CHAPTER 6

# Envisioning a Beautiful World

T HE LAST CHAPTER DISCUSSED THE IMPORTANCE of understanding how communities meet their needs and then form a new vision. Vision is important, but vision alone is not sufficient. The vision must reflect principles that will insure the continued health and vitality of the planet to support the goal of sustainable cities. In recent years, a truly amazing effort has been undertaken to develop and communicate a global vision for a just, peaceful, and sustainable future. This effort is the Earth Charter.[1]

The Earth Charter is a document that reflects a dialogue that has taken place in over fifty countries around the world, involving thousands of people. People from all walks of life — religious groups, businesses, schools and government, farms and indigenous communities, ghettos and slums, office buildings, huts, apartments, and from the north, south, east, and west — have come together to form a new vision for the planet. It is the first international treaty in history to be written by the people, instead of by a government or group of governments. It stands as a clarion call for a comprehensive Bill of Rights, including the rights of nature, at the international level, to counter the dominant values of free marketeering that drive most decisions at that level today. If cities want to have a master blueprint to use as a guide for their vision statements, the Earth Charter, and the Melbourne Principles for Sustainable Cities[2] — which were developed for cities as a way of interpreting the Earth Charter — are good places to start.

The Earth Charter contains 16 key principles and the practices that support them. The principles create a vision of caring for our world that establishes a sound ethical foundation for the community

## Preamble of the Earth Charter

We stand at a critical moment in Earth's history, a time when humanity must choose its future. As the world becomes increasingly interdependent and fragile, the future at once holds great peril and great promise. To move forward we must recognize that in the midst of a magnificent diversity of cultures and life forms we are one human family and one Earth community with a common destiny. We must join together to bring forth a sustainable global society founded on respect for nature, universal human rights, economic justice, and a culture of peace. Towards this end, it is imperative that we, the peoples of Earth, declare our responsibility to one another, to the greater community of life, and to future generations.[3]

and the four systems defined in this book: the social (care) system, the political (power) system, the economic (money) system, and the material (physical) world. The Earth Charter demonstrates it is possible to articulate a set of shared values that can inform action in any community context. It is a vision for ways in which all our needs can be met. The following discussion applies Earth Charter principles and practices to the communities and cities where you and I live.

### APPLYING THE EARTH CHARTER PRINCIPLES TO THE SOCIAL SYSTEM

The social system described in this book is the ways in which we meet our needs for care, for relationships, and for fulfilling and living our values. The first principle of the Earth Charter states the importance of having "respect and care for the community of life." This principle in turn is further supported with four practices: (1) to respect Earth and life in all its diversity; (2) to care for the community of life with understanding, compassion, and love; (3) to build democratic societies that are just, participatory, sustainable, and peaceful; and (4) to secure Earth's bounty and beauty for present and future generations.

Applying the principle "to respect Earth and life in all its diversity" to the needs identified within the social system, we can see how it applies to the needs for (1) safety and peace; (2) healthy and loving relationships; (3) belonging, a sense of community; (4) healthcare;

(5) education and childcare; (6) recreation; (7) creative self-expression; (8) aesthetic enjoyment; and (9) spiritual development. A vision that describes conditions for meeting these needs in an equitable way across society would include statements that speak to each of them in turn. What follows is a discussion of the various community needs defined in this book.

## Safety and Peace

The key Earth Charter principle that relates to safety and peace is the statement that we need to treat all living beings with respect and consideration. Treating other people, other life forms, and Earth with respect, not taking more than we need, giving back when we can, all are elements of a sustainable relationship. If we are treated with respect, we feel safe. If whole communities treat each other with respect, there is peace. Perhaps the whole social credo of the Earth Charter can be summed up in the principle that says we should recognize the ignored, protect the vulnerable, serve those who suffer, and enable them to develop their capacities and to pursue their aspirations.

The Earth Charter also states that we need to accept that with the right to own, manage, and use natural resources comes the duty to prevent environmental harm and to protect the rights of people, and asks us to affirm that with increased freedom, knowledge and power comes increased responsibility to promote the common good. Protecting people's rights and promoting the common good are two very important ways in which our needs for safety and peace are satisfied.

## Relationships

The Earth Charter asks us to recognize that peace is the wholeness created by right relationships — relationships that are mutually supportive, non-exploitative, based on mutual respect — with oneself, other persons, other cultures, other life, Earth, and the larger whole of which all are a part. All beings are interdependent, and every form of life has value regardless of its worth to human beings. For us to respect and care for the community of life, it is important to value all life, even life or beings that do not meet our direct needs.

To build a global community where right relationships are possible, we need to strengthen families and ensure the safety and loving nurture of all family members. So many government policies today erode the family, despite their ostensible support of "family values." To survive, most parents today have to work full-time jobs, and yet the national school system in the US is still set on a $19^{th}$ century clock, where women stayed home and 80 percent of families lived on farms. School gets out between two and three o'clock in the afternoon, despite the fact that parents often work until five or six. There are long summer vacations, while parents usually have only a few weeks off during the year.

In other countries, basic social supports like welfare and social security still have to be developed. The lack of social support often leads to families feeling as if their security for old age lies in having more children, which fuels the population problem. Supporting families is a critical element of any community development program. Without healthy families, healthy communities are not possible.

Other right relationships that need to be supported by communities are the relationships we have with animals. All cultures on this planet rely on animals for food, companionship, work, energy, and for transportation. The Earth Charter calls on us to prevent cruelty to animals kept in human societies and protect them from suffering. We need to protect wild animals from methods of hunting, trapping, and fishing that cause extreme, prolonged, or avoidable suffering. In hunting, we need to avoid or to eliminate, when possible, the taking or destruction of non-targeted species.

Communities that are founded on right relationships create a strong sense of community cohesiveness. The sense of community is identified as another need we have, addressed in the Charter "to care for the community of life with understanding, compassion, and love." If people are treated with respect and consideration, they have a sense of being cared for as part of a community. This sense of community is a very important factor for sustainable development.

### HealthCare

Healthcare is part of the practice of caring for the community of life with understanding, compassion, and love. In the United States, healthcare has become a product and service like all others — there to make a profit for shareholders, available only to those who can pay, and subject to the vagaries of the marketplace. What would it take for us to live up to the Earth Charter call to ensure universal access to healthcare that fosters reproductive health and responsible reproduction?

This means two things. One is that people would have a right to healthcare, so health is not a commodity only the wealthy can afford. It also means that women and families would have access to safe birth control, so their choices about having children could be informed and well-planned.

"We hold these truths to be self-evident; that we are endowed by our Creator with certain inalienable rights, these are the right to life, liberty, and the pursuit of happiness." Old words, yet we are still trying to meet this challenge. Right to Life has been taken up as a slogan by the anti-abortion movement so effectively that we shirk an exploration of what its deeper meaning might be. The Earth Charter reaffirms this basic right when it says that we need to uphold the right of all, without discrimination, to a natural and social environment supportive of human dignity, bodily health, and spiritual well-being, with special attention to the rights of indigenous peoples and minorities.

One other principle in the Earth Charter that speaks to health issues is the assurance that information of vital importance to human health and environmental protection, including genetic information, remains in the public domain.

## Education

One of the key ways we care for our young people, and for each other, is through the process of education. Humanity is not alone in this endeavor. Many other species exhibit some level of training or upbringing for their young. We need to honor and support the young people of our communities, enabling them to fulfill their essential role in creating sustainable societies — one of the principles of the Earth Charter. To be a function of caring rather than coercion, education that takes our differences and interests into consideration helps us fulfill our potential. In many cases education makes us conform to oppressive and outdated social structures. Recognizing the importance of education throughout our lives is not a new phenomenon, although it is gaining more attention as the skills and knowledge we need to be successful and sustainable increase with each passing year.

The Earth Charter holds education as a critical link to making sustainability a necessary part of our thinking and practice. It speaks to the need to integrate formal education and lifelong learning with the knowledge, values, and skills needed for a sustainable way of life. To do

this, we need to provide all, especially children and youth, with educational opportunities that empower them to contribute actively to
sustainable living. Through this process, we can transmit to future generations values, traditions, and institutions that support the long-term
flourishing of Earth's human and ecological communities. If our institutions and values don't support the kind of practices needed to care
for all of creation, we can't hope that our efforts will succeed in the
long run.

Educational systems are not the only way to meet the need of the
public for growth and development. Another avenue for increased
social development that the Earth Charter identifies is the media. It
states that we need to enhance the role of the mass media in raising
awareness of ecological and social challenges. Perhaps this statement
does not go far enough, however, if meaningful change is going to
occur on a global scale. Right now, the mass media is largely responsible for perpetuating overconsumption that is systematically destroying
the biosphere. Enhancement of the role of the mass media needs to go
hand in hand with a reduction in its role as consumption-monger.

Two other principles in the Earth Charter that relate to education
are to: (1) advance the study of ecological sustainability and promote
the open exchange and wide application of the knowledge acquired,
and (2) support international scientific and technical cooperation on
sustainability, with special attention to the needs of developing nations.

## Spiritual Development

The quest for a transcendent belief system and the practice of different spiritual disciplines has been a central feature of the human
condition throughout history. Today, perhaps more than ever before,
theologians and spiritual leaders from all religions and wisdom traditions are beginning to recognize the value and vitality present in the
diversity of faiths and beliefs we have on Earth. Culture shapes and
informs the spirituality of an individual, and community forms of
worship and practice are features of most civilizations.

Spiritual values are central to the interest we have in keeping Earth
intact for future generations. Our love of Earth, the compassion we feel
for all of creation, the wisdom we have to offer, and the courage to
stand up to the forces that would have it otherwise, are all gifts of the
spirit. Wisdom traditions worldwide speak of these attributes of the
human condition as sacred. To achieve our full potential as human

beings, we need to have the freedom and institutional support to pursue truth, love, and beauty in whatever way we feel is important for our personal and collective enlightenment. There are conditions and principles that can help insure that this is possible; some of these are described in the following sections.

The second statement under the first principle of the Earth Charter asks us to affirm our faith in the inherent dignity of all human beings and in the intellectual, artistic, ethical, and spiritual potential of humanity. This statement covers a lot of territory if you consider the horrific history we have had as a species, with the racism, sexism, slavery, oppression, and genocide that we have inflicted on each other. For a community to take this principle to heart requires some careful reflection about all the ways in which we work to keep people locked into undignified roles in our society, and about the ways that in our own minds we continue to classify people above and below us. A corollary to this, in fact, a requirement if this vision is to be realized, is the call to recognize the importance of moral and spiritual education for sustainable living.

The Earth Charter also asks us to recognize and preserve the traditional knowledge and spiritual wisdom in all cultures that contribute to environmental protection and human well-being, to affirm the right of indigenous peoples to their spirituality, knowledge, lands, and resources and to their related practice of sustainable livelihoods, and to protect and restore outstanding places of cultural and spiritual significance. The diversity of our various traditions needs to be preserved — the days of holy wars and violent attempts to make everyone conform to one religion need to end.

## Arts, Culture, and Recreation

The needs for aesthetic enjoyment, creative self-expression, and recreation, which are all needs within the social system, are not specifically addressed in the Earth Charter, beyond a statement that we should promote the contribution of the arts and humanities, as well as the sciences, in sustainability education. Yet, while these needs are very important to the vision of the Charter, they can be seen as some of the means to attain the vision that the Charter articulates. People can be touched in new ways through the arts and through recreational activities that they enjoy. Social development that neglects these aspects of our humanity does so at its own risk.

Artistic creativity comes from a place deep within the collective psyche. By using creativity to mobilize people to embrace a new ethic, artists can play an important role in moving society toward sustainability. A good example of this is in the amazing transformative work done by artists in Vermont for the Earth Charter. It all began with a small group of artists who got together to share their concerns about environmental degradation and the declining state of the world. They felt that by engaging with the arts, they could offer an alternative vision for the future of the planet and help people heal themselves.

Out of these dialogues, the artists developed the Temenos Project,[4] named after a sacred circle in the Greek wisdom tradition, where extraordinary events inevitably occur and special rules apply. Temenos Books are eight-by-eight-inch works of art that have been created with the principles of the Earth Charter in mind. The artists made some themselves and then developed a curriculum for Vermont schools to work with teachers and have students make their own books. Hundreds of the books were produced, and the artists decided that it would be a good idea to host an event to celebrate the Earth Charter and engage more people in the artistic affirmation of its principles.

The event, For Love of Earth, was held on September 9, 2001 — two days before terrorists flew airplanes into the World Trade Center. Two thousand people came to listen to Jane Goodall, Steven Rockefeller, and Satish Kumar; to sing; and to make the pages for the Temenos Books. It was inspiring and uplifting — many people left feeling like they understood the Earth Charter and shared its vision for the future. The event also served as a kickoff for a campaign to engage Town Meetings throughout Vermont in March in a discussion of the Earth Charter. Twenty-three cities and towns in Vermont voted to endorse the Earth Charter, and the artists' work played an important role in helping motivate and inspire people to participate.

The artists were still cleaning up after the event two days later, when the attacks in New York occurred. Hearing the news, they spontaneously decided to walk the Temenos Books and the Ark of Hope, a chest that had been made to hold the books, to the United Nations in New York City, so that the message of peace and sustainability could be heard throughout New England at a time when the nation was girding for a military response to the attacks. The artist who had created the Ark of Hope, Sally Linder, and friends, people who happened to join in along the way, and many volunteers, walked the Ark through four states, over 300 miles, arriving in New York on the Hudson River sloop *Clearwater* in early November. The artwork and the message of the Earth Charter touched thousands of people. Newspapers carried stories about it throughout its route.

In January, just in time for one of the preparatory conferences in anticipation of the World Summit on Sustainable Development, the Ark of Hope and the Temenos Books were accepted as an exhibit at the United Nations — cutting through an enormous amount of red tape, made more complicated by the security concerns raised by September 11. From there, the Ark traveled to Johannesburg for the Summit, bringing children from Diepsloot, a squatter settlement near Johannesburg into the World Summit for a side event with world leaders. The whole history of the artists' effort makes a clear case for how the arts can be used to advance the vision that a community has for a more sustainable, just, and peaceful world.

## THE VISION FOR THE WORLD OF POWER

The political system, and its many subsystems, is described here as the ways in which we meet our needs for power. We use power to control the events in our lives and our environment, to resolve conflict, and to gain access to resources we need. Justice is associated with the way power is used for all of these reasons, which is why our need for equity is placed in this system. If power is distributed equitably, then people will feel that the world is fair — there will be more equitable access to resources, to economic goods and services, to justice.

### Self-Determination

One principle in the Earth Charter that addresses the power system asks people to ensure that communities at all levels guarantee human rights and fundamental freedoms and provide everyone an opportunity to realize his or her full potential. Realizing our full potential is only possible in the context of freedom. Realizing the self-organizing properties of complex systems is likewise only possible with freedom. There are still many places in the world where people are enslaved in different ways — with very limited political, economic, or social freedom. Freedom is another word for self-determination — we all want to be able to decide what we will do with our lives.

With freedom of action, however, comes responsibility. The Earth Charter goes on to say that the freedom of each generation is qualified by the needs of future generations. We need to think about our grandchildren and their grandchildren before we exhaust the non-renewable resources we use. Before we lay waste vast areas that could have been productive otherwise. Before we buy that extra car, just to have a fun car to drive on weekends.

Our individual freedom needs to be reflected in the governance structures that we develop to manage our collective interests. For this reason, the Earth Charter asks us to strengthen democratic institutions at all levels and to provide transparency and accountability in governance, inclusive participation in decision making, and access to justice. These tenets of a democratic society are imperfectly realized in even the most democratic governments today. Given the dramatic rise in power over resources, services, and personal security that global corporations have, these principles are a long way from being implemented in what we consider to be the private sector. More democratic structures, more transparent accountability, and more stakeholder involvement in decisions is needed in every institution that has an impact on whether or not people meet their needs.

These additional principles in the Earth Charter speak to the need for self-determination:

- Support local, regional, and global civil society, and promote the meaningful participation of all interested individuals and organizations in decision making.

- Protect the rights to freedom of opinion, expression, peaceful assembly, association, and dissent.

- Strengthen local communities, enabling them to care for their environments, and assign environmental responsibilities to the levels of government where they can be carried out most effectively.

This last point, empowering local communities with the ability to manage local resources and empowering regional communities to manage regional resources, is very important to sustainable development. Every source of pollution is located somewhere. The local communities that are host to facilities and forms of hazardous development suffer the greatest damage and share many of the facilities' risks. Many resource problems around the world come from a lack of local control over how resources are used — whether it is in the Amazon rainforest, where oil companies with decision-making structures thousands of miles away are deciding to displace local populations and contaminate thousands of acres of pristine wilderness, or in Central Asia, where the demand for water in distant Soviet cotton fields forces localities upstream to sacrifice their ability to use water for their own purposes. Powerful, non-democratic institutions have forged ways to control resources that meet public needs. Empowering local communities with the ability to manage local resources more effectively would help counteract this trend.

## Equity

The dream of equality is at the root of the United States Constitution. The call of all men being created equal was a rallying cry of the revolution. Now, in hindsight, we know that even then many of the revolutionaries didn't really mean it. After all, the only men who were created equal at that time were white males. The slaves working on the plantations weren't equal. The Native Americans who were being systematically slaughtered weren't equal. Women didn't have equal rights — they were considered the property of their families and husbands. So when the Earth Charter calls for the elimination of discrimination in all its forms, based on race, color, sex, sexual orientation, religion, language, and national, ethnic, or social origin, it is as relevant today as it was 200 years ago.

Political, social, and economic equity is still a very controversial subject. Raise it in a discussion with political leaders today and you will be immediately accused of having communist sympathies. We know that doesn't work, you'll be told — look at what happened in the former Soviet Union. Communism was a failure. Without the profit motive, without the ability to climb the ladder to success, people don't work; they aren't motivated enough. Well, for every example you can cite of the failures of communism, there are equally compelling examples of the failures of capitalism. It's time that we looked beyond the outdated political labels and really opened discussion about how to achieve justice in a world that is increasingly divided between the ultra-rich and the destitute poor.

If we accept the premise that we are all born with equal rights, and that those rights include the right to life, liberty, and the pursuit of happiness, then it stands to reason that our equitable right to life includes a right to the resources we need to sustain life. The Earth Charter emphasizes this point when it calls us to guarantee the right to potable water, clean air, food security, uncontaminated soil, shelter, and safe sanitation, allocating the national and international resources required.

Some steps that the Earth Charter recommends for trying to bring about more equity on gender issues include affirming gender equality and equity as prerequisites to sustainable development and ensuring universal access to education, healthcare, and economic opportunity; securing the human rights of women and girls and ending all violence against them; and promoting the active participation of women in all aspects of economic, political, civil, social, and cultural life as full and equal partners, decision makers, leaders, and beneficiaries.

## Access

Issues of access are closely related to issues of equity; it is difficult to separate the two. But while equity can make access to power and resources possible for people, it is important enough to describe on its own. Whole new legal systems have been developed to make sure that people have access to government, to facilities, and to information. The Americans with Disabilities Act made it illegal to deny people with disabilities access to jobs, housing, and governmental facilities.[5] This means that government and employers are even required to reconstruct the way buildings and public infrastructure work. The Freedom of Information Act gives people the right to have access to all non-classified government information. Various sunshine laws and open meeting laws around the country make it illegal for governmental officials to hold meetings out of the public view. All of these legal requirements point to the importance of access as a human need.

The Earth Charter's statements about access include the idea that we should uphold the right of everyone to receive clear and timely information on environmental matters and all development plans and activities that are likely to affect them or in which they have an interest. It also calls for the elimination of corruption in all public and private institutions. Since corruption changes the way government works by distorting people's access to government and resources, it is appropriate to mention it here. The Earth Charter states that we need to institute effective and efficient access to administrative and independent judicial procedures, including remedies and redress for environmental harm and the threat of such harm. In many parts of the world, a judiciary that is truly independent of the dominant political party is still an ideal that hasn't been realized. When the place you turn to for justice is part of the same entity as the party that harmed you in the first place, your access to justice is impaired.

## Conflict Resolution

One of the four central principles of the Earth Charter is to promote a culture of tolerance, nonviolence, and peace. This is a tall order in a world that spends more on guns, weapons, and soldiers than it does on health, education, and welfare. According to a study by Ruth Leger Sivard, military expenditures in developing countries rose from U.S.$27 billion to U.S.$121 billion between 1960 and 1991. There are some promising trends; the level of military expenditures in industrialized countries dropped as a percentage of GNP in the late 1990s,[6] while proportional expenditures on health and education rose. The fact that some of the poorest countries in the world (Angola, Ethiopia, Mozambique, Myanmar, Somalia, and Yemen) still spend more on weapons than they do on education and welfare is a testament to the fact that poverty, and the inequity at its root, breeds hatred and causes conflict to escalate into violence.

Much can be done to promote a culture of tolerance, nonviolence, and peace. The Earth Charter lists several steps that can be taken to develop this type of ethic. The first step that calls us to encourage and support mutual understanding, solidarity, and cooperation among all peoples and within and among nations is a strategy that can be implemented and supported on the local community level. Many communities have student exchange programs, or sister cities, or other activities that help build intercultural relationships. The most effective way to help people understand humanity's common ground — we all love our children, we all get up in the morning and try to work to make our lives a little better, we all have hopes and dreams and values that we hold dear — is to have people meet each other and interact with each other as equals, as partners, as friends.

A second point that the Earth Charter makes about promoting peace is that we need to implement comprehensive strategies to prevent violent conflict and use collaborative problem solving to manage and resolve environmental conflicts and other disputes. This is relevant for communities as well. Violent conflict occurs in our communities every time someone is robbed, or raped, or abused or their property is vandalized. The increasing activity of gangs and organized crime has led to more violence in many cities. Prevention activities involve engaging young people from an early age in pro-social activities, so that they will be able to resist the pressure to join gangs or get involved in drugs and illegal activity that is often associated with criminal behavior.

Much can be done, as well, to change the way communities address disputes that arise between citizens or between citizens and the local government. In the United States, an inordinate number of these disputes end up in the judicial system, which is constructed as a win-lose model. Increasingly, alternative conflict resolution strategies are gaining a foothold, strategies that allow the disputing parties to engage in a mediation process, where the core interests are identified and a win-win solution can be found. Communities can adopt these methods as well, as a way of making sure the inevitable conflicts do not produce long-lasting divisions that can disrupt effective collective action in the future.

Many of the other actions called for by the Earth Charter are more relevant to the national level of government. These are listed below. Yet even for these strategies to be feasible at the national level, local people need to be aware of the importance of recapturing the community-level opportunities that are lost with the money that is spent on the military.

- Demilitarize national security systems to the level of a non-provocative defense posture, and convert military resources to peaceful purposes, including ecological restoration.

- Eliminate nuclear, biological, and toxic weapons and other weapons of mass destruction.

- Ensure that the use of orbital and outer space supports environmental protection and peace.

## THE VISION FOR THE ECONOMIC WORLD

They say that money makes the world go round, but that can't be true, because for money to make the world go round, you have to *love* money. The economic world that has evolved over several thousand years is a complex system that has had the benefit of a great deal of theoretical and practical study. To an economist, the idea of cyclical processes at work in a system with dynamics that produce a state of equilibrium is an accepted fact about the way the economy functions.

The discipline of economics claims authority over all of the subjects that are discussed in relation to our economic and environmental needs. Housing markets, commodities, communication, transportation, and goods and services are all part of the economy. The two needs that have been defined as purely economic needs are highlighted here because there is a difference between the way money and labor behave in our communities and the flows of natural resources and other material goods and services. There is no doubt that they are very closely related.

## Money

Our care and concern for all other people needs to extend to concern about their economic well-being. One of the more controversial statements in the Earth Charter is that we need to eradicate poverty as an ethical, social, and environmental imperative. This means empowering every human being with the education and resources to secure a sustainable livelihood, and provide social security and safety nets for those who are unable to support themselves. To do this successfully, we will need to promote the equitable distribution of wealth within nations and among nations.

Where does the rationale come from that dictates that a corporate CEO should earn millions of dollars per year, while his employees earn a fraction of that? In 1999, *Business Week* reported that in 1980 the ratio between the wages of an average worker and salaries of top management was 1:42. By 2001, it had grown to 1:531,[7] more than ten times what it was in 1980. The wave of corporate scandals that rocked the United States in 2002 poignantly illustrated the raw avarice behind this trend. Companies have been exposed in a series of accounting scandals that have sent giants like Enron and WorldCom into bankruptcy while the rank and file have watched their jobs, their pension funds, and their futures erased like the false profits reported to the stockholders. Meanwhile, top executives walked away with golden parachutes; bad business, bad policy, bad results. Rather than pointing blame at a few hapless corporate scapegoats — like the two Adelphia

executives who are facing jail time for fraud, it is important to identify what systems dynamics lead to this type of mess.

The flow of money takes place on many levels. The Earth Charter
asks the developed world to enhance the intellectual, financial, technical, and social resources of developing nations and relieve them of
onerous international debt. In the United States, we spend enough
money every year on chewing gum ($2.5 billion in 1995 dollars) to
make some serious progress toward eradicating childhood hunger in
the world. It is important to work to distribute wealth and benefits to
people more equitably all over the world — our future depends on it.

## Work

Human beings need to work. Work is not just the way we earn money,
it's also the way we feel like valuable members of a community, how
we express ourselves, and how we create an environment for ourselves
that we can live in comfortably. The Earth Charter asks us to promote
social and economic justice, enabling all to achieve a secure and meaningful livelihood that is ecologically responsible. To do this, we need
to ensure that economic activities and institutions at all levels promote
human development in an equitable and sustainable manner, to ensure
that all trade supports sustainable resource use, environmental protection, and progressive labor standards, and to require multinational
corporations and international financial organizations to act transpar-
ently in the public good, and hold them accountable for the
consequences of their activities.

## THE VISION FOR THE PHYSICAL ENVIRONMENT

When most people hear the words *Earth Charter*, they assume that the
document is primarily concerned with the environment. As previously described, its many ways of addressing the full spectrum of
human needs are important to one of its central tenets, namely, we
can't have hope for a healthy environment if we don't also have
respect and care for the community of life, social and economic justice, democracy, nonviolence, and peace. They are all inextricably
interrelated, not in competition with each other.

## Clean and Safe Environment (Air, Water, Soil)

The Earth Charter recognizes the central importance of a healthy
environment, and it calls for us to:

- protect and restore the integrity of Earth's ecological systems, with special concern for biological diversity and the natural processes that sustain life,
- adopt at all levels sustainable development plans and regulations that make environmental conservation and rehabilitation integral to all development initiatives,
- establish and safeguard viable nature and biosphere reserves, including wild lands and marine areas, to protect Earth's life support systems, maintain biodiversity, and preserve our natural heritage,
- promote the recovery of endangered species and ecosystems,
- prevent harm as the best method of environmental protection and, when knowledge is limited, apply a precautionary approach,
- take action to avoid the possibility of serious or irreversible environmental harm even when scientific knowledge is incomplete or inconclusive,
- place the burden of proof on those who argue that a proposed activity will not cause significant harm, and make the responsible parties liable for environmental harm,
- ensure that decision making addresses the cumulative, long-term, indirect, long-distance, and global consequences of human activities,
- prevent pollution of any part of the environment and allow no buildup of radioactive, toxic, or other hazardous substances, and
- avoid military activities damaging to the environment.

One of the most important shifts in environmental protection policy that is captured through these principles is the precautionary principle. The precautionary principle takes a more cautious approach to new technologies and initiatives, placing the burden of proof on the proponents to demonstrate that the proposal will not cause harm, rather than requiring opponents to demonstrate that it will. This principle has already been put into practice in Germany, and a growing body of theoretical and practical information can inform policy-makers on all levels about effective implementation without causing problematic consequences for people with innovative ideas for moving the economy forward. Several criteria have been advanced for its use, stating that a precautionary approach should be taken when:

- there are significant scientific uncertainties,
- there are scenarios of possible harm that are scientifically reasonable,
- the uncertainties associated with the proposed technology or initiative cannot be reduced without increasing ignorance of the issues,
- the potential harm is sufficiently serious and irreversible, and
- delayed action may make countermeasures more difficult.

Another important shift the Earth Charter calls for as a method governments use to assess new projects, technologies, or other initiatives is life cycle, full-cost accounting. This principle states that all of the costs associated with new initiatives should be factored into the decisions about whether or not they make sense — the long-term impacts, the natural resource costs, the indirect costs, any impacts that might happen over a long distance — as is the case with acid rain depositions, and any global impacts like $CO_2$ or ozone-depleting emissions.

The Earth Charter asks us to recognize the inherent value of all species, not only those that have been particularly helpful for human development. We must recognize that we need biodiversity as much as we need water, air, or other environmental services. Every species on the planet is precious, all part of the interconnected web of life that supports us, regardless of how insignificant it may seem.

## Housing

Our need for high-quality safe housing is an important driver of many national, state, and community laws and regulations. Most national governments play a central role in the provision of housing, whether through direct construction, subsidies, or tax breaks. One of the most significant government housing programs in the United States, for example, is the deduction that homeowners get on their income tax for the mortgage interest they pay to the banks. Monetarily, this is the largest housing subsidy the U.S. government offers, yet it is a rare day when you hear it being referred to as the same type of welfare assistance that lower income people receive.

On the community level, most community services are directly or indirectly connected with supporting the housing sector. Laws and regulations for land use, for constructing new developments, or building roads, or managing access to community infrastructure such as water and sewer services, solid waste facilities, and schools are all related to the need we have for housing.

The Earth Charter states that the universal need for housing should translate into a universal right to shelter, along with rights to potable water, clean air, food, uncontaminated soil, and safe sanitation. It calls for national and international resources to be allocated to meet this need and secure these rights for people.

## Energy

Of all the environmental needs we have, energy is one that underpins many others. We don't actually need energy, after all. We do need heat and hot water and the ability to get from one place to another. We need light when it's dark. We need to cook our food and to keep it from being contaminated due to improper storage. We need power to make things. All of these needs translate into our need for energy in some form or another. The production of energy is one of the key leverage points for the global environment, and recognizing this, the Earth Charter asks us to:

- manage the extraction and use of nonrenewable resources, such as minerals and fossil fuels, in ways that minimize depletion and cause no serious environmental damage, and

- act with restraint and efficiency when using energy and rely increasingly on renewable energy sources such as solar and wind power.

## Transportation

Like energy, transportation itself is not a fundamental need. Yet so many community systems have been developed to address the underlying need for people to move from home to work, to have access to goods and services, and to visit family and friends who don't live within walking distance, that transportation needs to be addressed when considering the community as a whole.

While the Earth Charter doesn't say anything specific about transportation, without fundamental changes to our transportation systems, we won't be able to achieve the goals of reducing and eliminating nonrenewable energy consumption, since so much of the fossil fuel we produce is used to power automobiles, trucks, and ships —

estimated by the World Resources Institute to be 60 percent of global energy use.[8] One way to reduce the amount of energy that is used for transportation is to reduce the need for transportation by locating work, goods, and services closer to where people live.

## Local Goods and Services

The production and consumption of all the goods and services we use to meet our needs is another significant leverage point for global environmental health. The Earth Charter speaks to the need to change our consumption and production systems substantially, focusing on both the quality and the quantity of the goods and services themselves. The following principles relate to this point.

- Control and eradicate non-native or genetically modified organisms harmful to native species and the environment, and prevent introduction of such harmful organisms.
- Promote the development, adoption, and equitable transfer of environmentally sound technologies.
- Internalize the full environmental and social costs of goods and services in the selling price, and enable consumers to identify products that meet the highest social and environmental standards.
- Adopt patterns of production, consumption, and reproduction that safeguard Earth's regenerative capacities, human rights, and community well-being.
- Adopt lifestyles that emphasize the quality of life and material sufficiency in a finite world.

The last point speaks to the value of changing our mindset about consumption. This is in stark contrast to the predominant consumer culture we promote now. Television advertisements convince millions of people to buy products they never knew they needed in the first place; in fact, some stations are dedicated only to shopping. Twenty-four hours a day, hosts of these shows promote a wide variety of products that be purchased over the phone. The Internet has also become an electronic marketplace. It is difficult to log on to the Internet without being bombarded with advertisements for all sorts of unnecessary products. Our continued willingness to purchase products that are harmful, unnecessary, and based on huge, undervalued inputs from the biosphere, is the main driver of this very unsustainable system. We have the power to change it with our economic choices.

## Water

Next to air, without which we would not survive for more than a few minutes, water is the most fundamental human need. Yet today, billions of people do not have access to safe, potable water. Millions of people die every year from preventable, waterborne diseases such as cholera, dysentery, and hepatitis. On a global level, our water delivery systems are increasingly being turned over to for-profit companies, even though they were not economic to operate on a non-profit, governmental level. The convoluted logic behind this is that for-profit institutions are more efficient, so they will be able to squeeze blood from the stones of impoverished communities and provide water for a price that includes an allowance for profit. Most of these communities can't pay any price for water — they literally have to trade off between buying water and buying food to eat. This is why many of the poor rely on unsanitary sources of water and die of diseases that could easily be prevented.

In addition to having potable water categorized as a human right, and directing national and international resources to guarantee this right for everyone, the Earth Charter asks us to manage the use of renewable resources such as water, soil, forest products, and marine life in ways that do not exceed rates of regeneration and that protect the health of ecosystems. Water is a renewable resource, if we treat it well. There is no need to have the level of contamination we experience today.

## Communication

The need to communicate with each other about our family lives, our work, our interests, and economic and political issues has been the hallmark of humanity's ascent from apes to Homo sapiens. Our communication systems weave a web of connection around the planet, even venturing into outer space. The vitality of a community is often dependent on having adequate access to the communications network, so more work is required to insure that communities all over the world are able to link up. While the Earth Charter doesn't speak to this point directly, access to communication is essential if we are going to achieve social and economic justice, democracy, nonviolence, and peace.

Communication between cultures, bridging old animosities, making new friends and trusted allies, and forging new networks that serve to support each other, is a critical leverage point for the success of sustainable development efforts worldwide. The media must be engaged in the dialogue about our global future in new ways. One example of this is in New England, where several established columnists have teamed up with activists, the Institute for Sustainable Communities,[9] and Mt. Auburn Associates, a Boston-based consulting firm, to research and write articles to be published in all the major papers about the sustainability issues facing New England. A coordinated approach is sure to raise the collective consciousness of the region to a new level, which will help inspire change.

## Waste Processing

Last, but not least, is the need we have to safely process our wastes. We must first implement the three Rs of waste management — reduce, reuse, and recycle. The more we reduce our need for waste disposal facilities, the more sustainable our community systems will be. The Earth Charter captures this strategy in the principle that says we need to reduce, reuse, and recycle the materials used in production and consumption systems, and ensure that residual waste can be assimilated by ecological systems.

## THE MELBOURNE PRINCIPLES

Partly in response to the efforts made by the Earth Charter, and partly due to a growing recognition that cities require guidance on how to become more sustainable, an effort was made by the International Environmental Technology Centre of the United Nations Environment Programme to develop sustainability principles specifically for cities.[10] Consultations were held in Canada and in Australia that brought experts together who had experience with cities, with sustainable development, and with the Earth Charter, to form a vision statement that could be adopted and utilized by cities all over the world.

The Preamble of the Melbourne Principles states that cities meet our fundamental needs for economic opportunities and social interaction, as well as cultural and spiritual enrichment.[11] Cities also damage the natural environment and exploit natural resources in an unsustainable manner, which can jeopardize long-term prosperity and social well-being. This is of global concern, as more than half of the world's population lives in cities, and trends indicate that this will increase.

The Preamble goes on to say that the transformation of cities to sustainability will require cooperation between various levels of government, resource managers, the business sector, community groups, and all citizens. Their collective and individual contributions are essential in achieving a common purpose. Improving the sustainability of cities will not only benefit their inhabitants, but also significantly contribute to improving the well-being of people around the world. The overarching vision of the Melbourne Principles is to create environmentally healthy, vibrant, and sustainable cities where people respect one another and nature, to the benefit of all. The text of the Melbourne Principles is as follows:

## Principle 1

Provide a long-term vision for cities based on: sustainability; inter-generational, social, economic and political equity; and their individuality.

### *Elaboration*

A long-term vision is the starting point for catalyzing positive change, leading to sustainability. The vision needs to reflect the distinctive nature and characteristics of each city.

The Earth Charter, an international treaty drafted by thousands of people in 51 countries, can serve as the basis for a city's long-term vision. The Charter recognizes the fact that ecological integrity, social and economic justice, respect and care for the community of life, and democracy, non-violence, and peace are inextricably linked. To achieve any of these goals, communities need to work to achieve all of them.

The vision should express the shared aspirations of the people for their cities to become more sustainable. It needs to address equity, which means equal access to both natural and human resources, as well as shared responsibility for preserving the value of these resources for future generations.

A vision based on sustainability will help align and motivate communities, governments, businesses and others around a common purpose, and will provide a basis for developing a strategy, an action program and processes to achieve that vision.

The entire community needs to be involved in crafting a vision for the city, which will ensure its relevance to their values and aspirations, and will generate the commitment and engagement of people who live in the city to realizing the vision.

## Principle 2

Achieve long-term economic and social security.
### *Elaboration*
Long-term economic and social security are prerequisites for beneficial change and are dependent upon environmentally sound, sustainable development.

To achieve triple bottom line sustainability, economic strategies need to increase the value and vitality of human and natural systems, and conserve and renew human, financial and natural resources. Through fair allocation of resources, economic strategies should seek to meet basic human needs in a just and equitable manner and as a priority eradicate poverty. In particular, economic strategies should guarantee the right to potable water, clean air, food security, shelter, and safe sanitation.

Cities are the incubators of human diversity; their policies, structures and institutions can significantly contribute to fostering cohesive, stimulating, safe and fulfilled communities.

## Principle 3

Recognize the intrinsic value of biodiversity and natural ecosystems, and protect and restore them.
### *Elaboration*
Nature is more than a commodity for the benefit of humans. We share the Earth with many other life forms that have their own intrinsic value. They warrant our respect, whether or not they are of immediate benefit to us.

It is through people's direct experience with nature that they understand its value and gain a better appreciation of the importance of healthy habitats and ecosystems. This connection provides them with an appreciation of the need to manage our interactions with nature empathetically.

Just as humans have the ability to alter the habitat and even to extinguish other species, we can also protect and restore biodiversity. Therefore, we have a responsibility to act as custodians for nature.

The best method to protect and restore nature is to avoid harm by taking a precautionary approach. Where scientific knowledge is incomplete or inconclusive and the consequences are not fully understood, decision making should seek to avoid the possibility of serious or irreversible harm. In these circumstances the onus of proof is on those who propose activity that could have an ecological consequences.

## Principle 4

Enable communities to minimize their ecological footprint.

*Elaboration*

Cities consume significant quantities of resources and have a major impact on the environment, well beyond what they can handle within their borders. These unsustainable trends need to be substantially curbed and eventually reversed.

One way of describing the impact of a city is to measure its ecological footprint. The ecological footprint of a city is a measure of the *load* on nature imposed by meeting the needs of its population. It represents the land area necessary to sustain current levels of resource consumption and waste discharged by that population. Reducing the ecological footprint of a city is a positive contribution towards sustainability.

Like any living system, a community consumes material, water and energy inputs, processes them into useable forms and generates wastes. This is the *metabolism* of the city and making this metabolism more efficient is essential to reducing the city's ecological footprint. In reducing the footprint, problems should be solved locally where possible, rather than shifting them to other geographic locations or future generations.

## Principle 5

Build on the characteristics of ecosystems in the development and nurturing of healthy and sustainable cities.

*Elaboration*

Cities can become more sustainable by modeling urban processes on ecological principles of form and function, by which natural ecosystems operate.

The characteristics of ecosystems include diversity, adaptiveness, interconnectedness, resilience, regenerative capacity and symbiosis. These characteristics can be incorporated by cities in the development of strategies to make them more productive and regenerative, resulting in ecological, social, and economic benefits.

## Principle 6

Recognize and build on the distinctive characteristics of cities, including their human and cultural values, history, and natural systems.

*Elaboration*

Each city has a distinctive profile of human, cultural, historic, and natural characteristics. This profile provides insights on pathways to sustainability that is both acceptable to their people and compatible with their values, traditions, institutions, and ecological realities.

Building on existing characteristics helps motivate and mobilize the human and physical resources of cities to achieve sustainable development and regeneration.

## Principle 7

Empower people and foster participation.

*Elaboration*

The journey towards sustainability requires broadly based support. Empowering people mobilizes local knowledge and resources and enlists the support and active participation of all who need to be involved in all stages, from long-term planning to implementation of sustainable solutions.

The people of cities are the key drivers for transforming cities towards sustainability. This can be achieved effectively if the people living in cities have adequate educational opportunities, are well informed, can easily access knowledge and share learning. Such knowledge will empower them to contribute actively to sustainable development, both at a personal and community level.

People have a right to be involved in the decisions that affect them. Attention needs to be given to empowering those whose voices are not always heard, such as the poor, religious and racial minorities, women, young people, and people with disabilities.

## Principle 8

Expand and enable cooperative networks to work towards a common, sustainable future.

*Elaboration*

Strengthening existing networks and establishing new cooperative networks within cities facilitate the transfer of knowledge and support continual environmental improvement.

The energy and talent of people can be enhanced by communities working with one another through such networks.

There is also value in cities sharing their learning with other cities, pooling resources to develop sustainability tools, and supporting and mentoring one another through inter-city and regional networks. These networks can serve as vehicles for information exchange and encouraging collective effort.

## Principle 9

Promote sustainable production and consumption, through appropriate use of environmentally sound technologies and effective demand management.

### *Elaboration*

A range of approaches and tools can be used to promote sustainable practices.

Demand management, which includes accurate valuations of natural resources and increasing public awareness, is a valuable strategy to support sustainable consumption. This approach can also provide significant savings in infrastructure investment.

Sustainable production can be supported by the development, equitable transfer, adoption and use of environmentally sound technologies that can improve environmental performance significantly. These technologies protect the environment, are less polluting, use resources in a sustainable manner, recycle more of their wastes and products and handle all residual wastes in a more environmentally acceptable way than the technologies for which they are substitutes.

Environmentally sound technologies can also be used to drive reduced impacts and enhance value along a supply chain and support businesses embracing product stewardship.

## Principle 10

Enable continual improvement, based on accountability, transparency and good governance.

### *Elaboration*

Good urban governance requires robust processes directed towards achieving the transformation of cities to sustainability through continual improvement. While in some areas gains will be incremental, there are also opportunities to make substantial improvements through innovative strategies, programs, and technologies.

To manage the continual improvement cycle, it is necessary to use relevant indicators, set targets based on benchmarks, and monitor progress against milestones to achieving these targets. This facilitates progress and accountability and ensures effective implementation.

Transparency and openness to scrutiny are part of good governance and good business practices. This includes the right of everyone to receive clear and timely information on environmental matters and all public and private development plans and activities which are likely to affect them or in which they have an interest. Furthermore, those making decisions in government and in businesses should be accountable to those affected directly or indirectly by those decisions. Corruption in public and private institutions needs to be eliminated.

It is important that environmental responsibilities, and adequate resources to achieve sustainable outcomes, are assigned to the level of government where they can be carried out most effectively.

On August 30, 2002, the Local Government Session of the World Summit on Sustainable Development at Johannesburg adopted Local Action 21.[12] This builds upon the worldwide successes of Local Agenda 21 since the Rio Summit and represents a move from plan to practice. Part of Local Action 21 includes a commitment to the Melbourne Principles and the Earth Charter.

One thing that is clear from both the visions of the Earth Charter and the Melbourne Principles is that sustainability is an integrated whole. It's not just about a clean environment, or economic development that minimizes environmental destruction. It concerns itself, by necessity, with our social and governance systems as well. Bringing all of these systems into a coherent and consistent vision for our cities is critical to the success of sustainability efforts worldwide. To do this, our cities will need to change.

## CHAPTER 7

# The Challenge of Change

*The very nature of change guarantees that at some point you will need to completely rethink your organization and move in a new direction.*[1]

Joyce Wycoff

A CITY IS NEVER A FINISHED PRODUCT. It is always changing. There is no end to the learning, development, and adaptation it requires to remain vital and responsive to the needs of its citizens. Making changes in a city is extraordinarily complex because the work of a city doesn't stop — it has to continue, 24 hours a day, 7 days a week. The people involved are not always rational; they are influenced by political forces, by their emotions, by their histories, and if they feel threatened in any way they will react against change, even if the change proposed would be a benefit to them.

When communities have learned to recognize and chart dynamic systems relationships, have gathered information and examples about how their systems work, have collectively come up with a vision for the future, and have created some future scenario possibilities, they will begin to understand what types of transformation strategies might be effective. But the facts are only part of the process. To work together to formulate a plan for using the information to improve the community is a challenge itself. It is important to understand the nature of change, the ways in which the change process can be supported, and to use group process skills that enable real learning, trust, commitment, and accountability and that help the group manage the conflict that inevitably arises.

Change itself is not the goal, because change is a constant and can work either for or against improvement. Communities need to direct change toward their vision and to do it effectively. This means gathering the data on how a community's needs are met, developing a shared vision, planning strategies that address the needs so that the vision can be realized, implementing the strategies in a way that is consistent with the values and the vision, and then constantly reflect on and evaluate the progress that has been made. None of the work involved in changing community systems can be done without understanding how change occurs.

## THE NATURE OF CHANGE

The word change has its roots in the Celtic barter system, implying that something is exchanged for something else of equal value. Metamorphosis might be a better metaphor for the kind of change we are talking about in cities. The word metamorphosis has interesting roots. Morph is from the Greek word *morphe* meaning form. The *meta* part of the word implies a nature of higher order or more fundamental kind; there is even a hint of supernatural forces at work. Metamorphosis means the action or process of changing in form, shape, or substance, especially by supernatural means. Whole systems change that relies on shared vision, and that seeks to create new emergent properties, is tapping into the transcendent values and heart of the community to bring about a new reality. These uplifting, transforming capacities help insure that the change will be meaningful.

There are many kinds of change. Growth is change. Destruction is change. The seasons change in a cyclical pattern. The growth of healthy organisms typically follows an incremental path, changing slightly over time to accommodate the slowly evolving creature. Incremental change is often the way large, complex systems move forward and evolve.

Cyclical change is different from incremental change. Since cyclical conditions fluctuate over time, the ways in which systems adapt to cyclical change are often temporary, going back to a previous state once the cycle has passed again. We put storm windows on in the winter and take them off in the summer. Utility companies brace themselves for summer cooling season, and then the demand for services is reduced again with cooler temperatures.

Often, when we are looking to make whole systems more sustainable, we are less interested in incremental or cyclical change, but more interested in major, long-term structural change. Major changes don't happen in the same ways as incremental changes. With incremental change, it's easy to map out a step-by-step process, develop a budget, and move forward. Major structural changes often have to proceed in a more flexible, open-ended way, guided by a vision and a plan, rather than by old patterns of behavior and outmoded practices.

The process of guiding and working through a major structural change requires different skills and different mindsets than incremental change does. The difference between a manager and a leader is that a good manager knows how to do things right, but a leader knows how to do the right things. Good managers are needed for incremental change, but good leaders are needed for major structural change. Major change doesn't demand the ability to use all the old techniques well to get a job done. It often means reinventing processes as you go, taking risks, groping in the dark, yet always being able to use the vision and ethical framework as a touchstone to keep the often chaotic and scary process on track. Creativity is more highly valued with major change, as is flexibility, openness, and adaptability.

## SERVANT LEADERSHIP

Much attention has been paid to *servant leadership* over the past twenty years, and its effectiveness is well documented. Robert K. Greenleaf, the founder of the Robert K. Greenleaf Center for Servant Leadership, describes it this way:

> The servant-leader is servant first … It begins with the natural feeling that one wants to serve, to serve first. Then conscious choice brings one to aspire to lead. He or she is sharply different from the person who is leader first, perhaps because of the need to assuage an unusual power drive or to acquire material possessions. For such it will be a later choice to serve — after leadership is established. The leader-first and the servant-first are two extreme types. Between them there are shadings and blends that are part of the infinite variety of human nature.

The difference manifests itself in the care taken by the servant-first to make sure that other people's highest priority needs are being served. The best test, and difficult to administer, is: do those served grow as persons; do they, while being served, become healthier, wiser, freer, more autonomous, more likely themselves to become servants? And, what is the effect on the least privileged in society; will they benefit, or, at least, will they not be further deprived? [2]

Larry Spears, in an article titled "Servant Leadership: Quest for Caring Leadership," describes ten characteristics of a servant-leader:

1.  Listening receptively to what others have to say.

2.  Acceptance of others and having empathy for them.

3.  Foresight and intuition.

4.  Awareness and perception.

5.  Having highly developed powers of persuasion.

6.  An ability to conceptualize and to communicate concepts.

7.  An ability to exert a healing influence upon individuals and institutions.

8.  Building community in the workplace.

9.  Practicing the art of contemplation.

10. Recognition that servant leadership begins with the desire to change oneself. Once that process has begun, it then becomes possible to practice servant leadership at an institutional level. [3]

Leadership with service as its primary objective is fundamentally different from leadership where self-promotion is the underlying motivation. The former is based on a deeply caring relationship with those served, and the latter is often based on a desire to control, to gain advantage or personal prestige. When egotism is an important motivator for people who seek leadership positions, the cast of characters that give politics a bad name grows ever larger. What is at the root of egotism? Many psychological studies and theories from the last century suggest that, at its core, fear is the motivator of egotistical behavior. Fear and its companion, a lack of trust, is a major contributor to many dysfunctional community systems. These two emotional responses trigger impulses that make people seem like control freaks. Overcontrolling behavior, sometimes referred to as micromanagement, severely limits the kind of creativity and spontaneity that can make for successful innovations in systems.

Another important concept for even the best leaders to recognize is that one person can't really change anyone else. It is true that a lot can be done, and is done, to try to impose changes on other people. We educate them, lock them in jail, preach to them on Sundays, and we go door-to-door to talk to them about important issues. We advertise products for them to buy, we go to war to change the way their country works, and we pass laws that all people have to follow. All of these actions represent one group of people trying to impose change on another group of people. Yet anyone who has worked with any of these efforts to change other people knows that those efforts are only successful when the people on whom the change is imposed agree to it. Education works best when the student wants to learn something. Laws only work when the people agree to them. This means that our methods of making changes have to be inclusive; they have to involve all the affected parties. The ways changes are made are as important as the goal itself ... the means are as important as the end. Regardless of how enlightened a particular strategy or technology or new idea, unless it has broad support, it will go nowhere.

Lao Tse may have said it best when he wrote: "A leader is best when people barely know he exists, not so good when people obey and acclaim him, worse when they despise him. But of a good leader who talks little, when his work is done his aim fulfilled, they will say: 'We did it ourselves.'"[4]

## GUIDING AND SUPPORTING THE CHANGE PROCESS

For the most part, people don't like change, especially when it comes from a direction they perceive as being outside their control. It is very important to recognize this basic fact in any planning process and to adapt to it in several ways. For one, the more people are engaged in the discussions about the direction change will take, the less they will feel like the change is outside of their control. If people involved control what happens, change can happen much more easily than if it is imposed by outsiders.

Another strategy is to consciously recognize the emotions triggered by change, making space in the planning and implementation process to support people who are experiencing fear, grief, loss, confusion, and conflict. Bring these reactions into the open; maybe even include special times during meetings to speak about the emotional barometer of the group. Often, the people who are pushing for the change are so enthusiastic that they fail to recognize and honor the feelings of those who are slower to make changes.

There are limits to change that people can tolerate, so it is important to prepare them for it and invite their participation. The best way for people to influence the future is to help create it. Their participation will moderate the degree of change that occurs so they will adapt to it in a timely way. Participation brings a higher level of energy and time to achieve the vision, and while these levels of energy and time are being expended, the motivation generated is relatively high. Yet once the community assimilates the new processes and practices they will experience their effort less as change and more as the way things are. Stress will turn into excitement, creative tension — even fun. It will be comforting to expect there will come a time when what seemed to be such a huge challenge will later be perceived to be completely normal.

## Innovation Diffusion

In his book, *Believing Cassandra*,[5] Alan AtKisson describes a game he has developed called the Amoeba Game, based on Everett Rogers' work on innovation diffusion. The game is a good way of conveying the dynamics of introducing a new idea, technology, or system change. Rogers and AtKisson identify several ways in which people respond to a proposed change. These personal response patterns do not always describe one person, but rather characterize how people react to change — any individual may embrace certain kinds of changes and resist others. The ways in which these personal attributes manifest themselves in any given change process depends on the success of the implementation effort. In the examples below, we've use the general response patterns that Rogers and AtKisson identified to characterize people in relation to the community, to clarify how they fit in with the implementation plan.

The person who comes up with a new idea, a new approach to how the community can do something, is the Innovator. The word *innovator* conjures up a mental picture of someone who's brilliant, and maybe a little crazy, who doesn't socialize much, and is often a hopeless perfectionist with respect to their work. People perceive them as being out on the fringes of society and are not likely to give them the level of credibility they would need to be successful at making change in a community. In reality, masterminds can be someone as prosaic as a store clerk who finds a new way to market a product, but the nature of change and innovation itself is likely to marginalize them within a given organizational context.

The second group of people, the Change Agents or Opinion Leaders, has the social skills and connections necessary to introduce the innovation to others. They are the sales people who are able to take complex new ideas and explain them in words of one syllable and make people believe that the new idea is a good one. They are particularly effective in introducing new ideas to the next group, the Early Adopters (Trendsetters), the people who are willing to try new things in any given population or organization.

The Trendsetters are a critically important group of people for the introduction of an innovation. These people go out and buy the first pet rocks or the first desktop computers. They like new things, they are not resistant to change, and, best of all, they tell their friends about it. With any given innovation that is proposed, they are not a large group of people, but there are more of them in any community than there are Opinion Leaders. Making the link between the Trendsetters and the Opinion Leaders on the community level means doing things like holding neighborhood meetings in the homes of the Opinion Leaders, who then invite their Trendsetter friends to hear about the new community development strategy. Or they ask the Opinion Leaders to write letters to the editor of the local paper in support of a new initiative.

A group that tends to be even larger than the Trendsetters and the Opinion Leaders combined is the Conservatives, or the Maintreamers, as AtKisson described them. These people are more resistant to change; the label does not reflect a political orientation but rather their receptivity to a particular innovation. They are satisfied with the way things are and are likely to wait a long time before they buy a new desktop computer or that new automotive technology that reduces gas consumption. They are a big part of the reason that significant change is so hard to achieve. Yet, when you consider that all change is not necessarily good, these people are also responsible for a certain level of stability within a community system. Any implementation effort needs to consider this group and to factor in a strategy and timeline to help them adopt whatever is being proposed. This group needs proof that an innovation will not only succeed but will benefit them in some way. They need to see a clear demonstration of the benefit before they are likely to sign on.

There are a few other types of people who need to be taken into consideration as part of an implementation plan: Iconoclasts, Reactionaries, and Curmudgeons. Iconoclasts are the outspoken social critics, people who are not afraid to fight with city hall or protest something they think is wrong. These people do not generate new ideas; they challenge old ones. If they can be included in the implementation plan, their energies challenging the existing basis for the proposed change, they can be very effective, especially if their work distracts the next group of people, the Reactionaries.

Reactionaries fight any change that comes along. They defend business-as-usual, and the status quo. Set against the Iconoclasts, the Reactionaries can be engaged, as they defend the status quo. Often in doing so, the Reactionaries undermine their own credibility. Some of their underlying biases and dysfunctional motivations come to light, and they lose supporters, moving them unhappily, but nevertheless steadily, in the direction of the change that is being proposed.

The Reactionaries are not far from the next group, the Curmudgeons. These people are against everything — at least the Reactionaries are in favor of the status quo. Curmudgeons can be miserable, bitter people, and their efforts often work to make other people miserable as well. It is best to avoid them at all costs, because their negativity can be a real poison for any implementation of transformation. If avoidance is impossible, one strategy that occasionally works to defuse Curmudgeons is to actively recruit them for some sort of decision-making role, although it would be best if the decisions that they had to make were not central to the success of the effort. Often, if they feel that they play an important part in something, they can turn around.

The final group that is worth mentioning is the Spiritual Leaders. Spiritual Leaders can help the public transcend forces that might work to resist change. They call people to a higher consciousness and can be very important, if not critical, to solidifying a vision that addresses the need for change in the first place. While they are not always easy to pull into a program for change, they should be invited to be part of the process. Historically, exemplars of this group are Martin Luther King, Gandhi, or the Dalai Lama. By seeking out local Spiritual Leaders to inquire of their opinions and input, they can be invited to contribute. Sometimes, depending on the issue, Spiritual Leaders will bring their followers along.

All of these personality types must be considered and involved in the implementation plan. For example, knowing the Conservatives often need clear demonstrations of the benefits of an innovation, the strategy might include highly visible examples of Trendsetters using it. Providing incentives for people who are willing to use the innovation for a trial period, or simply inviting neighbors to a demonstration are useful approaches. Recognizing that different people in the general population have very different reactions to change is very important for the development of a successful implementation plan.

## The Respectful and Caring Group Process

The stakeholder group will have to discuss information, share opinions, resolve disagreements, and gain an understanding of all the points of view that are offered. The more a diverse group can interact successfully, the more robust and meaningful will be the result. The group needs to create conditions for respectful meetings where everyone will have an opportunity to speak and to be heard, where there is fairness, and everyone feels of equal value. A few approaches to cultivating group meetings with these values will be discussed next.

When anything goes in a group setting, respectful and insightful discussion may be very difficult to achieve unless there are some ground rules and guidelines on which people can agree. It is important to consider how group discussion will happen and to have an adept facilitator to guide the process. In any planning process there will be strong opinions and special interests. People are not always comfortable in a group, stating their opinions, or questioning others, or arguing points of disagreement. As a result, many people will often sit quietly, not participating for fear of confrontation or of breaking some unwritten rule about how the group is supposed to work. Displaying, discussing, and agreeing to the rules or guidelines before you begin your work will encourage participation, and the process will be much more successful.

Nine guidelines to consider:

1. Speaking: Speak so everyone can hear you; one person speaks at a time. Speak the truth without blame or judgment. Pay attention to what has meaning for you and speak that meaning.

2. Listening: Give the speaker your full attention; stay open to new ideas, stop the mind chatter, and listen without making assumptions or judgments; please do not have side conversations while one person is speaking.

3. Using Time: Make an agreement with each other, a contract with time — to begin and end the meeting on time as agreed. Show up on time prepared to share the results of your effort.

4. Focus on the system as the problem, not the people.

5. Be open to the outcome; we don't usually know what the results of group process will be until it's done.

6. Keep your agreements, be impeccable with your word.

7. Be present oriented. Try to stay connected to how things are in real time, in the now.

8. Avoid hypothetical instances to make your point but do formulate scenarios that create opportunity pathways to where you want to go and what you want to accomplish.

9. Always do your best.

## Effective Meetings

It is useful to consider the questions, What is an effective meeting? How do you know the meeting was successful? Effective meetings improve productivity; people were able to confront difficult issues; participation increased, meetings were efficient and effective, issues were discussed and decisions were made. An excellent resource for managing effective meetings is the book *How To Make Meetings Work: The New Interaction Method* by Michael Doyle and David Strauss.[6] It is a small, inexpensive paperback with very readable information on holding meetings for the layperson and professional manager. Many leaders have used this method for over 25 years with great success.

Very briefly, the Interaction Method separates the *what* (the content) from the *how* (the process) by first clarifying for the group that the process is how the group works through issues. Some examples of processes are: making a list, evaluating, solving, and discussing. The content is *what* you list, evaluate, or discuss. In a group you must agree on a common what (content) and a common how (process) or the whole thing will fall apart. The meeting can become a shambles of individuals trying to be heard and can easily deteriorate into an angry mayhem. Think of a traffic jam, and you will get the picture of a group out of control.

Managers often try to anticipate this control problem and develop an agenda and schedule ahead of time to control the meeting. That approach may ensure efficiency but not effectiveness, because the creativity and spontaneity of the group can be squelched. The book shows you how to build an agenda on the spot to include the latest information. Every meeting needs a sensitive moderator who will keep an open and balanced conversation and who will be able to adjust to the moment-by-moment needs of individuals in the group without letting any one person dominate. The Interaction Method also details the roles necessary to make meetings work, the Facilitator, the Recorder, and the Group Member.

The Facilitator's job is to clearly define the roles, to get agreement on a common process and content, to reflect questions to the group, to help educate the group about options for enriching the process, to encourage people to participate, to protect them from attack, and to coordinate pre- and post-meeting logistics.

The Recorder's job is to create a group memory from what the participants are saying. This helps to focus the group on a task, acts as a record of a meeting's content and process, frees people from taking notes, assures people that their ideas were heard and recorded, and helps prevent needless repetition. The recorder writes the words of the speaker and listens for key words and phrases to capture the essence of the meeting.

When a group discusses issues that affect a large number of people, it is important to accurately record the information in a way where everyone can see it. Charting it with marker and newsprint is the usual way. Using a computer and projector is becoming more common. Each person in the group might have information to share about a particular issue. This information might come from gossip, from newspapers, from extensive personal research, or from local authorities, all of which will have differing levels of credibility. It is important to record the sources of the information as a standard practice as they are presented and then to follow up by checking their accuracy. A person could be designated to follow up on questionable information or to do further research on a particular topic. This person also might agree to keep minutes, making a knowledge repository open and accessible to the community, perhaps in a website.

Everyone else is a Group Member. The Group Members lead and the Facilitator assists. The Facilitator may need to coax the group along until people feel comfortable participating. The quality of the meeting depends on the Group Members and their contributions; everyone needs to take responsibility for it being a high-quality experience. The Facilitator will take care of the process. Being a good listener is very important, and it's useful to practice listening skills such as active listening, dialogue, conflict resolution, and high-impact discussion.

## The Retreat

When a diverse group of strangers gets together for the first time to discuss something as important as sustainable community development and the future of their community, a retreat that includes a cordial, relaxed social time will help them to get to know each other. The retreat is a good time to discuss some guiding principles and ground rules for the group process. It is advisable to set aside time for the stakeholder group to focus exclusively on designing the groundwork for the community sustainability project. Ideally, it is good to get people away from their normal setting for two or three days together to get acquainted, to share meals, and have some fun as well. But even if the retreat can only be a day long, it is well worth the time it will take to do it. All the subsequent work will be easier as the people begin to build trust and camaraderie.

During the retreat, it is important to describe the scope of the project, so people have an opportunity to comment on the sustainability planning process itself. In group activities participants can learn about, and determine, how the process will work. Each phase should be discussed — the needs assessment, vision, strategy development, implementation, and evaluation. Realistically, each of these steps will require more time than allotted for the retreat, but it's a good start, and people can continue to work together in teams. An action plan with goals, timelines, and a schedule for regular meetings should be determined. Subcommittees or teams can be established, and all individuals ought to determine what roles they will play in the process. It is important for everyone to have a role and that they be perceived as important to the group process.

Roles and guidelines for interaction can be determined and agreed upon. Other issues must be decided. Where will meetings be held? How will disagreements be handled? How will conflict be resolved? How will final decisions be made, and by whom? How will subcommittees give their input to the whole group? Who are the leaders? How will meetings be run? There is a lot to discuss organizationally, especially for people who have never worked together. If there is a municipal mandate for the group to follow, such as laws that require meetings be open to the public, or a special charge to the committee, or limits set on the scope of its work, then all these should also be discussed. For many of the questions, there are no right answers, only the answers that the group itself determines. Leaders can suggest certain methods to use, but the group must decide to use them or not.

## Common Patterns of Group Behavior

It is important for a people to know they are not the first group in the world who got together and worked on improving their community. Studies of different groups have revealed a common pattern of group behavior: Forming-Storming-Norming-Performing. In the Forming stage, the people don't know each other very well, and they tend to avoid conflict, preferring instead to defer to others, maybe to a natural leader, and to keep their opinions to themselves. This only lasts for so long, and if individual members of the group have experienced being suppressed in groups, the next phase, Storming, might be quite disruptive. In the Storming phase, the gloves come off, and people start to make their egos and suppressed opinions known, engaging in conflict, and not shying away from confrontation. This phase can be so severe and unpleasant that groups break up and stop their work. In a community planning process, you want to prepare people to work together through this phase by acknowledging at the outset that conflict is inevitable and establishing some guidelines and decision-making strategies to address it.

In a typical group process, open conflict might happen before people realize they need to agree and develop rules for interaction. This is known as the Norming phase — when the group sets standards and rules, so they can manage the conflict of Storming. Storming is also an opportunity for the testing of ideas, of listening carefully and respectfully without reacting or judging; all skills worthy of mastery. Group work will provide many opportunities to practice. After the norms have been established, the Performing phase begins where people work together effectively to reach their goals. With training, orientation, and a retreat at the start of the process, it is possible to manage conflict and to make it productive rather than destructive, by agreeing in advance on how to work together.

## Conflict Resolution

Conflict is inevitable in any group process, and its qualities and quantities either can reinforce a healthy group dynamic or can undermine it. If the conflict management skills are used diligently, then the conflict that does emerge should be productive and will help the group move in a synergistic direction. If not, then the conflict can escalate, egos can be bruised, feelings can be hurt, and a negative reinforcing loop can dominate the group dynamics. Conflict can, and does, tear good working groups apart, more often than not.

What is conflict? At its most elemental level, conflict is a function of power and of competition. Conflict emerges in a group setting when there is competition for something — ideas, money, control, space, affection, time, or resources, to name a few. Earlier, self-determination was identified as a strong human need that we all share. In group settings, satisfying our need for self-determination often hinges on our ability to get the group to agree with us. When several autonomous, headstrong, and capable people get together, there are bound to be times when each of their individual propensities to control the outcome of the group process will be stymied by others in the group, and conflict will result.

The key to making conflict a positive force in group dynamics is to recognize that it is inevitable, not an unexpected and unpleasant phenomenon to be avoided at all costs, and to plan for it in advance, *before* the conflict emerges. It is helpful to adopt some conflict resolution rules at the outset of a group process, so that there will be a safe and productive procedure to follow when it happens. It is helpful to have decision-making structures articulated in advance, so conflict won't emerge simply because the decision-making process is unclear or ineffective. The exact form the conflict resolution procedures and decision making will take will vary depending on the group involved, along with any existing laws, regulations, or procedures that govern the situation. Part of any procedure should be a clear articulation of the vision statement, mission, and the conflict resolution criteria. Agreement on criteria in advance is an important way to guide decisions through later conflict.

## SELF-ORGANIZATION AND PUBLIC PARTICIPATION

Self-organizing systems exhibit the capacity to create process struc-tures and responses that fit the time and circumstances. Self-organization comes easily when the actors in the system are free to do things that help meet their needs. In self-organizing adaptive organizations, the task determines the organizational form. Organizations that develop their capacity and readiness to respond are structured around core competencies and can produce expertise, teams, and projects in rapid response to a need. Yet even in unorga-nized situations, the capacity for self-organization overrides even some of our institutional attempts to block it.

When housing is in short supply, for example, and more jobs are in urban rather than in rural areas, informal settlements spring up around large cities as immigrants from rural areas move in. Where free enterprise has been outlawed, black markets spring up spontaneously because, in part, of the important role the market plays in meeting human needs. Human needs are powerful drivers of self-organization; community leaders and national policy-makers ignore them at their peril.

All human community systems depend on the capacity to self-organize. The capacity of these systems to change, or to reproduce or sustain themselves, depends on the structures put in place as processes evolved. Some elements of governance systems are more rigid than others. It is more difficult, for example, to change the constitution of a country than it is to introduce a new set of regulations. Religious systems remain virtually unchanged for thousands of years. College and university curricula can either remain intact or be reinvented reg-ularly, adapting to the needs of students, the changing times, and the demands for knowledge.

Two actions to consider when designing an implementation strat-egy for transforming a community system are: (1) identifying the elements of a system likely to resist change, and (2) providing open-ings to external influences that might facilitate change. On the first point, a needs and systems analysis can often identify balancing feed-back cycles in a community, which tend to be systems that seek equilibrium and have a powerful resistance to change.

On the second point, it is important to involve the public in the plan as it is developed. Managers may think they have the right ideas and the solutions to the problems, but unless they work with people who are part of the community, countless opportunities for creativity, new ideas, and strategies will be missed. Community members will be much more supportive of any decisions the governing body makes if they have a level of ownership in the proceedings. Thoughtful strategies developed by administrators seem fine until the staff or public gets wind of the plan. Then the divergent interests that are active in city politics and government come into play, and the process of achieving widespread buy-in has begun.

Public participation is a two-way street. It means talking — and listening — to the people in the community. It means finding new ways to get people appropriately involved in whatever project is underway. At the heart of any implementation process is the recognition that we are all in this together, everyone matters, and everyone's opinion counts. Authentic public participation is a radical sharing of power over our common future.

The public participates in decision making and implementation within their communities in many ways, from relatively passive to very active involvement. The design of a public participation plan requires a variety of strategies for involving people and will be important to the implementation of any sustainable community effort. What follows is a description of each stage of this spectrum of community engagement in the decision-making process.

## Public Information

At the most passive end of the public participation spectrum are efforts by governing bodies to inform the public of the initiatives they are taking through one-way communication — TV programs, radio ads, newspaper articles, brochures, mass mailings, or other media. The word gets out to the people, whether or not there is any way for them to respond. For many years in the U.S., these public information strategies were the dominant form of public participation that many government agencies supported, forgetting that the public also had a mind of its own. While one-way communication is a very important component of any public communication plan, a participation strategy can't be limited to it.

## Public Meetings

At the next level of involvement, government officials hold a public meeting to initiate an informational exchange, dialogue or conversation.

If the meetings are formal public hearings, the government invites comments from the public on a proposed law or policy. Sometimes the meetings take the form of roundtables or focus groups, where people offer opinions in a less structured, more open-ended way. In both cases, the government is usually listening to people (a step up from simply talking), yet not really involving them directly in decision making.

## Stakeholder Groups

Stakeholder groups have become a popular way to involve the public in decision making through proxies. Proxies are people who are asked to represent particular interests on a board that will help the government make decisions. These groups often become formal links to government agencies or offices, and, if the selection of proxies is not done in a democratic fashion, they can also serve to limit participation, if special interest groups become the sole form of public participation. For example, in the informal settlements outside of Johannesburg, South Africa, several successful projects have been done with the help of stakeholder groups from the settlements. Yet since the settlements themselves have not been formalized and incorporated as self-governing entities, the existence of the stakeholder groups has served over the longer term to limit participation in decision making to the stakeholder groups, rather than extending the votes and control over decisions to the residents of the settlements.

## Direct Democracy

In New England, direct democracy has been practiced for nearly three hundred years in the form of annual Town Meetings. These allow registered voters to participate in an annual meeting where the budget is set, new laws are passed, and other business is conducted. There is a representative body, the Selectboard, who functions in the place of Town Meeting over the course of the year. Citizens can approach the Selectboard with issues or comments. When issues come up, in the interim, that require a Town Meeting vote, a special meeting can be called to address the issue. Direct democracy means that all citizens have a direct role in decision making.

## Citizen Initiatives

Citizens can take the initiative and make proposals for government action in many U.S. states, through a petition process that results in a general election. This is another form of what is called direct democracy. For example, citizens in California presented citizen initiatives calling for more funding for the construction of public schools and water pollution control projects. In 2002, citizen initiatives won $2.6 billion of general obligation bonds to conserve natural resources (land, air, and water), to acquire and improve state and local parks, and to preserve historical and cultural resources.[7] Citizen initiatives can be a powerful way to redirect resources to things that people care about.

Using these strategies and others is a way to release the amazingly creative potential of the community. The more people who can be touched and motivated as part of an overall planning process, the more successful it will be. Innovation is not something that happens overnight; it often is very difficult to move forward. To help new strategies and mindsets find a foothold in a community, it is helpful to understand both how to reach and involve people, and how people will react to new ideas.

### CONCLUSION

When we speak of community change as metamorphosis, it will always be an extraordinary journey. The result will be far more beautiful than can be imagined. The essence of a community depends upon establishing relationships and exchanges in the form of feedback loops and recursive learning processes that become fundamental to its very functioning. If it freezes into rigid institutionalized and routinized structures it will not be able to evolve to its potential or to adapt to changing conditions and offer vital responses to the needs of the community. Communities must continuously break down old patterns and systems and establish a culture of learning and change.

An example of how the participatory learning process can work in a city is the story of the blind men and the elephant. Several blind men approached an elephant and tried to describe to each other what the elephant looked like. Each perceived only a part of the elephant and thought they knew what it was. To one man, at the tail, it was like a rope. To another, who felt the toenail, it was like a hard object. The man who felt the hide said that it was like a suitcase. When the blind men got together and shared their knowledge, they experienced real synergy as they discovered a new meaning — the whole elephant. Transformation happens when participants share, listen, and respond. Imagine what difficulties the blind men would have if each of them tried to get the others to only see their narrow perspective, missing the opportunity for a more complete view.

It is important to create the context for the possibility of transformation that happens as community members express their views and experience and listen to those of others — all in the pursuit of making things better for everyone. Whole systems change comes about through co-creating a shared vision, generating a constancy of purpose, and germinating new emergent possibilities.

## CHAPTER 8

# Whole System Strategies

ONCE THE COMMUNITY ASSETS ARE IDENTIFIED, and a vision is developed, and the process of change is understood, it's important to try and develop strategies that can transform the existing systems into more sustainable systems. Systems dynamics offers two main tools for strategy development — leverage points and systems strategies. Leverage points offer insight into where a small amount of effort can change the way the systems dynamics are working — they have the potential to turn a system that is spiraling out of control in the wrong direction into one that is moving in the same reinforcing way in a beneficial direction. They will be discussed further in Chapter 9.

Systems strategies are larger strategies that draw on lessons from many years of systems modeling, which can often lead to leverage points, but that are not necessarily leverage points themselves. Systems understanding also offers important insights on why some of the current strategies for solving problems don't work or actually make the original problem worse.

## CHANGING SYSTEMS, NOT SOLVING PROBLEMS

The idea of systems strategies and leverage is fundamentally different from the analytical, problem solving orientation. For example, the problem solving orientation might take on the problem of homelessness as a target for a community development project. With this orientation, the problem is stated as: "We have a growing homeless population in the city." Solutions are proposed — more homeless shelters, more transition facilities, more housing subsidies. The problem of homelessness is seen as a series of isolated, individual events that culminate in a group of people who need housing, not an issue that has systemic or structural roots.

Taking a whole systems approach would look quite different. Once the need for housing is identified, all of the ways that the community provides housing to its members can be explored. For example, the research might find, as it did in Vermont, that many homes built recently are very large and full of expensive features — the economy has been booming, and people are upwardly mobile. Construction of lower-priced, middle-, and lower-middle-class homes has virtually stopped. There are a limited number of construction firms in the area, and their profit on the high-end homes is much higher than on lower-priced homes. The research might also show a low vacancy rate in the rental housing in the community. The existing homeless shelters and transition housing are also reviewed — the increase in homeless people has placed a real burden on these services. The hotels in the area are filled with homeless people as a result.

People who have some understanding of systems dynamics might notice that there is a bottleneck in the housing market. Large homes are being constructed, but the people moving into these homes are a small number of highly paid executives. People who need middle-income housing are filling the rental market because there are no new homes being built, and few being vacated, that meet their needs. The low vacancy rate in the rental market, in turn, is forcing people into homelessness, because the lack of supply causes inevitable higher prices.

Then one day, during an interview with a woman who works in the homeless shelter, she asks the researchers a hard question: What do you think is the leading cause of homelessness in this city? They swallow hard. They don't know. Unemployment? That doesn't fit, because there are jobs available in the local area. There are stories about families with two parents working but who are homeless. High prices? That might be it. No, she says, neither of those things. The one thing that causes more homelessness than any other factor is that people smoke cigarettes. Cigarettes are getting more and more expensive, and so they can be the one thing that stands in the way of being able to afford an apartment or not. She tells a story about how she's been able to work with the people at the shelter to give up alcohol, to give up drugs, but has had the hardest time of all getting them to give up cigarettes.

It would take many years of research and the production of fairly sophisticated models to prove the specific role that the cost and habit of cigarettes play in homelessness, but this systems approach to the community development process has yielded two important points. If instead of building homeless shelters and transition housing, a proactive campaign was initiated to get low-income people to quit smoking, this might have beneficial impacts beyond the issue of homelessness and housing. The analysis of housing services in the local community indicates it would also seem that encouraging the construction of middle-income housing might help reduce the homelessness in the area and encourage people in the middle-income sector to move out of the rental housing.

The two strategies described above are quite different from the usual reaction to homelessness with building more shelters, providing more subsidies, and making more transition housing available. Assuming that the two alternatives proposed are strategies that would work, they also illustrate another truth about using a systems approach to make communities more sustainable. In this case, the leverage point might be the cigarette smoking habits of low-income people. Now, to most people, conducting an anti-smoking campaign as a way to alleviate homelessness in the area is not intuitive at all. Leverage points are often like this — they are hidden from a superficial view of the situation. The other strategy, creating more middle-income housing as a way to alleviate homelessness, is also not the first thing that people would think about. It is a larger, systemic strategy that is only discovered after reaching a fuller understanding of how the entire system works — another characteristic of using systems to take positive action. Is it a leverage point? Not really — implementing a policy to create more middle-income housing can hardly be described as taking a small action to have big results; building moderate-income housing on a large scale is not a small task. Yet large tasks that have a systemic foundation are much more likely to be successful than those that are based on a fragmented and incomplete understanding of the issues.

## STRATEGIES FOR SYSTEM CHANGE

Donella and Dennis Meadows made history when they created the first computer model that dared to simulate the entire world system in the 1970s. Their simulation produced some alarming results, which they described in a book titled *The Limits to Growth*, published in

1972.[1] Since then, hundreds of researchers have spent entire careers developing computer models that imitate and track real systems, to try and determine how they work, to predict how they will behave in the future, and to increase our overall understanding of complex systems. Out of this voluminous and ponderous work has come some new understandings of the places to intervene in a system. Donella Meadows published a short article on this subject, in 1999, called "Leverage Points: Places to Intervene in a System."[2] In this article, she identified twelve parts of a system that are sensitive to change:

1. Constants, parameters, numbers (such as subsidies, taxes, standards).

2. The size of buffers and other stabilizing stocks, relative to their flows.

3. The structure of material stocks and flows (such as transport networks, population age structures).

4. The length of delays, relative to the rate of system change.

5. The strength of negative feedback loops, relative to the impacts they are trying to correct.

6. The gain around driving positive feedback loops.

7. The structure of information flows (who does and does not have access to what kinds of information).

8. The rules of the system (such as incentives, punishments, constraints).

9. The power to add, change, evolve, or self-organize system structure.

10. The goals of the system.

11. The mindset or paradigm out of which the system — its goals, structure, rules, delays, parameters — arises.

12. The power to transcend paradigms.[3]

Each of these intervention points identified by Meadows will be discussed with respect to community systems, to provide some insight into systems strategies and the use of leverage points for effecting positive change in a community.

## 1. Constants, parameters, numbers (such as subsidies, taxes, standards)

Meadows listed the intervention points in reverse order of their effectiveness, so on the scale of places to intervene, this one is the weakest point. Changing these elements of a system is the least likely way to produce the desired change. Yet, paradoxically, this is the first type of strategy that people think of when they are trying to solve a problem. In the earlier example of homelessness, the traditional response to homelessness has been to increase housing subsidies. Yet increasing the housing subsidy does not address the structural problems that were discovered when people evaluated the whole housing system in the community. The subsidies only provide more money for the people without housing to attempt to buy into the rental market. This in turn, given the laws of supply and demand, is more likely to drive the cost of rental housing up in a market where there is limited supply, and not bring the cost down. It could very possibly create more homelessness, not less.

If a community wanted to protect its open space, it might pass regulations that require large developments to set aside parts of their land for common space, or green space. This would be an example of a parameter change. Would it protect green space? Yes. Would it do so in the way that the community envisioned, while maintaining wildlife corridors, watersheds, and viewsheds? Probably not. Rather, it would add small parcels of green space into an increasingly fragmented form of urban sprawl.

Let's consider the earlier example of the road repair system. Spending more money fixing the worst roads in town is not going to improve the town roads overall. In fact, just like changing any parameter that is blind to the system as a whole, it may make it worse. What needed to change wasn't the money spent on the worst roads; it was the orientation of the town leadership toward maintaining the roads that weren't in bad shape.

When parameters are used within the context of a comprehensive understanding of the system, they can have more influence on the way it changes. But they are still a very weak point. For example, if a community imposes impact fees to moderate the cost of new development on public infrastructure, this is a parameter change that will actually target the systemic impact it is trying to mitigate. If a shopping center is being built that will have a serious impact on a particular intersection in town, and the impact fee assessed allows the town to take action to correct the situation by adding lights or turning lanes, then there is a direct causal link between the parameter change, the impact fee, and the issue, traffic congestion at a particular intersection. If the developer of the shopping center doesn't have the will or the money to provide the town with the impact fee, the project doesn't happen; so, again, the traffic flow is stabilized.

As a society, we spend a lot of time and energy playing with numbers and parameters. The impact that these changes have on the whole system is minimal, and unless they fit into an understanding of the way the system works (which would place them in another category of system interventions), they are more likely to have the opposite effect than was intended.

## 2. The sizes of buffers and other stabilizing stocks, relative to their flows

A buffer, or stock, is the existing amount of a particular resource that is held in storage. Using the example of homelessness, the existing *stock* of housing in a community is the *buffer* against homelessness. One of the systems strategies used in that example was to create policies to increase the stock of moderate-income housing as a way of addressing the problem of homelessness in the community. This is an example of a strategy that adjusts the buffer or stock as a way to change the system. As it demonstrated, changing the stock can be a costly and long-term prospect. It doesn't provide instant gratification of the unmet needs, like the money savings that might accrue from a homeless person kicking the cigarette habit. This is why it is listed at the least-effective end of the spectrum of places to change systems, rather than at the most effective end.

In northeastern cities and towns every fall, the highway department spends one month working to stockpile road sand and gravel for winter. Creating this buffer for the community means that when the storms come, there will be sand to put on the roads and sidewalks to keep them open. In the spring, when dirt roads in rural communities become impassable mud holes, the gravel set aside the year before will allow the road crew to make those roads passable. Stocks and buffers are important.

But, at the same time, there would be no point in spending many months each year putting sand and gravel aside for several years' supply. The impact of the gravel withdrawal would be higher, more space would be needed to store it, and even though mobilization time would be saved by the highway departments, the costs would exceed the benefits. Increasing the supply so that it would cover several years might cause other problems, as other routine maintenance was ignored for another month to create the sand pile. So, even though stocks and buffers are important, there is a limited amount of good they can do to make any system more sustainable.

### 3. The structure of material and non-material stocks and flows

Communities build systems to manage their material and economic flows, the flow of information, relations, and caring services. There are sewer pipes, road systems, libraries, banks, hospitals, schools, churches, water pipes, stores, and all kinds of structures. Sometimes the way the physical structures are put together makes a huge difference to the behavior of the system they are built to accomodate.

For example, when sewer systems were put in many cities and towns in the early 1900s, all of the wastewater was directed into them. This included the wastewater from toilets, washing machines, sinks, car washes, industry, street runoff, roofs and gutters; everything that used or touched water in the course of the day. The sewage treatment plants at the end of the pipe often have their operations seriously compromised by events, like rainstorms, that put a lot more water through the system. These plants were not designed for peak flows, so the result is that, during storm events, raw sewage flows into the rivers and streams that receive the plants' effluent. Sewage plants are always located on rivers and streams to discharge treated effluent; only smaller innovative systems have developed the capacity to discharge the treated effluent to groundwater.

This is a simple example of how the structure of a material flow has a serious impact on the water system as a whole. If communities downstream from sewage treatment plants rely on the river for water supply, they are not able to use it after storm events. The United States Environmental Protection Agency (EPA) devised a solution for this problem; they provide towns with zero-interest loans to construct combined sewer overflow (CSO) facilities. This separates the sanitary sewage pipes from the highway drainage system, as a first step, and often provides some primary treatment for the highway runoff. These projects are enormously expensive, as is any structural reconstruction project, which means that they are not a leverage point, per se, but rather are a strategy undertaken with the whole system in mind.

Structures exist to manage the flows within all the community systems, and often these structures are part of the problem, not part of the solution. Banking structures, with customs and rules that have been in place for hundreds of years, have an important influence on who has access to financing for new ventures, and who does not. Information systems — the booming new area for our culture as a whole — have complex structures; computers, the internet, websites, libraries, and cyber cafes, that direct and manage the flow of information. The suburban neighborhood, with its neat fences and large yards to keep people apart, is a built structure that has an enormous influence on the ways in which we know people, and care for them, in the community where we live. It would be better to design these structures and systems right before they are built, because rebuilding them is almost impossible due to the expense involved.

Once the structure of a flow and its capacity is understood, another strategy is to devise ways that the flow won't be causing bottlenecks or be put under pressure. This is impossible in the case of rainwater entering the sewer system, but there are flows that are more manageable. Computer applications are always devising new ways to stop the viruses that overload the Internet's capacity to work effectively, and this is possible with other human inventions as well. Making the vast information on the Internet available to people who can't afford computers by putting computers in local libraries is an important leverage point for information dissemination.

The expense of retrofitting a physical structure is the reason that this systems strategy is one of the least effective interventions. It is much easier to design the system right in the first place than it is to change it once it's in place. For non-material flows, however, there are a lot of possibilities for effective change, if the structural elements are taken into consideration.

## 4. The lengths of delays relative to the rate of system changes

Delays were discussed in Chapter 4 — their occurrence in systems can cause oscillations over time, as the system tries to stay in equilibrium when the system conditions are overshooting the goal or underperforming because the information required to meet the need is delayed. Public infrastructure development is always going to have long delays that make it hard to meet needs perfectly over time. In western Massachusetts, for example, a building boom in the 1980s led to severe school overcrowding. In some schools, classes were held in hallways, principals moved their offices to the foyer of the school to make room for students. Yet the delay inherent in the process of building new schools meant that it took years to address the overcrowding, and by the time the schools were built, some towns found themselves in the midst of another baby bust, with more capacity than they needed.

Reducing the delay in responding to the system changes can be a leverage point for meeting needs more effectively. Some schools used prefabricated modular classrooms to take the overflow — modules that could be returned later when the student body was reduced. These were not optimal, but were better than hallway instruction for meeting the educational needs of the students.

Yet another way that some towns responded to the influx of new students points to a more effective strategy than reducing the delay in school construction. In Heath, Massachusetts, for example, the town moved quickly to pass a building permit cap, to slow the rate of growth in their student population so the delay in building new infrastructure could take better account of long-term trends, rather than responding to an immediate need. This is part of the reason that delay is still one of the least effective interventions. Sometimes delays are unavoidable — public infrastructure is probably always going to take a long time to plan, finance, and construct.

When you can reduce or increase a delay, it is important to consider the effects of this change. Even though the planning process lengthens the time it takes to build public infrastructure, this time is often put to good use; public priority setting, votes on capital bond issues, and public procurement processes all insure that the public good is being served. Shortening the process in the name of efficiency might open it up to more closed, corrupt, or elitist practices.

Sometimes delays can help keep the system in balance. The plodding and often Byzantine process of making municipal expenditures ensures that the public money is spent correctly and within budgetary and fiscal constraints. If the checks and balances that cause these delays were eliminated, it could cause much more difficulty for the financial managers in municipal government to control cash flow and insure fiduciary due diligence.

## 5. The strength of negative feedback loops relative to the impact they are trying to correct

A negative feedback loop is found in the basic balancing system archetype that was discussed earlier. Its purpose is to keep a system in balance, to help it avoid too much change in any direction. It could be called an opposite feedback loop, because its function is to move in the opposite direction from a destabilizing influence. So, if I get too hot, the negative feedback loops built into my complex human body system trigger the perspiration process that cools me off. Negative feedback is the process of keeping a system in balance — homeostasis, achieving a particular system goal. A sprinkler system in an office building, a smoke alarm in your house; all of these systems provide information, or reactions, to things that would push the system out of balance in a harmful or dangerous way.

Negative feedback loops are everywhere. If the elected leaders stray too far from the values and expectations of the voters, they are voted out of office. The spiritual leaders and practices in a community help balance relationships among people — what better control on our human tendency to sink into destructive spirals of revenge and hatred than the healing power of forgiveness and mercy? In the economic system, negative feedback is found in the pricing system — if products get scarce, their price goes up; if they are too abundant, the price comes down. It is also found on a macroeconomics level in the interest/inflation balance. If inflation starts to go up, interest rate adjustments make money more scarce; if inflation is low and unemployment or productivity is a problem, interest rates come down. In the environmental system and physical infrastructure, feedback controls are ubiquitous. The air pressure systems that chase each other around the globe producing our weather patterns, the emergency response systems we design for our buildings, these are both part of the complex dance that keep systems in balance.

To develop a strategy for sustainability, strengthening the existing negative feedback or creating new negative feedback where systems are unprotected are ways to help achieve new kinds of balance. For example, many communities have developed extensive emergency response plans to reduce the negative impacts of natural disasters. These plans strengthen the existing systems to counteract the impacts of floods, or snowstorms, or hurricanes. Either through improved equipment, or early warning systems, or coordination with other nearby emergency response providers, the community is strengthening the negative feedback loop in relation to the desired effect.

## 6. The gain around driving positive feedback loops

Negative feedback loops keep a system in balance by providing an equal and opposite reaction for every action. The positive feedback loop acts to provide momentum for an action that is already underway — it increases what was already increasing. So, if you put money in the bank earning interest, the more interest you earn, the more money you have, the more money you have, the more interest you earn; a positive feedback loop at work. In the case of money in the bank, we like the continuously increasing effect that positive feedback can provide. In other cases, the growth of a cancer cell, nuclear fission, the spread of an epidemic, positive feedback loops are not so appealing.

On the level of social development, we often try to create positive feedback loops. The more educated people are, the more education they want. If we reach out with compassion to care for our neighbors, there is hope that they will do the same for others. The more beauty people experience — through the arts and music and cultural activities — the more they want, and the better they are at creating it. Sustainability strategies can help enhance the gain around the positive feedback loops in these cases. In cases where positive feedback loops produce negative results, the cycles of hatred and violence that can throw a country into civil war, or worse, we would look for ways to intervene with strategies designed to slow the gain around the positive feedback loops.

On the environmental level, positive feedback loops can also be a blessing and a curse. Environmental health can improve or deteriorate depending on whether the positive feedback is moving in a beneficial or deleterious direction. The fact that it's called *positive* does not imply an inherent value judgment. Positive only means that the cycle of feedback is moving in the same direction as the initial action.

One local example of how environmental health can deteriorate because of positive feedback is the eutrophication process in lakes and ponds. The more phosphorous pollution there is, the more algae growth will occur. The more algae and plant growth there is, the less dissolved oxygen is available for fish and other life forms. As the natural forces that would keep the lake or pond in balance decrease, the more the eutrophication process continues, until what was once a clear, pleasant lake looks like a swamp.

Another cycle of positive feedback is the growth in urban sprawl that is taking over so much of the countryside worldwide. As population is drawn into larger cities, the cities themselves get more congested, which causes many people to look for housing and land outside the city. The congestion that results from the increased commuter traffic results in the local communities widening roads and adding transportation amenities to address the problem. As they build more roads, the development potential in an area increases, which in turn contributes to increased urban sprawl.

Yet environmental health can also produce positive feedback that brings more health. Take riparian management as an example — if the erosion along river banks is corrected through carefully understanding the river flow dynamics, and buffers are created to allow the normal flooding and recovery to occur, the damaging force of the river can be substantially reduced, which in turn leads to less erosion. If trees grow overhead, the temperature in the river can be moderated, to allow for more life forms and more dissolved oxygen, which in turn make for a healthier ecosystem. Riparian buffer zones allow for more natural absorption of pollutants, create habitats for diverse species dependent on the river system, and protect the banks from erosion and degradation. Healthy practices and management lead to more health, more species diversity, more clean water.

Finding the driving forces behind positive feedback loops is an important system strategy, both for creating positive feedback when it's needed, and for putting the brakes on when it's not. This can also be a place to look for leverage points, because there is often a very fine point between what makes a system spiral upward in increasing well-being, and what can make it spiral downward into deterioration. The dynamics in an office environment is one example. If employees are treated well, they will perform better at work, which will make the organization perform better overall, which in turn can lead to higher pay, better benefits, and increased opportunities for advancement. But all too often, some small change in working conditions can trigger the opposite positive feedback loop. Employee morale goes down, which means that the organization doesn't perform as well, which means fewer pay raises and opportunities. There is a positive loop at work in both scenarios, and finding the point that can turn it around, if it's an unhealthy situation, is critical to sustainability.

## 7. The structure of information flows

Earlier, the structure of the flows of material through a community was described as a way to address problems. If you change the physical structures that catch storm water, so that the peak flows don't go into the wastewater treatment plant, you can significantly improve the performance of the treatment plant, as it stops dumping untreated sewage into the river. The same is true of information — if you change the structures that determine where, what, and when information flows to people, the reaction to the new information can have a dramatic impact on the system.

The movement to create community indicators is one example. If communities can arrive at a set of conditions they want to implement, and develop indicators to monitor and to evaluate the community performance on achieving those conditions, then this provides a new feedback loop where there was none before. So, if they are concerned about the people in the community who don't have access to primary healthcare because of a lack of insurance, and they start monitoring the number of visits to the emergency room for primary care, this new flow of information can help identify an unmet need. One community set up a free medical clinic as a result of new information about health services that were needed. The costs of emergency room care went down, and people who had previously relied on the emergency room for healthcare started to get better treatment in a more timely and less costly way.

The structure of information flows is all about accountability. The Wall Street scandal in 2002 where many large U.S. corporations were using faulty accounting practices *to hide information* about expenses and losses clearly illustrates this point. The stock market took its largest loss in history over the time period when the faulty accounting practices were revealed. Congress took action to improve the accounting practices, so that correct information about the companies would be revealed to investors and customers in a timely way. How, when, and to whom information flows is an important system strategy to consider in the search for leverage and sustainability.

New structures of information flow, however, do not always work in the best interest of the system. Witness a new government program launched by the Bush administration called TIPS, the Terrorism Information and Prevention System. With TIPS, the government was trying to create a huge population of informers — over one million nationwide, who are prepared to report any activity they deem suspicious to the federal government.

According to the government website, "TIPS will be a nationwide program giving truckers, letter carriers, train conductors, ship captains, and others a formal way to report suspicious terrorist activity ... The program will involve the millions of American workers who, in the daily course of their work, are in a unique position to see potentially unusual or suspicious activity in public places. The goal of the program is to establish a reliable and comprehensive national system for reporting suspicious, and potentially terrorist-related, activity."[4] Do we want so much information flow that we are willing to live with Big Brother in our midst? Some feedback loops are best left incomplete.

## 8. The rules of the system

Human systems have rules — rules of conduct, rules of conflict, rules of operation. Within a community, rules include the ways decisions are made, the laws that the citizens have to follow, and thousands of unwritten social rules, but they are followed with little or no thought by the majority of citizens.

The invisible social rules become quite visible when people find themselves in a different culture. In Vermont, for example, Norwich University accepts students for its military training program from all over the world. Recently, some recruits from a small, wealthy, foreign country came to town, and it was immediately clear that their social rules were not the same as those in rural Vermont. When they went to the Dunkin' Donuts for breakfast, for example, when they finished the meal, they pushed all the used napkins, dishes, etc. onto the floor — in their country, the women or servants would be expected to clean it up. Needless to say, the Dunkin Donuts employees did not take kindly to the foreign rules.

Rules are boundaries: they are goals; they define the size of the system and the freedom within the system. In biological systems, the boundaries are often tolerance points that cannot be exceeded — the rules of our bodies require that we breathe whatever is in Earth's atmosphere without interruption. In a municipality, rules will dictate how fast we can drive on the roads, how development proposals are processed, how leaders are elected, how they make decisions (Robert's Rules of Order), how someone can hook up to the municipal water or sewer system, where certain types of development can be located, who can live in subsidized housing developments, who has licenses for serving alcoholic beverages, how to keep pets, how to dispose of solid waste; all of these subsystems are shaped by the rules of operation.

Rules like the New England states' Open Meeting Laws, where public leaders are required to allow the press and public access television into their meetings, can help systems by providing information flow and feedback to the voters. When leaders of government resist public scrutiny, they are stopping the flow of critical information that can help maintain the health of the system.

Rules are powerful points to effect system change. For example, before recycling became mandatory in the 1980s, a very small percentage of people separated their trash for recyclables. After the rule, some areas have achieved over 90 percent compliance — almost everyone separates their trash for recyclables now. Laws protecting wetlands, watersheds, endangered species, rivers, and lakes all have had an impact on the ways in which our environment is treated. Laws about marriage, religion, education, and health care have an impact on the way the social system functions. Laws that govern conflict resolution, voting rights, electoral rules, and discrimination all have an impact on the way the political system works. There are also laws about banking, employment, contracts, insurance and others that govern the way the economic system works.

Rules, while powerful, often try unsuccessfully to counteract system dynamics that are more powerful, which is why they are not the most effective interventions, and why some of the very well-intended laws and regulations we put into place don't accomplish their goals. If a rule is put into place to protect wetlands, while the other dynamics of the system encourage development anywhere, no matter what the cost, the wetlands will not be protected. When property values far exceed the value of a fine for filling wetlands, and the existing rules encourage people to make as much money as they can, regardless of the harm they cause, people will fill in wetlands, pay the price, and still realize a profit.

## 9. The capacity of a system to add, change, evolve, or self-organize its structure

Systems are alive — they change and evolve. This capacity of any system is directly related to its resilience and sustainability. When systems stop changing and evolving, they die. The universe is a dynamic place to live in, so systems are always pressured from one direction or another to adapt to new conditions. When this happens to species over time, we call it evolution. When it happens through technological innovation, we call it human creativity. It is all a function of a remarkable and miraculous capacity that systems have — their ability to self-organize. Systems self-organize by drawing on the raw material from the gene pool, from collective knowledge, and from cultural traditions that have evolved over millennia. They use the raw material to test new patterns, new ways of being, new ideas. When an innovation fits and improves the system's functioning, the system uses it to perform better.

This self-organizing property is obvious in many community systems. They change and evolve regularly, as new demands are placed on their resources. In Vermont, there are two recent cases of a community's decision-making system changing in response to pressures — the examples are interesting because the two systems changed in opposite directions.

In Randolph, the Selectboard was responsible for making decisions on a wide variety of issues including the recreation program the town offered its residents, police department activities, maintenance of roads, operation and maintenance of the water and sewer system, and operation of a state-of-the-art landfill. Five people served on the Selectboard, and during their regular meetings, they would discuss all of the information pertaining to the required decisions, they would make a decision, and then move onto the next item. The meetings would often run very late as a result, and the decisions that were being made at two a.m. were often not good decisions. Bad decisions have consequences, and so their decision-making process added to their workload. It caused a vicious cycle, where decision making deteriorated over time. See the related diagram in Chapter 4, Figure 4.19.

Some new members came onto the board, and, with the Town Manager's help, they suggested that a committee system be established to help process the information that was needed for the decisions, and to have the committees make recommendations to the Selectboard for action. Residents had grown increasingly frustrated with the bad decisions, and so many people were quick to step forward to volunteer for the committees — the Water and Sewer Committee, a Police Committee, a Landfill Committee, a Recreation Committee, a Highway Committee, and several others. The committees met regularly and made recommendations to the Selectboard for action on different issues. Within a month of the committees being in operation, the Selectboard meetings started adjourning no later than ten p.m. The increased involvement by the committees in decision making also resulted in less opposition to the decisions over time, as residents became more familiar with all the different factors pertaining to the issues.

In Burlington, Vermont, the opposite adaptation occurred, just a few years after Randolph introduced the committee system. In Burlington, they were all too familiar with this form of decentralized decision making. In fact, the city's various commissions had a fair amount of independence from the city administration — the mayor no longer had the power to hire and fire department heads; in fact, those decisions were made by the commissions that were established to oversee the different departments. This made it very difficult for the mayor to exercise any direction over the different departments. Although he was seen by the large majority of the population as the person responsible for city services, he actually had less control than he needed to effect meaningful change. So, the mayor initiated a campaign to convince city voters that the structure of the city needed to change. All of the independent commissions needed to come under the authority of the city council, and the mayor needed to have hiring and firing authority over the department heads. The campaign was successful; the city charter was changed by the city and passed by the legislature during the following session.

Of these two adaptations by community decision-making systems, one brought citizens into the process by involving them on committees; the other curtailed some of the independence that the citizen commissions had exercised. Both changes came about based on models used by other similar decision-making entities, and both changes responded to their own unique circumstances. Neither change was imposed from above in some way, but was part of the self-organizing capacity that exists in a democratic context where municipalities have some freedom and flexibility to design their own structure.

The freedom to be self-organizing is a powerful leverage point for systems. If communities don't have the flexibility to choose their own way of doing things, then the capacity to self-organize, so that the systems improve, will be limited. Yet, when you look at communities worldwide, they are, for the most part, severely constrained by rigid state systems that do not allow for creativity and change at the municipal level. Municipalities in many countries, especially throughout the former Soviet Union, do not have independent sources of revenue that they can use for local services, but are completely dependent on the state budget. Often, the structure for decision making is dictated by the central government, not left up to the local authorities. Even in Vermont, if a city or a town wants to change its charter, it needs to go to the legislature for approval. States dictate the kinds of laws that municipalities can enact, and, in some cases, the local government is little more than an extension of the central nation-state.

Massachusetts has some of the most liberal and enabling statutes for local municipalities. The Home Rule Law in Massachusetts allows towns to pass any laws they want, providing that the laws are not specifically prohibited by state statute. Towns can't enact zoning bylaws that require lots greater than two acres — this is considered *snob zoning*. Towns can't enact laws governing the use of pesticides. So, when communities in Massachusetts were faced with out-of-control residential and commercial growth, they could enact laws that limited building permits. In Vermont, where state law only allows municipalities to enact laws that they are specifically permitted to pass, this is not possible.

## 10. The goals of the system

This book started with the premise that the goals of community systems are to meet human needs. Many examples have been given to demonstrate this basic fact. All of our needs for material goods and services, such as water, sewer, housing, transportation, food, clothing, shelter, and energy, are met through community systems. Our needs for economic security, and for meaningful work are met through the community economic systems. Our needs for a certain level of power over our environment, for conflict resolution, and for equity are met through the community political systems. Most importantly, our needs for spiritual fulfillment, for care and relationships, for education and healthcare, recreation, and arts and culture are met through the social systems that we have developed in our communities.

A powerful leverage point for changing community systems can be found in how we meet our human needs. If needs are being met in an unsustainable way, then it is important to go back to the basic need, and see if there is another way to satisfy it. For example, if our need for food and nourishment is being met through a food industry that is increasingly filling prepared foods with sugars, fats, genetically modified food, and other unhealthy ingredients, we can choose to meet our needs in different ways. We can buy other kinds of food. The companies wouldn't be profitable if it weren't for the money we spend on their products. If our need for transportation is being met through cars that use larger and larger amounts of fuel, adding to global warming, then we can pressure our communities to improve the existing public transit. We can reduce the need for transportation by locating homes nearer to the businesses where people work. But every strategy that looks at the need first, rather than the problems caused by meeting needs in unsustainable ways, will have an advantage over the types of band-aid solutions that are often proposed with the problem solving approach.

It is true that other system goals can conflict with the basic goal to meet human needs. The goals of profit maximization, of personal glory, and of ever-increasing dominance over others can, and do, hijack the community systems that have been developed to meet our needs. When a municipal leader starts to take bribes and favors specific companies that bid on municipal contracts, this takes resources that could be used for human needs and uses them against the goal. When municipalities concern themselves more with controlling the opposition and don't listen to the diverse voices available to them, they are limiting the capacity of the system to make needed adaptations that may meet needs more effectively. When companies use government monopoly powers to control markets and maximize their own profits at the expense of the city's residents, this reduces the resources available for these residents to meet their other future needs. All of the laws and policies that have been enacted to stop this kind of practice are there for good reasons, both from a moral point of view and from a systems perspective.

## 11. The mindset or paradigm out of which the system arises

Mindsets and paradigms form the background, subconscious, and extraordinarily powerful forces at work to form the systems we establish to meet our needs. History shows us that these mindsets and paradigms change over time. In fact, looking at history can be a way to understand how they might change, even now.

What is a mindset or paradigm? Paradigms are the theory behind the practice. If the business management paradigm says that the highest and best good for society is to maximize profit, this drives business and individual decisions. If the educational paradigm says that children will learn better in groups with the same level of abilities, then classes will be structured accordingly.

How are paradigms and mindsets established in the first place? It happens in a variety of different ways. In a book called *The Structure of Scientific Revolutions*,[5] Thomas Kuhn stated that the paradigm has been the operational theory under which the work of science is done. So, when Newton advanced his theory of the physical sciences, most of the research done after that was working within the parameters he had established. Paradigms only change, in science, when anomalies occur; when phenomena like stellar parallax can be observed that challenge the theory. (Stellar parallax was the phenomenon observed through a telescope that first offered concrete evidence that the sun did not revolve around the Earth — the stars were observed in slightly different positions in the sky at different times of year.)

In society, paradigms work differently than they do in science, although there are similarities. Looking at ancient history, we can observe a few interesting paradigm, or mindset, changes. One was the transition from a primarily nomadic economy, based on raising animals and moving around to find forage for them, to an agricultural economy, where property rights and governmental structures were important. This is illustrated in the Bible's description of the two lifestyles. In the earliest stories, the fight between Cain and Abel was over the type of offerings they made to God. Abel kept flocks, and Cain worked the soil. God looked with favor on Abel's offering, but not on Cain's. So what does Cain do? He kills Abel, a metaphor for the real tensions that were occurring at the time between the nomads and the farmers. If you fast-forward to the time of Jacob and Esau, however, the paradigm was changing. In that story, Esau was the hunter and Jacob was the farmer. Yet Jacob manages to trick his father into giving him power over his brothers, leaving Esau, the rightful heir, with nothing. The ease and speed with which Jacob was able to provide his father with food was a critical factor in the switch. Our socioeconomic evolution was shaped in a real way with the advent of agriculture as the dominant paradigm.

Over time, technological and social innovation have brought about sweeping changes to the agricultural mindset. In feudal times, people lived in an economy that is very different from the one we have today. Individual property ownership was not common — lords owned the land, and the serfs worked it for them. As time passed, serfs increased their ability to own land, as freeholders, and this gave rise to more mobility and trade among the population. With the independence of land ownership, people felt that they should have more of a say in the decisions of the commonwealth. It can be shown that the seeds of modern American democracy can be traced to the part of England that was known as the Danelaw in the first century.[6] This region was ruled for a long time by the Vikings, who had an egalitarian orientation towards fellow Vikings, and so the land ownership patterns in that part of England — to the north and east of London — had a much higher percentage of freeholders than anywhere else in the country at the end of feudalism. This area in England gave rise to the Jacobeans and the Puritans, both cultures exerting a powerful democratizing force on England and on the colonies overseas.

A paradigm changed. People no longer accepted the inherent domination of kings and lords, but wanted more of a voice in the government. A revolution had begun, one that would end in violence, on English, French, and American soil. The doctrine of human rights was disseminated, and tracts began to circulate that spoke of the Rights of Man. Change was slow, and it took time. Religious leaders spoke of it from their pulpits. Illicit pamphlets found their way into people's hands. Discussions occurred, in the taverns, in the market squares, among friends and family. For a people long accustomed to their place in society, the idea that all men were created equal was radical.

With the industrial revolution and expansion in world trade, we see another paradigm shift. People are no longer tied to their land. They can venture to the cities for jobs that pay cash. Industry and trade needed an expansionist mindset; the dynamics of capitalism require growth at an increasing rate for the possibility of larger prof-its to be maintained. Large disparities started to emerge between the people who owned the factories — the means of production — and the people who worked there. These inequities produced their own tensions. Marx came forward with his epic theory about capital, labor, and government that ignited a major paradigm shift in a large portion of the world and pitted capitalism against state socialism as two com-peting operative mindsets.

We've come beyond that now. Yet a new mindset for the post-polarized era has not been firmly established. The weaknesses and tensions inherent in both the capitalist and the state socialist (a.k.a. communist) model are leading to increasing problems — climate change, widespread corruption, bankruptcy of enormous firms in the U.S. and abroad, and an increasing and dangerous disparity between the rich and the poor, both within countries and globally. We need a new model, a model that works for people around the world. We need to challenge the paradigm that world trade is the highest and best goal for international government. Right now, the powerful international government that is in place through the World Trade Organization has the power to overturn national laws if they infringe on free trade — no other values have emerged as counterbalances to this dehumaniz-ing mindset.

If the mindset changes, the system changes. This is a powerful place to work, and one where the highest degree of leverage can be exerted. The values we have as a society are critical to the way our society works. Another major paradigm shift in history that is partic-ularly relevant to the Western world was the advent of Christianity. The Christian ethic permeates Western government and systems, even in places where the separation of church and state is clear. Our bankruptcy laws that allow the forgiveness of debt are not always found in countries where Christianity is not a dominant religion. The service clubs, the volunteer organizations, the social fabric of Western culture all are profoundly influenced by Christianity, even in a society that is increasingly secular and distanced from formal religion.

How did that shift take place? One man offered himself up as a living sacrifice to share the message that God is love. To tell us that we all have access to God, and that access is not limited to a chosen few who are descendents of particular clans or bloodlines. Forgiveness and mercy are God's way of connecting with us. This was a powerful message, and it spread like wildfire. While it is true that over time people have misappropriated this and other messages to fulfill their own ambitions, and have constructed religious power structures that have worked in direct opposition to the inherent spiritual truths of our wisdom traditions, the simplicity of love, forgiveness, compassion and service always finds new ways to come to life for people everywhere.

We have the same powerful messages and new paradigms available to us today. The way to move forward is to spread them around, one person, one meeting, one pamphlet at a time. It is happening — the Earth Charter effort that has now involved thousands of people in 51 countries worldwide is one example. If we can change the world's dominant paradigm from one where attributes like greed are honored to one where attributes of respect, care, and compassion are honored, we will change the systems at work so that they are more effective at meeting human needs.

## 12. The power to transcend paradigms

In her typology of leverage points for system change, Donella Meadows added one last item on her list, one that she ranks as the most important.[7] While the power to change paradigms is extremely important, this point is a reminder that all of our human ways of understanding are necessarily limited. All unifying theories, all new conceptual frameworks, are merely analogs, maps, artificial constructs, that try to accurately imitate reality, but none of them ever get it comprehensively right. Once we understand this, and take a dose of humility along with the understanding, we can start to perceive the magnitude and majesty of the universe in new ways.

With the rapid change that our culture is experiencing now, the ability to adapt to new ways of seeing, precisely because of the understanding that no way of seeing is correct, is an important and potentially powerful insight. This includes the theories about systems we have discussed and all the other mindsets or paradigms that have been generated over the millennia. The possibility does exist that if you want to effect change in a positive direction, it is more important to be willing to let go of old ways of seeing, of all ways of seeing, than it is to look for leverage points with an eye toward manipulating them. Real power comes from a profound weakness, from a place of surrender, more often than it comes from having a position of control.

## CHAPTER 9

# Leverage Points

COMPLEX SYSTEMS OFFER A TANTALIZING HOPE that large systemic changes can be achieved with relatively small actions, known as *leverage points*. An example of a leverage point would be where a hunter finds the exact spot on his prey to bring it down with relatively little effort. The silver bullet, the magic formula, the moment in life when the future hinges on one small decision; the idea that there might be an easy way out of our predicament is appealing.

Leverage points are not always good. The O-ring in the space shuttle *Challenger* was a leverage point. Achilles' heel was another one. We've all heard the sayings: For want of a nail, the horse was lost; or, a stitch in time saves nine. All are reflections of the basic understanding that small actions can have big consequences.

Some of the most powerful leverage points for complex human systems are found in the systems strategies described in the last chapter. They are the underlying drivers of systems evolution: the goals of the system, the mindset, or paradigm that guides activity within the system, and the power to transcend existing paradigms.[1] One way to access these powerful leverage points in a community is to develop a collective vision for the future — any planning effort is blind without it. Energizing people through their creativity and their native wisdom in ways that promise novelty and a degree of excitement, that provide outlets for compassionate action, and that develop and inspire new leaders will capture many of the intangible elements of community behavior — these are the ingredients for successful community transformation.

### LEVERAGE POINTS FOR COMMUNITIES

Leverage is a powerful systems tool that can be used to move community systems that resist change in directions we want them to go. The problem is that finding the place where the most leverage can be achieved is not easy, nor is it likely to be well received when it is found. Leverage points are not always obvious, and they tend to be counterintuitive. In some ways, we are always looking for a leverage point when we try to change the way things are done in any system. We often find it, but as researchers like Jay Forrester point out, if we do find it, it is likely we are pushing it in the wrong direction.[2]

If the strategies described in Chapter 6 are whole systems strategies that can help us find leverage points, then where are the leverage points? If a community started to implement one of the systems strategies, it is possible that they would happen on a leverage point in the process, since the strategies listed have been developed with the whole system in mind. Another way to find leverage points is to take the time, resources, and energy to put together a complex input-output model of the community system and hire a systems analyst to calculate exactly where they are. Most communities will not be able to do this, however, so we need an easier way to begin.

Common sense and folklore offer many leverage points to contemplate. By matching leverage points that we know intuitively with strategies for communities, we can make the magic of leverage work, without sophisticated models or complex theories. The way to find leverage is to look for places where small amounts of effort can yield big results. The concept of leverage itself brings to mind the ability a person would have to lift a very heavy object using a long lever and a fulcrum. The common sense leverage points described below are not an exhaustive list. Communities can come up with their own strategies with these common leverage points in mind.

## MEDIA'S MESSAGE

We can go back to the earliest human communities — the small clans that gathered together to protect themselves, hunt, and raise their children and try to imagine how they met their needs as a clan. After all, their needs back then were similar to our needs today, even though we've developed ever more sophisticated ways of meeting them. It's possible that critical leverage points for our ancient ancestors would be important for us as well, although they might be easier to discern in the older, less sophisticated society.

Let's say that one of their young men had discovered a herd of wild antelope migrating just to the east of their small settlement. He knew that if the clan acted quickly and effectively, they wouldn't have to worry about food or clothing for many moons. He probably ran back to the clan, gathered all the hunters into a prehistoric focus group, told them all about the herd of antelope just over the hill, and then they devised a strategy to get the antelope. Mind you, they probably didn't strategize for a week or two; the conversation probably lasted less than an hour. Then they would have collected their hunting gear and moved forward to kill some antelope and meet their collective needs for food, for skins to make clothing, and bones to make tools.

Back then, the young hunter didn't need television news to announce the antelope's presence, or posters and radio ads to convene the focus group, or commercials to let the other clan members know about the availability of skins and bones. Life was a lot simpler. Today, however, the media is the critical communication channel that we have as a large human family. The messages and strategic direction that the media gives us are critically important, as important as the words and conversations that the young hunter had with his clan thousands of years ago.

If you look at the media's messages today and imagine that they have the same effect on us as the young hunter had on his clan, then it's hard to discount the pervasive violence, consumerism, and Western cultural dominance that the media churns out as mere entertainment. One of the most important leverage points for change is to change the media messages. The media shapes the values we have as a society, gives us direction for meeting our needs, and now more than ever, creates new needs, or wants and desires, that we never had before, and that accelerate the drive to global destruction.

Jacqueline Ottman, author of *Green Marketing, Opportunities for Innovation*,[3] worked in the advertising industry for many years before she started her crusade to help businesses reinvent themselves through sustainable innovation. She described how advertising firms are the largest incubators for new product ideas, continually coming up with proposals to feed to the manufacturers and producers. This is because the largest advertising budgets available are for the launch of new products. Simply keeping the old products on the shelves does not require the same level of advertising investment.

This demonstrates a fairly simple reinforcing cycle at work. New product ideas mean larger advertising budgets, larger advertising budgets mean more people employed by advertising agencies, more people employed can in turn lead to more new product ideas, etc. On an aggregate scale, the advertising, manufacturing, consuming, disposing snowball is rolling down the mountain at ever increasing speeds every year.

In other ways, the violent side of the media is also serving a reinforcing cycle. Media analysts have done studies that show that before they graduate from elementary school, most children in the U.S. see 100,000 acts of violence on TV, including 8,000 murders. These numbers double to 200,000 acts of violence and 16,000 murders by the time they reach high school.[4] While having the unanticipated side effect of desensitizing the children to violence, it also produces a culture of fear. The more fearful we are as a culture, the more likely we are to resort to violence. The more fearful we are as a culture, the more appeal the violent shows on television have, where the good guys always win in the end, despite the trail of blood they leave in their wake.

What if the dominant media messages were to change? The importance of our collective communication systems cannot be understated in terms of the leverage that they offer for real system change. Media messages form an invisible force field that guides and directs mass consciousness. Changing their orientation from one of promoting violence and consumerism to one that promotes resource conservation, social and economic justice, non-violence, and peace is the metaphorical equivalent of reprogramming a computer, or changing the standing orders for a giant army.

## THE MAGIC FORMULA

One leverage point that is described in folklore is the idea of a magic formula — a spell or potion that could change whatever it is used on into something else. Our attraction to magic and our attraction to leverage points share a key characteristic — people want to be able to make changes without going the usual long, plodding route that entails a lot of heavy lifting. Magic formulas offer such a shortcut.

One type of community strategy that can have an almost magical effect on people's ability to get things done is the effort to build community spirit, or what has sometimes been described as social capital. What is community spirit, exactly? One feature of it is that people identify with a place in a way that makes them care about its future. It might be a particular neighborhood in a large city, or a section of town, or even a large apartment block. The size of the community is not important. The connections between people in the community and the relevance that the particular place has for whatever is being done are important factors. So, if the efforts made concern an entire watershed, developing a sense of community connections within the watershed would be important. If the efforts being made concern improving living conditions in the old, state-owned housing blocks in the former Soviet Union, building connections between people in apartment blocks might be more appropriate.

Once the relevant place has been identified, researching the types of activities that might bring people together informally would be a good place to start. In a rural watershed, some type of regional event, like a river festival, might be effective, whereas in a large apartment block the event might be more like a street picnic on a sunny summer day, complete with activities for children and people of all ages. Efforts to build connections between people can also be linked to a particular strategy. Crime Watch programs, for example, where neighbors get together to help protect their homes from criminals, are often great ways to both build community spirit and accomplish a specific objective.

## Alternatives for Youth

Alternatives for Youth galvanized its program in 1982 when two Hispanic youth were shot and killed by the police. This tragedy polarized the Hispanic and Anglo populations. El Comite, a Hispanic organization, worked with these communities on a healing process. As a result, both sections of the community were very grateful for the support AFY's staff provided. This success story led to a group of community members who came together to form the first board of directors for Alternatives For Youth and established it as a non-profit.

In Longmont, Colorado, the Education and Community Spirit Project of the Alternatives for Youth organization provides academic support, tutoring, life skills development and service-learning projects to middle school students in the city. In its first year after beginning in 1999, this project served 215 students. Of these, 99 showed improvement in grades, and 17 are holding down As and Bs.[5]

One example of a project that was designed to build such community connections is Burlington, Vermont's Public Safety Project.[6] This assists Old North End residents in developing self-sustaining neighborhood organizations, which work to increase the real and perceived safety in this historic neighborhood. Neighborhood leadership is fostered, as residents are encouraged to identify and resolve issues that are important to them.

The goals of the project are to (1) strengthen and create neighborhood associations, (2) create and coordinate skills development through training on public safety issues, (3) facilitate community-driven, neighborhood-based improvement projects, (4) provide information, referral, and technical assistance to citizens, and (5) educate public officials and hold them accountable to neighborhood needs.

The Public Safety Project currently assists 27 neighborhood associations and is working to spur leaders and invigorate new groups daily. In the past five years, over 500 residents have been trained, $25,000 in grants allocated for neighborhood improvement projects, and over 96 tons of trash and recyclables removed from Old North End streets.

Much can be accomplished when people trust each other and work together to make their community a better place. Activities that build trust by bringing people together and that build a sense of shared destiny or pride in place can successfully create conditions where projects that might have seemed impossible are suddenly manageable. Resources are available that weren't there before; connections can make things happen.

### THE SILVER BULLET

The idea of a silver bullet comes from folk tales about werewolves. Werewolves are normal human beings who turn into horrible, hairy, wolf-like monsters at the full moon, terrorizing innocent citizens and generally wreaking havoc. As legend has it, the only way to kill these beasts was with a pure silver bullet. So, a silver bullet is a leverage point in the quest to conquer a normal person who has suddenly changed into something awful.

What community strategies might be likened to the silver bullet? Arguably, worldwide energy consumption is an example of a normal human process that over time has been transformed into something horrific, as we face the certainty of global warming that is already threatening the welfare of many island states. During the World Summit on Sustainable Development in Johannesburg in August 2002, President Leo A. Falcam of Micronesia summed up his despair this way:

> The current state of the science tells us that any hope we had of averting disaster [from rising sea levels caused by global warming] for low-lying countries such as my own in the longer term is now gone. Even if we all came to our collective senses this week in this beautiful city and agreed to immediately begin meeting the earlier targets and timetables, it is too late for most of the federated states of Micronesia. However, it may not be too late for slightly less vulnerable areas of the world, such as Manhattan or Calcutta. For nations such as my own, we will need the assistance of the international community in adapting to the rising seas and developing relocation strategies.[7]

Energy conservation is a community strategy that might demonstrate silver bullet leverage. If generating energy using renewable sources is one way to reduce the impacts of global warming, energy conservation goes even further by eliminating the need to generate the energy in the first place. Energy conservation strategies have been recognized as some of the most significant energy sources ever since residents, businesses, and industry started to implement them seriously during the energy crisis of the 1970s.

One example of a community using energy conservation as a key component of its sustainable development strategy is Burlington, Vermont, where, in 1990, voters authorized an $11.3 million bond to fund the Burlington Electric Department's (BED) energy-saving programs.[8] The majority of these programs have involved local contractors and resulted in job growth and reinvestment in the local economy. Since then, BED has worked on more than 14,950 individual energy-efficiency installations, which have saved customers 42,860 MWh or $4.3 million annually on their electric bills.

A host of programs are available to BED customers to help save money on their electric bills. For example, homeowners and renters can save through the Heat Exchange Program, where BED offers assistance and financial subsidies to convert homes from electric heat to other heating sources. Through the Energy Advantage Program,

BED delivers energy efficiency measures to medium-sized and smaller businesses, with 340 retrofits completed to date.

In environmental terms, these programs and others prevent the release of 32,439 tons of $CO_2$ emissions into the air every year, or 489,064 tons of emissions over the life of the programs. This is equivalent to the removal of 6,500 cars from U.S. highways, or the planting of 134,000 acres of trees.

Silver bullet strategies seek to end a practice that's degrading the system, rather than looking for ways to clean up the mess. Don't make the plastic packaging to begin with, rather than trying to build more trash incinerators that can burn all the plastic safely. Rather than chasing consumer demands with more and more products, find ways to transform the demands to practices that meet needs without all the stuff.

## THE STITCH IN TIME

Ben Franklin, philosopher, statesman, and inventor, wrote many lists of pithy sayings that were used to instruct young men and women in the virtues. He ran a printing press, and used it to disseminate *Poor Richard's Almanac*, replete with saying such as "Early to bed and early to rise makes a man healthy, wealthy, and wise," and "Well done is better than well said." One of his aphorisms that points to a leverage point is "A stitch in time saves nine." This means that if you sew a tear in a garment early, you can avoid more tedious sewing later. Again, it illustrates the idea of leverage because it is a small effort that makes a larger effort unnecessary.

If an alternative form of energy, which didn't produce $CO_2$, could be developed and rapidly deployed, that might be an effective way to slay this particular dragon. Amory Lovins of the Rocky Mountain Institute sees fuel cell technology as being one way to eliminate the use of fossil fuels in transportation and buildings. He estimates that with appropriate investment, we could convert from fossil fuel to a hydrogen economy within five to ten years.[9]

Even on a local level, efforts can be made to convert to renewable forms of energy that don't produce $CO_2$. Water, wind, and solar power are all economically viable given certain local conditions; communities can do much to change the ways in which energy is produced. Iowa has taken this challenge very seriously. The Iowa Energy Program began in 1985 as an ambitious effort to reduce dependence on energy imports. Since that time, aggressive investments have been made in wind power, which has produced over $150 million in energy savings in over five years.[10]

Stitch-in-time strategies do something to avert new damage that could emerge along the same path as the strategy itself. Preventative health care, addressing health problems when they're small, so they don't grow into something serious and expensive, is an example of this. Preventative maintenance of facilities and equipment would be another example. It's better to buy that computer protection software than it is to have your hard drive wiped out by a virus. Likewise, early education programs that prepare young people from poor communities for schoolwork may be more effective than the remediation programs for older students.

## THE SECRET PASSWORD

Another leverage point of folklore, the secret password, is the word that opens doors that had previously been closed tight. One word and the passageway to the inner chambers swings open, solving mysteries, or finding treasure, or revealing access to esoteric truths. For communities everywhere, it is possible that one key secret password might be the practice of forgiveness.

Forgiveness is not a word that is typically associated with public discourse, yet if you could see the roots of many community-level social and political problems, a lack of forgiveness would stand out as a key causal factor. There are extreme examples, like the ongoing violence in Israel and Palestine, the Balkans, the Caucuses. The Hatfields and the McCoys, perhaps the two most famous feuding families in the Appalachian Mountains, on a smaller scale, typify long-standing lack of forgiveness. Yet even when a lack of forgiveness is not so extreme as to cause violent conflict, it still festers within the hearts of many communities, making collective action toward a better life very difficult.

For all of the most widespread wisdom traditions, Christianity, Judaism, Islam, Buddhism, and Hinduism, forgiveness is an essential element. For Hindus, forgiveness is the highest virtue. For Christians, it is the core message that Christ brought to the world. Yet, for all its importance to spiritual leaders, there is precious little that anyone learns about it in school. There are very few examples of institutionalized processes that encourage forgiveness — US bankruptcy laws and the Truth and Reconciliation Commission in South Africa being notable exceptions.

What would it take to have society start to consider forgiveness as an important facet of their lives? What skills are needed to help people practice this very difficult emotional and intellectual process? The current cultural dominance of consumerism and economic gratification makes difficult questions like forgiveness seem like something from another planet, but it is a serious issue for communities to consider.

By incorporating an effective conflict resolution process into every effort that involves collective action, communities can reduce the potential for the types of serious conflict that would result in a need for forgiveness on the part of participants. Learning and practicing active listening skills from an early age can also help people try to take the other side of the argument to heart.

Forgiveness can be a collective healing process. One example of a community level strategy that has been used to encourage collective forgiveness is in Burlington, Vermont, where the Community Justice Center initiated the Neighborhood Action Project (NAP).[11] It is a demonstration project that grew out of Burlington's Community-Based Policing Task Force. Located in Ward 2, the NAP brought together neighborhood residents, merchants, landlords, police officers, and members of Burlington's Public Safety Project. Participants identify neighborhood problems and concerns and engage in problem solving strategies.

There were a lot of complaints about noise, litter, and petty vandalism in Ward 2. The residents blamed it on the fact that their neighborhood was located between downtown and the University of Vermont campus. Students would walk through the neighborhood at all hours, on their way home from activities downtown. Since the onset of the NAP, noise complaints are down 50 percent.

As part of the NAP, offenders who receive a ticket for violating the noise ordinance are given the restorative justice option, in addition to their choices of paying the ticket or appearing in court to contest it. With this option they contact the Community Justice Center and meet with community members in a group conference setting as part of the NAP's weekly meeting agenda. The conferences are facilitated by trained community members with the goal of reaching a negotiated restorative contract for the offender to complete (apologies, community work service, etc.). Successful completion of the contract results in the ticket being voided.

Another important part of the NAP is the SWAT teams organized by the Community Justice Center to intervene in cases of residential break-ins and vandalism. When the Justice Center learns of such cases, it brings in a SWAT team to immediately repair the damage, to the extent possible, and act as a support group for the person who was harmed. This strategy developed out of a growing concern for victims' rights, which are often lost in the morass of the criminal justice system that focuses more on punishing the offender than it does in caring for the victim.

Working to make restitution when people are violated in some way is an important step toward making the practice of forgiveness a part of our institutional structures. Bringing the violators face to face with the people they have harmed has also proven to be an effective way to stop crime from recurring. In every case where violence is escalating out of control, there are lost opportunities to practice forgiveness on an individual and collective level. This potential to turn the self-reinforcing system of hatred and retribution into the opposite self-reinforcing system of healing and reconciliation marks forgiveness as a critical leverage point for communities everywhere. It is the secret password that opens the door to a new future.

## THE WRENCH IN THE WORKS

Another leverage point that has captured imaginations and led to a wide variety of interesting and controversial activities is the idea of throwing a wrench in the works. A strategically aimed wrench, popular wisdom dictates, can shut down an entire manufacturing process, if it is thrown in the right location at the right time. Again, it is a small action that has large consequences — a leverage point.

Identifying weak points in the system that you are trying to change and acting to take advantage of those points can be an effective way to change a system. When Greenpeace sailed into the forbidden zone surrounding atmospheric testing sites, knowing that the bombs wouldn't be tested if people were within the range of the nuclear explosion, they were taking advantage of a leverage point in the testing system. When Mahatma Gandhi decided to challenge the British government's unjust control over India by leading his people to the sea to make salt themselves instead of continuing to pay the salt tax and abide by laws that gave the British a monopoly on salt production, he was throwing a wrench in the works at a strategic leverage point.

Non-violent direct action against an unjust, inflexible system has a long and relatively successful history. Sometimes it is impossible to work within the system to bring about the kind of change that is required. Civil disobedience uses a higher order as a reference point, rejecting the premise that all laws are inherently just. When Rosa Parks was arrested for taking a seat that only white people could legally occupy, she was acting on the basis of this higher order. When Greenpeace activists are arrested for violating the Canadian Seal Protection Act, dictating that the only people who can be within 100 feet of the seals are the people hunting them, they are illuminating the injustice that can be perpetuated by our institutions.

The notion of non-violent resistance to injustice can be traced back to some of the ideas of Jesus Christ, specifically stated in Matthew 5:39-41: "If someone strikes you on your right cheek, turn him the other also. And if someone wants to sue you and take your tunic, let him have your cloak as well. If someone forces you to go one mile, go with him two miles."[12]

Theologian Walter Wink examined these passages in his essay titled "Jesus' Third Way."[13] After carefully researching the historical and cultural context of the passages, he came up with a completely different interpretation than the passive surrender they seem to imply.

The first statement about turning the other cheek is further explained when you know that for people of the time, the left hand was considered unclean and could not be used to touch another person. So, if someone had been struck on the *right* cheek, this was the backhand slap of a master to a person below them in stature, perhaps their slave or servant. To offer the other cheek was to invite the master to strike with an open hand, which would not only be considered an illegal assault (which could get the master arrested), but would also acknowledge the other person as an equal.

The second statement is similar. It was not uncommon during these times for creditors to take someone's tunic in payment of debt. To give up the cloak, as well, would be to be left with nothing, stark naked. What we didn't know until recently was that the legal system of the time made it illegal to view someone who was naked, not to be naked in the first place. By going the extra step, the person harmed would be placing the offender in a precarious legal position. But more than that, the act would force the creditor to see their action in a very human light. It would demand that the other person's humanity be taken into account.

The third directive reflects on the common practice of Roman soldiers to demand that people carry their loads for them. Under the law, if a soldier asked you to do this, you were legally required to do so for exactly one mile. If after the mile is up, you go on to carry the load for another mile, the soldier could actually get into trouble with his superiors if it was reported, and you are once again taking the initiative and making the oppressor see you as a human being, rather than an object.[14]

Non-violent direct action, resistance, and monkey-wrenching all have the potential to provide critical leverage for change. This is because they appeal to a higher ideal; they ground people in values that are important for everyone, and often expose unjust and intolerable practices for what they are.

## PRESSURE POINTS

If you have a headache, you can relieve the pain by pressing the point between your thumb and your forefinger, just where the bones come together in a V. Most systems have places where a variety of forces converge, making them more sensitive than other parts of the system, and also points where change can more easily occur. These pressure points also can be leverage points, if they are pushed or pulled in the right direction.

Community systems often exhibit several pressure points, places where a variety of forces converge. One area that communities all over the world have in common is the education system. The education system is a place where children are cared for, where values are transmitted, where citizens can have some input into the way a governmental service is delivered, and that is also an important source of employment and income. Schools have an environmental impact as well, in terms of the wastes they produce, the resources they consume, and the effect that their location has on surrounding properties and on the growth of the whole community.

Schools can be important leverage points in communities and should not be overlooked when strategies are being designed to make communities more sustainable. Sustainable development projects can involve students in design, data collection, and strategy development.

Students can survey their families to get a sense of the issues within the community. Schools can serve as demonstration sites for different technologies, strategies, or information dissemination that the community decides is important. Almost everyone in a community is touched by the school system in some way, and if they aren't, it's important to find ways that they can be. As a society we are increasingly aware of the importance of lifelong learning. If schools aren't providing members of the community with some type of educational service throughout their lives, the community is missing enormous opportunities for human development and change.

Pressure point leverage is a strategy that identifies where a variety of forces come together in a community and finds a way to work with the pressure point so that it moves the entire community in the right direction. Another example of a pressure point might be the downtown area of a community, where many different types of public and private services are provided. It might be that improving the downtown area goes a long way to making people feel more positive about the community as a whole.

## THE KEY

The key is another leverage point. In addition to being a small object that can often unlock huge doors, removing insurmountable barriers with the turn of the tumblers, the key has another meaning — on a map, it gives people the information they need to understand the data. Both of these meanings are important to understanding the idea of leverage and using leverage as a strategy in communities.

Keys that unlock things are interesting in that they are often made at the same time the lock is made, specifically for the purpose of unlocking it. Their design is completely compatible with the lock; the lock is useless without the key. Strategies that use keys as leverage points are strategies that take advantage of the specific design of the system and use the way the system was designed to open it up to new ways of doing things. In a democracy, a key leverage point would be to involve people in community decision making in new ways. Following the strategies identified in this book — establishing stakeholder groups, conducting extensive community surveys, and using innovative involvement techniques to propose new programs for change — would be using the system exactly the way it was designed to achieve sustainable development.

The other type of key, a map's legend, the guide a reader needs to understand the information in front of them, also has relevance to the transformation of community systems. Having an understanding of systems dynamics and seeing systems at work within communities, gives people who are responsible for designing strategies for transformation important information to help them understand the material presented to them. If you are given a topographical map and you don't understand the contour lines that describe where the mountains and valleys are, or the scale that tells you the distances involved, you may end up on a long and arduous journey in the wilderness. With that information, however, you can often find the easiest way to navigate the territory and find the path that will bring you to the correct destination.

Key leverage points, then, are twofold. One uses the way the system was designed in the first place to open it up to new possibilities. The other provides important information that helps people understand the systems they are working with. These two types of leverage might be some of the most important for municipal managers who are working to improve their community systems, since they are often in the best place to take advantage of the existing system design and to interpret data in new ways.

## CONCLUSION

The discussion about systems strategies and leverage points is designed to provide conceptual tools for communities that help them develop strategies once they know where they are and where they want to go. Much of the discussion of leverage points illustrates that the idea there might be a shortcut to change is tempting but doesn't avoid the need for broad public involvement and ownership of whatever is being proposed. This in itself is a lot of work, work that can't be avoided if the strategies are going to be effective. No shortcuts there.

Another unavoidable task is the effort it takes to really understand the whole community system before making any attempt to change it. This doesn't necessarily mean that years of research are needed before anything can be done, but it does mean that it's important *not* to start with a narrowly defined problem and work from there. Even if a problem seems like it can't be ignored, take a few steps back from it and try to identify some of the structural issues that have created the problem in the first place. All problems are symptoms of something else, and if the ineffective band-aid solutions we have developed over the years aren't indictment enough of the analytical, problem solving approach, then maybe all the unintended consequences of our actions are.

We must meet needs, not solve problems. We must understand whole systems, not isolated data sets. We must work together to make sustainable communities, not separately, locked into distinct disciplines that never speak to each other. We must share, care, and take personal responsibility for the success of a given project. Ben Franklin put it well when he said that we must all hang together, or, most assuredly, we shall all hang separately.

With this in mind, creativity, hard work, and inclusive participatory processes will certainly find ways to use leverage in the community when sustainability strategies are proposed. Even people who have studied systems dynamics for years acknowledge that all the fancy computer models often tell people what they know already — leverage points are intuitive, as well as being the results of sophisticated modeling. Once you find them, it is important to figure out if they're being pushed in the right direction.

## CHAPTER 10

# Initiating Action

THERE ARE LESSONS FROM SYSTEMS DYNAMICS that inform efforts to move from planning into implementation with strategies for sustainable development. Unfortunately, most strategic planning is linear, where the planning process moves into implementation in a step-by-step fashion, often using top-down, command and control forms of governance. In this type of linear strategic planning, feedback is often separated from actual action planning. Strategic planning will benefit immensely by incorporating the holistic approach of systems thinking.

A linear process is perceived in the same way we perceive time, as a long line of actions that are supposed to produce a desired outcome. A systems thinking process perceives cycles of activity with no end, only with changes in the quality and characteristics of the process. Systems thinking has demonstrated the benefits of involving the community and giving everyone opportunities to learn by doing things together. The use of systems thinking to inform strategic development is intimately connected with the dynamic nature of the cycles of process and change.

Systems thinking challenges us to see the whole picture and the capacity to respond, then becomes the basis for intelligent, informed action and intervention. Systems are continuous cycles of cause and effect, or causal loops, where today's problems are really yesterday's inadequate and shortsighted policies, and yesterday's solutions for those problems will be tomorrow's headaches. On the other hand, today's interventions and decisions made in the light of the systems understanding with foreknowledge of the effects of an intervention avoid creating new problems and headaches.

185

The next question is "How do we initiate action so our vision can become reality?" A strategy may appear to be perfectly suited for whatever change is contemplated, but if it is not implemented wisely, many pitfalls and problems can arise. It is important, therefore, to understand the nature and difficulties of the relationships involved in implementing changes and then to create an action plan with careful attention given to all sectors of the community.

The key to an effective implementation process is the development of an action plan that takes into account all of the resources, needs, strategies, criteria, specific implementation efforts, and feedback mechanisms (monitoring and evaluation). The action plan is an outcome of the community's efforts to understand current realities and to plan for the future.

Effective action plans include a clear sense of what resources and actors are needed to make change. Financial planning, management and decision support systems, life cycle design and accounting, and sustainable procurement policies all play important roles in an effective implementation cycle, and all of these techniques are based on a cyclical and systems-based understanding of the community, and the concurrent need to develop learning communities and learning organizations.

## OUTLINING ACTION FOR CHANGE

An old Chinese proverb tells us that the journey of a thousand miles begins with one step. Once the stakeholder group has an idea of where they are going and how to choose effective strategies based on a systems understanding, they still need to carefully consider the specific strategies and the implementation plan. The plan needs to be prioritized, so that steps are taken in an order that can build on each other. Strategies that interfere with, or complement, each other need to be identified, so that maximum synergy can be achieved. Feedback systems need to be established to continuously monitor the way the strategy is moving forward. The transformation, or metamorphosis, that the stakeholder group wants to see happen in the community needs to be planned as carefully as any sort of campaign.

One exercise that can help the participants begin to imagine how the action plan will proceed is to envision the action they want to take with all the community sectors in mind. This technique can jumpstart a group's creative process by helping them see connections and factors affecting the particular community system before specific ideas are put forward for the action plan. The idea is to identify the community system that needs to change. Maybe it's the transportation system, or the downtown businesses, or the education system in town. Once this has been agreed upon as the focus of the discussion, the next step is to brainstorm all of the ways in which that system is part of the community — to identify all the linkages, effects, actors, resources, and other factors that could have an impact on the transformation of the system.

It can be helpful to put these linkages into the general community system categories — social, governance, economic, and environmental systems. This can be done by putting the diagram shown in Figure 10.1 on a large flip chart and connecting everyone's suggestions to one arm or another, building on all the different facets that are discovered through the dialogue.

Figure 10.1 Diagramming the Community System

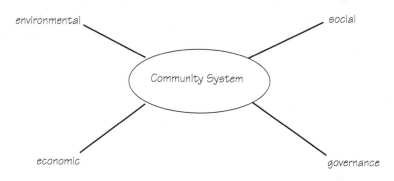

The following questions can help the group to start the diagramming process:

1. What does the transformed system look and feel like?
2. What needs are being met by the system?
3. What means are used to meet these needs?
4. What is the impact of the means that are used?
5. What resources and actors are involved?
6. Can any feedback loops be identified that either cause the system to spiral out of control, or cause it to stay the same despite your best efforts?
7. What emergent properties does it have?

The facilitator of the group should try to keep several types of linkages and factors in mind when drawing the group's answers on the chart. These are important when the group tries to design a strategy for change.

## Actors

Actors are individuals or institutions that have a role to play in the system in question. So, if the system being discussed is the transportation system, the car drivers, the public transit company, and the municipal highway department are all actors.

## Resources

Resources can be material, like water, or housing, or communication infrastructure. They can be particular types of information or knowledge, financial or legal agreements, or services that are provided, like health care or education. The money that is needed to move forward with a strategy for change is a very important resource; the action plan can identify and help secure the financial support for the project.

## Constraints

If the transportation system is being discussed, one constraint might be the lack of energy-efficient automobiles in local markets. This might accurately be attached to the drivers that were identified as actors, for example.

## Values and Mindsets

If the transportation system is being discussed, then perhaps the prevalent attitudes about automobiles as sex symbols, or icons of power, or champions of freedom might be identified.

## Opportunities

For the transportation system, the introduction of the hypercar, made of carbon fiber and powered by a fuel cell, might be an example, or new carpool programs or public transit incentives initiated by area businesses.

Once this exercise is completed, the next step is to prepare an action plan that charts a course for change. Change doesn't just happen. It is a complex combination of factors, including finding key actors and connecting them with critical resources, preferably in an area where there is already momentum building for positive change in the desired direction. Making sure that there are going to be opportunities for feedback as the process moves forward is one way to complete the loop and to use a systems understanding to inform action. Knowing the constraints in advance can inform strategy development. Identifying mindsets that need to change, or that might work to your advantage, is another important element of the strategy.

Here is a simple way to look at this: Actors combined with Resources produce Change. Working backward, try to imagine the transformation that is desired, the goals of your activity. This might be the implementation of environmentally sound technologies, or it might be the establishment of a cultural center for local youth to have a place to express their creativity and talents. Focusing on the transformation — culturally active youth, a reduction of chemicals used for sewage treatment — can help people start to identify the other factors that are prerequisites to get there. Once the transformation itself, the goal, is clearly defined, then it is important to find the actors that have the ability to use the appropriate resources, to take advantage of opportunities, and to overcome constraints.

## THE ACTION PLAN

The action plan itself can take many forms, but at a minimum it should describe:

1. The needs and assets that were identified in the beginning with the needs assessment, asset identification, and visioning.
2. The goals and objectives of the action plan.
3. The public participation process that will be undertaken.
4. The criteria that the community has developed for making decisions.
5. The resources: money, staff, partnerships, etc., that will be used to meet each objective.
6. The key actors: participants, organizations, and institutions that have accepted responsibility for moving forward with the plan.
7. The activities that the people using resources will undertake to meet the objectives.
8. The short- and long-term results that are expected, in terms of increased knowledge and skills, or changed behavior, or improved environmental, economic, governance, or social conditions.

9.  The specific implementation strategies that will be used.

10. The efforts that are planned to institutionalize the strategies, such as a sustainable procurement policy or the introduction of different accounting techniques.

11. The indicators that people have selected to monitor progress.

12. The evaluation plan for the project, including the processes of reporting to decision makers and the public about the success (or failures) of the strategies.

Goals and objectives are important when it's time to develop a step-by-step plan for taking action. The process of defining goals and objectives can devolve into the linear process of the old strategic planning paradigm if the other factors listed above don't play a role. It is helpful to realize that the initial conception of the project will change over time, and so flexibility and possibilities for innovation need to be included in the project design right from the beginning.

### PROJECT LOGIC MODELS

To think clearly about how the action plan will work, it is often helpful to use a project logic model to outline the ways all the elements listed above fit together. This model provides a closed-loop planning process for municipal decision makers, so that specific needs can be correlated with results that reflect improved need satisfaction from the action strategy. The needs and assets that have been identified are the bases for identifying goals and objectives for the sustainable development strategy. In turn, for each objective, the inputs, activities, and results are listed, with the long-term results always referencing the original needs that were identified. The following example illustrates how the project logic model works:

Need:       Education

Goal:       To educate local citizens — youth and adults — so that they develop living skills that are compatible with the goals of sustainable development.

Objective:  To complete 15 neighborhood demonstration projects where groups of people come together to discuss sustainable lifestyles and then work to support common and individual efforts to live more sustainably.

Figure 10.2 A Simple Project Logic Model

| INPUTS (partners, $, staff, resources) | ACTIVITIES (what does the program do with the inputs?) | RESULTS (Changes in knowledge, skills, behavior, social and environmental conditions, etc.) | | |
|---|---|---|---|---|
| | | Short-term | Medium-term | Long-term |
| • Workshop Leader<br>• Printed materials | • Identify neighborhoods and participants.<br>• Convene discussion groups.<br>• Establish support networks.<br>• Hold regular follow-up visits. | • Increased knowledge about sustainable livelihoods. | • Changed behavior: more energy conservation.<br>• Fewer vehicle miles travelled,<br>• Use of clotheslines instead of dryers. | • Improved social networks in neighborhoods.<br>• Improved neighborhood safety.<br>• Improved local environmental conditions.<br>• Money savings for participants. |

The action plan should identify specific organizations or staff who are responsible for every element. If everyone is responsible, no one is responsible. When specific people make a commitment to implementation, accountability is much more straightforward.

Finally, the action plan should be easy for people to read and should be written to inspire people to join in and be part of the plan. While it's important to think through things like systems dynamics and project logic models and complex implementation strategies, these are for the benefit of the people who are designing the project, not necessarily for the public. The public needs to see that the action plan reflects the priorities they set as part of the public participation process. They need to resonate with the values that the document espouses. They need to feel ownership of it and feel a level of pride in the fact that their own municipality is concerned about their well-being and the well-being of future generations. If the action plan is truly the public's action plan, the effort will be more likely to succeed.

## MANAGEMENT AND DECISION SUPPORT SYSTEMS

The long-term success of any city's effort to implement sustainable strategies hinges on its ability to create an iterative management process that continually reviews the progress of its implementation. Based on the values, vision, strategies, and indicators developed as part of the initial planning process, the managers continually develop new strategies to address the changing situation. There are several management and decision support tools that can help cities do this, ranging from very simple, low-tech ideas to fairly complex, computer-intensive modeling systems.

Where planning, implementation, and evaluation operate as linear models, many opportunities for learning and improvement are missed. Systems thinking challenges communities to make the process cyclical and iterative rather than linear, as illustrated in Figure 10.3.

Figure 10.3 Community Action Planning Cycle

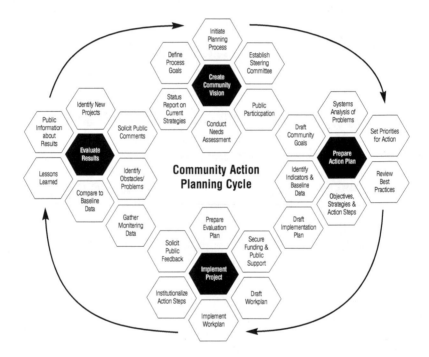

Once systems thinking approaches are demonstrated and accepted as useful tools for city planning, management must develop core competencies in a variety of skills. These skills of facilitating and optimizing the gathering and assessing of information in the form of feedback are the vehicle for moving through the planning process. At first, this can feel quite risky. Feedback is not always positive, and facilitating the process of honest feedback requires a level of trust and vulnerability that is often difficult to achieve on a corporate level. This is why the idea of servant leadership, and the accompanying skills, is so important to the sustainability planning effort.

On a very basic level, information is critical. Management and decision support systems help supply the decision makers and the community at large with continuous feedback on the results of any implementation efforts. This enables them to modify the program or develop new strategies as needed. If a municipality does not have the dedicated computer staff and database to continually enter, interpret, and distribute the data, it doesn't negate the need for continuous feedback. The city can set up a process where decision makers get periodic status reports describing progress made on both the strategies and activities proposed, and on the indicators that were selected to monitor the strategy's success. At least one staff person, possibly working with a subcommittee of the stakeholder group or decision makers, should have the responsibility to keep on top of the constant stream of feedback and report to the appropriate groups or subgroups. Progress reports that describe the systemic impacts of the implementation effort will bring clarity and more certainty to the actions taken because the focus will be on how the innovation affects the entire process.

Margaret Wheatley in her wonderful book, *Leadership and the New Science*, writes:

> An organization can only exist in ... a fluid fashion if it has access to new information, both about external factors and internal resources. It must constantly process this data with high levels of self-awareness, plentiful sensing devices, and a strong capacity for reflection. Combing through this constantly changing information, the organization can determine what choices are available, and what resources to rally in response. This is very different from the more traditional organizational response to information, where priority is given to maintaining existing forms and information is made to fit the structure so that little change is required.[1]

Another part of the planning process that can be very helpful for decision makers is the creation of specific criteria for handling information, making decisions, or communicating with the community.

Criteria help guide standards, protocol, or policies consistent with an overall sustainable development plan. Codifying the criteria into policies, laws, regulations, master plans, and development plans is one effective way to institutionalize them. Periodic reviews of the criteria will insure they will continue to be relevant and supportive of the sustainable development efforts.

At the more sophisticated end of the spectrum, cities with information management staff and resources can consider investing in management and decision support systems that compile and analyze a wide variety of complex data to make computer models of scenarios that are being considered for further action. These models simulate reality and reduce uncertainty as proposals are made for new strategies. The models can also help decision makers identify leverage points, as scenarios are tested and variables are changed to reflect different policy options and outcomes.

The value of management and decision support tools is the degree to which they serve to build a cyclical, iterative process for planning, action, implementation, and evaluation. Investing in a sophisticated computer system for data analysis will get you nowhere if the results are never reviewed by the decision makers.

Open and forthright communication between people who are actually doing the work and those who are making decisions is one of the most critical elements of successful action plans. If people who manage the system do not accommodate and use this important flow of information, huge mistakes can result. One good example of a failure to communicate important information was evident in the space shuttle *Challenger* disaster. The engineers working on the launch were vocal and pointed about their concerns. Instead of provoking a learning process, their supervisors became defensive, and the information failed to reach the people making the decisions.

Open communication and the importance of all data — successes and mistakes — must be part of the culture in a city committed to sustainability. If people are hesitant to report things that did not turn out as planned, for fear of shame or poor performance review or whatever else might be a disincentive, the organization will not learn, the management and decisions will be inferior, and the community will suffer. People usually try to do the best they can and sometimes make mistakes. A culture that looks to blame individuals for mistakes creates fear and uncertainty in the workplace.

Most mistakes are either a result of a faulty system in which a person operates or are the legitimate and necessary errors of people who are working to innovate and change the system. Once the attention is off someone's mistake or failure and on the whole system or process that was at work, the roots of problems can be uncovered, and a more supportive culture will emerge, where mistakes are viewed as learning opportunities instead of failures. This culture of permission to make mistakes is important for a learning organization, for innovation to thrive, and for community systems to be adaptable and resilient.

## LIFE CYCLE DESIGN AND ACCOUNTING

We are on the threshold of a new paradigm of designing for wholeness, which takes the life cycles, unintended consequences, and the quality of life for future generations into consideration. Standing on the threshold of this new paradigm, we can envision not just new accounting methods but the creation of a whole new ecological economy where businesses and public institutions succeed economically while protecting vital natural resources and enhancing human communities.

In the fields of designing and accounting, careful consideration of the objects being designed and how they fit with the environment is essential. Whole systems include the environment in which a project or product is manufactured and the interactions that are likely to occur in the process. The old paradigm considered only the object being manufactured and the individual product's useful life. Most of us are numb to the real effect our consumption has on Earth. We don't perceive the wholeness of systems; we perceive isolated objects. Design and accounting are just beginning to catch up to the idea of integrated wholeness.

Life cycle design is one way that the idea of whole systems is being taken into account. This mental model of a system begins by noticing how things, people, ideas, and organizations fit into the ecology. It also looks at the whole system involved in the design and construction of infrastructure, buildings, and products — including all aspects of manufacture, construction, disposal or demolition, and reconstruction or remanufacture, rather than the discrete parts of a process that suit our needs for an individual product's useful life.

The belief that resources are unlimited and the lack of market signals promoting resource conservation leads municipal decision makers to implement programs and processes that are more wasteful of

resources than they need to be. This belief and practice is changing —
road construction methods are being introduced that recycle asphalt
rather than treating it as a waste product. Recycled tires show promise
for use in road construction. Several states now have construction and
demolition debris programs that encourage recycling. In Santa
Barbara, California, for example, a program is in place to recycle
wood, asphalt, metal, concrete, gypsum wallboard, metal, carpet, and
carpet padding from construction and demolition.

Yet, all of this is only a baby step toward a design system that envisions the reuse and recycling of building materials before the building
is built, so that demolition and reprocessing will be an integral part of
the process. In a revolutionary book, *Natural Capitalism*, Paul Hawken
and Hunter and Amory Lovins described several private companies
that have taken advantage of the potential for remanufacture to dramatically change the way they do business, to the mutual benefit of
the environment, their customers, and the companies. An example of
this is Interface, a carpet company that moved from providing carpet
as a product to providing floor covering as a service. Interface leases
carpet to companies and uses tiles that can be easily replaced in worn
spots. They reuse the tiles that are changed in the production of new
carpet, thus closing the loop between initial manufacture to recycling
and reuse.[2]

Along similar lines, new accounting practices are being introduced
which consider the whole cost of products and services, including the
hidden costs of resource use associated with production, use of the
product, the waste generated by the product's life cycle, the costs of
reprocessing, and the cost of any impact on the environment. While
the new paradigm has not yet been able to overcome the laws of thermodynamics (it is not possible to completely eliminate entopic
processes through reuse and remanufacture), there is significant
promise these new perspectives of design and accounting will move
public and corporate decision making in sustainable directions.

The Enron and Arthur Andersen corporate scandals in the United
States in 2001 and 2002 have demonstrated conclusively the effect
that accounting practices have on the overall economy. Clever
accountants figured out a way to circumvent rules that dictate how
profit and loss is measured, the key indicators investors rely on to
determine investment choices. Accounting practices are based on economic theory. One significant problem with our current economic

theory is the assumption that natural resources are completely free and they are not assigned a value in economic formulas. Distortions resulting from this egregious error lead the entire economic system to prefer strategies, technologies, and options that promote growth through increasing exploitation of natural resources.

Donella Meadows spoke of the high leverage value of paradigms — that is, the way we think — and the mental models, or mindsets, we carry around inside our heads. She pointed out our collective outmoded understanding of the value of natural resources. Changing our thinking is the most effective way to intervene in a system, and is the leverage needed to create huge change with minimal effort. A relatively simple shift in human consciousness — one that places a value on the natural resource base that sustains life on the planet — would have profound implications for the implementation of sustainable development strategies.

Some of the regulatory systems introduced in recent years attempt to change mindsets to this new model of adequately pricing the natural resources and services that Earth provides. The carbon tax, which imposes a tax on oil and gas because they add $CO_2$ to the atmosphere, the air pollution credits scheme introduced by the US Environmental Protection Agency under the Clean Air Act that carry an assumption about the value of clean air, and to a certain extent, the systems which have been invented for the transfer of development rights in land use planning are examples of this. These ideas are the seeds of innovation largely outside a dominant thought system that still favors unhindered exploitation of natural resources. The difficulties these ideas have encountered in being enacted in many places are a clear result of their challenge to the dominant paradigm.

On the accounting side, new ways of thinking are making inroads, especially in areas where the real costs of natural resources are not distorted by subsidies or other artificial factors favoring resource depletion. New accounting tools take into account previously ignored and undervalued factors that have a significant impact on sustainability. Some of these new tools are: Total Cost Accounting (TCA), which looks at liability, risks, hidden costs, and intangible costs like customer acceptance; Full Cost Accounting (FCA), which looks at the social costs like harm to the ozone layer and other effects that would not be automatically monetized by a company's analysis; and Environmental Life Cycle Accounting (ELCA), which looks at the costs of the environmental impacts of a particular product. Obviously, all of these forgotten and ignored costs are important to take into account when considering how profitable a particular new venture might be. Some of these costs are taken into account; for example, when the costs of disposal are already available to a company, they do tend to factor these into their determination of which technology to promote.

## Ecobudgeting in Heidelberg

The City of Heidelberg, Germany, has adopted a new form of municipal budgeting developed by the International Council for Local Environmental Initiatives (ICLEI), called EcoBudgeting. According to ICLEI, EcoBudgeting "applies periodic financial budgeting processes, mechanisms and routines to the management of natural resources so that city managers devote the same amount of attention and concern to these resources and to environmental quality." The environmental budgets don't set monetary values on natural resources, but they do account for how the natural resource budgets within a community are "spent" over time. In Heidelberg, the city accounts for carbon dioxide emissions, water consumption, and waste generation in their EcoBudget, as well as several other resources.[3]

Costs do not equal value. Financial valuing of natural and social benefits is not the whole solution to the sustainable management of natural and social resources. The introduction of the types of whole systems approaches to design and accounting described here, however, might help mitigate the dramatic and harmful effects of the distorted practices we currently have in place.

### SUSTAINABLE PROCUREMENT SYSTEMS

When the strategy is finalized, the funding is secured, the next step is to procure the products and services which are needed to move an effort forward. Understanding the life cycle questions for both accounting and production can also help municipalities rethink the ways their procurement systems work. Municipalities are mega-consumers, and the ways in which this consumption impacts the social, financial, and natural fabric of a community are critical to any strategy that envisions a sustainable future. It is estimated that in developed countries, governments alone consume 15 percent of Gross Domestic Product (GDP).[4] If communities make a conscious choice to purchase products and services based on an analysis of their environmental, economic, or social impact, this will have a dramatic effect on the product and service providers themselves, as they work to remain competitive in the municipal market.

There are many books and guidelines that help companies and municipalities implement green procurement and sustainable procurement strategies. Organizations that are working towards compliance with ISO 14001 are already taking steps to make their procurement practices more sustainable.[5] In Manitoba, Canada, the province has even passed a Sustainable Development Act[6] that requires organizations that receive funding from the government to institute green procurement regulations.

Sustainable procurement makes for sound fiscal practice as well. Products that use natural resources efficiently can reduce the total costs to a municipality by using less energy, by being easily recycled, by being healthier for employees, by lasting longer, and by producing less waste, especially less hazardous and toxic waste, which can be very expensive to dispose of or recycle.

The City of Santa Monica, California, has taken several steps to implement a sustainable procurement program. The City passed several laws and ordinances related to their purchasing policy, including:

- Recycled Products Procurement Policy
- Administrative Instruction Pertaining to Office Paper
- U.S. Conference of Mayors/CALPIRG Buy Recycled Campaign
- Janitorial Products Purchasing Criteria
- Tropical Rainforest Wood Purchasing Ban
- Ozone-Depleting Chemical Purchasing Regulations
- Reduced-Emission Fuel Policy of City Vehicle Purchases
- Print Shop Purchasing Policy

The benefits they have been able to measure since the policies have gone into effect include the following examples from the janitorial purchasing criteria:

1. Replacement of toxic products throughout the city with less toxic or non-toxic alternatives in 15 of 17 cleaning product categories.
2. The elimination of approximately 3200 pounds of hazardous materials in products purchased annually.
3. A cost savings of approximately five percent resulting from the purchase of more concentrated products having lower packaging and shipping costs; lower cost per application of the alternative products; and better, less wasteful use of products due to improved custodial training.
4. A proven and effective set of procurement specifications that can be adapted for use in future Toxics Use Reduction efforts.
5. Increased morale of the custodians, who recognize the City's concern for their health and working conditions and who appreciate the opportunity to participate in making decisions about their work.[7]

Santa Monica saved money, improved morale, developed good governance strategies, and reduced environmental impact. That's a win-win-win-win strategy — all four sectors of community life were improved.

## INDICATORS

Indicators, described in more detail in Chapter 11, are very useful for two parts of sustainability planning — identifying areas where work is needed and tracking the way a system behaves. If indicators have been gathered over time, they will point to specific parts of the system that need attention. Tracking the way a system behaves provides important information for design innovations.

Indicators are also critical for evaluating whether or not a developed strategy is successful. One thing that indicators are not particularly useful for, however, is in designing effective strategies for change. Indicators are like the gas gauge on your car, they can tell you that you are running out of gas, but they won't tell you to buy a bicycle. For strategy design, it's important to have a solid understanding of systems dynamics, so that interventions can take advantage of the existing momentum in the system and can avoid unintended consequences.

The implementation effort should include a plan for identifying, monitoring, and publicizing indicators, so that the people involved in implementation will know how their efforts are working, and so the public can receive regular reports on the effectiveness of the planning and implementation effort.

## ENDS AND MEANS

Ends and means have been debated for centuries. Perhaps one of the most famous treatises on the subject was by Machiavelli in the 1500s when he instructed leaders to use any means available, ethical or not, legal or not, to consolidate and maintain their power, since he saw the state as necessary for people's peace, security, and happiness. With Machiavelli, the idea that the ends justify the means came into common parlance.

A key insight gleaned from understanding whole systems is recognition of the value and necessity of integrity. Mahatma Gandhi said, "We must *be* the change we wish to see in the world." Here is a firm and final rejection of the notion that actions and ethics not consistent with the goals can somehow achieve those ends. Gandhi also said "There is no *way* to peace; peace *is* the way." The idea that a violent, or top-down, or inequitable strategy could produce a peaceful, democratic, or just result lacks the integrity necessary to cause the result. When a person or organization is in integrity they are the result. Time and space collapse the instant we realize that we are the cause of our reality. There is no longer putting the future out in front of us — there is no way to the future — we are the future. We express our values through our behavior in the present. This expression is our gift to the future. We are completely responsible in the present, now, for the results we will reap in the future. The paradigm shifts from looking out there somewhere for the way to peace to causing peace by being it — here and now.

Relating this ethical thinking to sustainable development, the paradigm shifts in this way: sustainable living in the present enhances the local capacity to meet future needs. Actions in the present that are eroding the local capacity to meet future needs are unsustainable. Using systems thinking, we ask a simple question, Are we practicing sustainable living in the present? Then we look to see if we are, to see how we are acting. The resulting feedback informs us to what degree we are living in integrity with our world. Then we can correct our next actions to improve our relations to be in integrity with the natural world. It's a circular process. I create it creates me/I create it creates me ... and so on.

After realizing that we, collectively, are causing the results we get, we can seriously ask, How are we doing that? It doesn't take any time to recognize if we are causing the erosion of our ability to meet future needs, that we can cause something better to happen. Here is where the value of relating comes in. We cannot change our behavior alone, that is, by ourselves. We need each other in conscious and supportive relationships to change the habitual thinking of the past to the vision all our hearts desire. In this vision we would seem to be a world being peace, acting out peace, and forgiving all the rest. Various governmental systems have developed with all good intentions to help us act in concert to meet the needs of all. But the problem of government can become one of control and power, and altruistic intentions get lost in a scramble for power and control. The reason people scramble for power is they don't feel they have enough. Enough what? The what doesn't matter because feeling a lack of anything tends toward hoarding, whether it is food, money, or power.

This ends-and-means discussion cannot be complete without mentioning all the poor, homeless, and starving people who are not getting their basic needs met. Are they too causing their condition? They find themselves in this condition because humanity must act as a whole, not in isolation. The condition in which the poor and hungry find themselves is one of separation from a caring humanity. The promise of a healthy community only comes with the caring and sharing of our resources with those who do not have the capacity to share. The poor acquire and learn their capacity to care and share from their community as it helps them meet their needs. The community, in all good intentions, provides an educational system to provide youth with skills for earning a living when they grow up, but it does not usually provide the knowledge that we, in each moment, are an expression of that which we value. If we don't like what we seem to be, or cannot communicate our value to others because we don't believe we have any value to offer others, we often contribute to an escalating suicide rate — the ultimate separation from humanity. We may, in our separation, in our lack of a stable relationship, lose ourselves in self-absorption, self-pity, drugs, wild partying, and bizarre behavior. Instead of self-destructive behavior, we may turn to crime or violence, war, and push our suffering onto others. In the paradigm change, in our new perception that comes with the shift in thinking, we will perceive that what's required is always present. It's a matter of matching resources and needs.

There's an old saying, Home is where the heart is. Home is the community of caring and support we all need. All of us are indebted to others for our very existence. The Native Americans would say all ground is holy. Everywhere you step you make sacred or profane. It's your choice — you do it — and you do it in every moment of your life, in every thought you think, in every breath you make, and in every step you take on this long learning expedition. As we are practicing peaceful values and expressing these values in our behavior, we are causing a community life we love. We need to recognize that integrity is a shift from searching for the answer to being the answer.

Systems thinking and linear thinking create different results. Linear thinking includes linear causality; for example, we look for the way to peace instead of expressing peace in our every action. In such thinking, the thought does not occur that an action might come full circle to confront the actor once again. Systems thinking, on the other hand, honors cyclical, systemic causality. For example, violent acts are most likely to produce more violence, not peace. Top-down controlling strategies are most likely to produce additional consolidation and centralization of power, not empowered citizens and grassroots action. The methods used to pursue sustainable community development must have integrity, that is, to be congruent with the ends that they are trying to achieve. This requirement for integrity demands that we look hard at how we intervene in communities and their systems, to align innovative strategies with the ethics of respectfulness, justice, ecological integrity, and democratic non-violence.

## CHAPTER 11

# Success

SUCCESS: IT'S A SWEET WORD. We all want it. Failure, on the other hand, feels like a curse. Success denotes a state of being where the resources we have used, the energy we have expended, and the money we have spent were put to a productive use. We have achieved something. The world is a better place for our having been here. Failure means that for all our efforts, nothing has been accomplished; if anything, things have deteriorated. We have fallen short. We try so hard to avoid anything that feels like failure that, often, real failures are thinly disguised as successes.

How do you know if the community's planning and implementation efforts to improve sustainability are successful? This chapter will describe tools and techniques communities can use to accurately evaluate programs and practices. It includes some stories about communities that have implemented sustainability programs and how they evaluated their success.

It is difficult to define the success of a community sustainability effort because sustainability itself is a dynamic concept, involving the interplay between our needs and the capacity that Earth and our community systems have to meet them. We can succeed by modifying our needs; we can succeed by improving our capacity, or some subtle combination of the two. Yet a hard look at current consumption, growth, militarism, and population trends would suggest that for all our best efforts, the sustainability movement is a dismal failure on the global scale, despite bright spots in some places.

The statistics tell the story. Efforts to implement the Kyoto Protocol to reduce carbon dioxide emissions have been underway for several years — public consciousness about the issue is growing. Yet in

2001, carbon fossil fuel consumption and $CO_2$ emissions increased one percent worldwide, setting new records.[1] Global energy use has grown by 70 percent in the last three decades, with North Americans as the leading consumers, using five times more than Europeans per capita.

The land that grows the food we eat is being degraded at an accelerating rate, with 10 to 20 percent of the world's 1.5 billion hectares of land already degraded by 2002. In the poorer parts of the world, this figure rises to 25 percent, due to inappropriate practices, erosion, overgrazing, and other factors. Even though the introduction of artificial fertilizers and pesticides made some land appear to be more productive, farmland degradation has reduced global food production by 13 percent over the last several decades.[2] If this isn't bad enough, in the United States, urban sprawl is paving over more than one million hectares of arable land every year.[3]

The water story is even more frightening. The World Water Council estimates that by the year 2025, over one half the world's population will live in countries where there is high water stress.[4] These trends are the hallmarks of failure, not of success.

We are already outstripping the planet's ability to support us. A lot of work has been done to estimate the amount of resources we have available compared to the resources that we are using. Using the ecological footprint methodology pioneered by Mathis Wackernagel,[5] it is estimated that there are currently 3.8 hectares available to support each human life on the planet, whereas the worldwide average footprint is 4.25 hectares.

The human species is generally good at devising new activities and programs to try and solve problems. Over time, we have also become more and more conscious about the need to evaluate these programs. One unfortunate consequence is that we often spend more time trying to evaluate whether or not the programs were conducted according to their design, if all the activities actually happened as planned, and if all the money was spent. If everything was done the way it was proposed, then the project is considered successful. What is often ignored is whether these activities actually changed the conditions they set out to improve. Grant funding, reporting expectations, changing conditions, personality conflicts; there are many factors that can make people forget their original objectives. As one popular saying states, When you're up to your ass in alligators, it's hard to remember that you came to drain the swamp.

A review of so-called success stories published by organizations who are working toward sustainability reveals the three main flaws in the evaluation of success: (1) the difficulty defining success, (2) the tendency to evaluate activities rather than outcomes, and (3) the lack of a holistic approach — too much emphasis on solving problems. The following passages are excerpts from stories that illustrate these flaws.

### IS THIS SUSTAINABILITY?

This project description comes from a website sponsored by the United Nations Environment Programme Regional Initiative on Information and Communication Technologies and the Environment. It describes an effort in India to "tackle the challenges posed by fragmented farms, weak infrastructure, and the involvement of numerous intermediaries in Indian agriculture."[6]

> The Indian farmer is generally trapped in a vicious cycle of low risk-taking ability to low investment to low productivity to weak market orientation to low value addition to low margin to low risk-taking ability again. This makes him and the Indian agribusiness sector globally un-competitive, despite rich and abundant natural resources.
>
> To enhance the competitiveness of Indian agriculture and trigger a virtuous cycle of higher productivity, higher incomes, enlarged capacity for farmer risk management, larger investments, and higher quality and productivity; a market-led business model, e-Choupal, is conceived.
>
> Appreciating the imperative of intermediaries in the Indian context, e-Choupal leverages Information Technology to virtually cluster all the value chain participants, delivering the same benefits as vertical integration does in mature agricultural economies like that of the US. The idea is to see a kind of growth in rural incomes that will also unleash the latent demand for industrial goods, which has a direct implication on the continued growth of the Indian economy. This will create another virtuous cycle propelling the economy into a higher growth trajectory.[7]

This discussion of vicious and virtuous cycles indicates an understanding of systems principles, but is the type of growth described the goal of sustainable development efforts? Grow, grow, grow, is what they appear to be saying. Let's create a new demand for industrial goods — like fertilizers, pesticides, tractors — that the agricultural sector can unleash if only they were more competitive globally.

## THE ACTIVITY TRAP

Many, if not most, of the efforts to promote sustainability find it difficult to measure their absolute impact on either the human community or the planet's natural systems. Since this is so difficult, they tend to fall back on secondary measures, such as the aggregate number of people who were trained or the quantity of fluorescent light bulbs installed. Stories describing sustainability efforts are full of examples of projects that are measured by the level of activity, rather than real impacts. This is not to say that the activities are problems in themselves, or that project resources should be diverted to measure the immeasurable. But it does raise legitimate questions about how we define success in relation to sustainability. Here is an example, from California, of a group called Common Ground that is reporting about its success based on its activities, rather than real impacts.

### Common Ground Co-Sponsors Walkable Neighborhoods Workshop

In January, Common Ground co-sponsored a workshop on designing walkable neighborhoods. Featured guests included Dan Burden, a national expert on Walkable Communities, Shelly Poticha, the Executive Director of the Congress for New Urbanism and developers and architects with experience in building walkable, infill developments.

### Common Ground Supports Transportation Funding Incentives for Infill Development

In December, Common Ground wrote to the Transportation Agency of Monterey County (TAMC) to encourage the use of a portion of available transportation funding as incentives for local communities to produce more infill housing and compact forms of development.

> The goals are to promote the use of mass transit, walking and biking. The use of Community Investment Funds and Housing Incentive Programs modeled after Bay Area programs were encouraged to meet these goals. [8]

This is not to say that hosting a workshop on walkable neighborhoods is not worthwhile. But a true success story in this area would be a neighborhood that added sidewalks and traffic calming measures. Promotional activities are fine, they have a place; but, without implementation, they do not constitute successful sustainable development projects. In the second example, the question of impact could be answered by determining if any actual infill or compact housing was created; or, by evaluating the impact the transportation incentive program had on people's decision to build compact development. The difference between activities and outcomes is sometimes clearer when the activities don't produce the desired results.

## SOLVING PROBLEMS, NOT CHANGING SYSTEMS

When policy-makers focus on a narrow definition of a problem and try to solve it without considering all of the ancillary impacts of the solution, they can often cause more problems instead. The following example, taken from the United Nations Sustainable Development website, gives a good overview of what can happen when the narrow problem solving approach is taken, and also how this group worked it out to take more of a whole-system approach.

> The New York City (NYC) water supply system is the largest surface storage and supply complex in the world, yielding 1.2 billion gallons of water daily. Within this watershed is the Catskill Mountain region of New York, an area primarily agricultural and forested but facing development pressure. The U.S. Environmental Protection Agency's (USEPA) 1986 Safe Drinking Water Act required filtration for all US water systems, including NYC's. The potential cost for the implementation of a filtration system for NYC's water supply was enormous, approximately $6 billion for the construction and an annual operation and maintenance cost of $300 million. Fortunately, the USEPA granted NYC the opportunity to

seek alternatives to the filtration system through watershed protection.

NYC's Department of Environmental Protection (NYCDEP) proposed a series of watershed regulations in 1990. In an effort to limit pathogens and nutrients entering the watershed, severe restrictions were placed on agricultural runoff. These restrictions would have devastated livestock agriculture in the watershed and probably resulted in the closure of several farms. Increased urban development would inevitably necessitate the construction of a filtration system. The Catskill farmers saw their way of life threatened by New York City's overbearing regulations. NYCDEP saw no alternative but to regulate farm activity in the watershed.

The political stalemate resulted in confrontation, but both parties eventually realized that open dialogue offered the only possibility of resolution. From these dialogues, some key principles for an agreement were affirmed. The parties acknowledged that agriculture is a preferable land use in the Catskills watershed, and maintaining well-managed agriculture is the best method of watershed protection.

The farmers also recognized that agricultural pollution was a problem that needed to be addressed. And NYC offered to welcome and address any constructive responses from the farming community. From these guiding principles emerged the New York City Watershed Whole Farm Program. All aspects of the program were to be implemented by the farmer-led Watershed Agricultural Council. The first phase of the program included developing, testing, and demonstrating the whole farm plan approach on at least ten farms.

A whole farm plan can be viewed as an extended farm business plan that includes management and structural steps to reduce pathogen, nutrient, sediment, and pesticide runoff. The second phase involved recruiting volunteer farmer participants into the program. NYC agreed to provide cost-share assistance for the implementation of agricultural best management practices in the watershed. Each farmer chose for him or herself whether to participate. The Watershed Agricultural Council was responsible for delivering an overall rate of 85 percent participation within five years of implementation.[9]

If the New York City DEP had gone forward with the regulatory system they had proposed, farms would have folded and been sold to residential development. The regulations they had suggested covered agricultural pathogens, not residential contaminants, so the resulting urban runoff would have made their existing problem worse. This is a classic case of how the problem solving approach can cause more problems than it solves. It was only when they entered into open dialogue with the farmers and worked to meet their needs that a solution that worked for everyone was eventually designed and implemented.

In recent years the need for measurable success has emphasized indicators as tools for pursuing sustainability. If we can measure the variables that will show whether or not we're succeeding, we can monitor progress and insure that resources are being used appropriately. While this is true, it can often be as much work to gather and maintain the data as it is to do the work in the first place, so it is important to select indicators that measure real change in the system and that are possible to monitor without diverting substantial resources from the efforts to make the change. There are also some types of community improvements that are not easy to measure with indicators, so other techniques also need to be explored for assessing success.

## INDICATORS

Indicators are data that tell us something about a system's behavior. Indicators are chosen because people feel that the data being gathered is relevant to a particular concern they have or a value they cherish. When the City of Seattle worked to select indicators that would help them monitor the overall health of the ecosystems around the city, they chose to measure the number of salmon going upstream to spawn every year as a critical one, partly because the health of salmon is a good gauge of the ecosystem's health, and partly because citizens of Seattle cared about the return of the salmon.

The study of indicators has grown into a science, with volumes published on it all over the world. Indicators have been used by cities, by national and international governments, and by businesses to help plan for sustainability. As the science of indicators has grown more sophisticated, people have identified particular types of indicators that correspond with system characteristics to produce more meaningful data for people who are interested in a desired change in the system.

Indicators can be developed to track the drivers that human activities exert on a system, such as all the needs we have for transportation, food, energy, shelter, voting rights, spiritual growth, income, education, work, and recreation. The needs we have are the root drivers of all the systems we have developed to meet the needs. This might be comparable to measuring the demand for a particular product — how much demand is there for the type of food that causes environmental damage, or that contains toxins and mutagens that adversely impact health?

The second layer of indicators might monitor the pressures that are produced when these drivers take action. There is a need for food, so the agricultural system responds, growing crops in an increasingly capital-intensive way, with huge inputs and large transportation costs, as food is shipped to a global market. The indicator chosen to monitor the pressure the agricultural system exerts on the system might monitor the pesticides applied to the fields, or the quantity of food shipped out of a poor country to a rich country.

A third layer of indicators can track the effect that these pressures or drivers have on the natural systems and the other human systems that are being used to meet these needs. We can monitor air quality, water quality, the rate of inflation, the rate of unemployment, the number of people participating in recreational activities, the number of children in the school, the dropout rate, etc. All of these track the state of the system and, when monitored over time, can track the changing state of the system.

The fourth layer of indicators can measure the impacts that the changes in the state of the systems have on their ability to continue to function adequately to meet the needs that drive the system pressures. This level of analysis starts to give us information about the sustainability of the system in question — is the capacity to continue to meet our needs being enhanced or eroded by the actions we are taking? Maybe the impacts of a changing system state are deteriorating health, or loss of biodiversity, or economic recession, or, conversely, an increasingly stable economy as the variations and natural regeneration rates are taken into account, or an educational system that is helping children be creative, valuable members of society because it is funded adequately and has adopted new ways of teaching and learning.

Still another level of indicators can measure the responses that the system makes in attempting to ameliorate these impacts. The number of people taking public transit when subsidies from industry are introduced, the number of municipalities who are implementing energy conservation measures to fight global warming, the companies that have begun to take back their products to recycle them into new ones, the number of people participating in a new, participatory form of government; there are numerous ways to measure the strategies that are used to increase sustainability. We need to find indicators that measure the rate of change in a system, rather than focusing too much on more static elements.

The creation of indicators at the outset of a strategy to increase sustainability accomplishes another important function with respect to effective action. It gives us a clear vision so that we know, as we move forward, whether or not we're getting closer to, or further from, our goal.

## PROJECT EVALUATION STRATEGIES

The evaluation of a project needs to be laid out before the project begins. Selecting indicators that help define success and that inform strategy development is one obvious reason, but there are others. Baseline data must be collected, so that a clear picture of the existing conditions can be compared with the conditions the project is trying to create. A strategy for collecting data on an ongoing basis must be developed, so that evaluators will have the information they need for assessing progress. Clear expectations for the type of evaluation that will be done also must be defined. There are many levels of evaluation, and selecting the appropriate form of evaluation for the type of strategy that is being implemented is important.

Some evaluation projects are oriented toward a more superficial analysis of a strategy that's being implemented. The evaluation is designed to describe the completed activities to document the level of effort that was made on a project. This is the least in-depth analysis, and the problems with it have been described earlier. In some cases, it

Figure 11.1 Systems Indicators: Calgary's Sustainability Trends[10]

Sustainability Trend Legend
Sustainability trend information about each indicator is located in the upper right-hand
    corner of the indicator pages. The following symbols are used.

☺     Trend is moving toward sustainability

☹     Trend is moving away from sustainability

😐     There is no discernible trend

There are six "Indicators in Progress" for which a satisfactory measure does not yet
exist or a measure could not be obtained for our second State of Our City Report.

**Community Indicators**
- 😐  Crime Rate & Rate of Victimization
- ☺  Leisure Activity
- 😐  Membership in Community
        Associations
- ☺  Number of and Attendance at
        Public Festivals
- 😐  Sense of Community
- ☹  Valuing Cultural Diversity
- 😐  Volunteerism

**Economy Indicators**
- 😐  Economic Diversification – Oil
        and Gas Reliance
- 😐  Food Bank Usage
- ☹  Hours Required to Meet Basic
        Needs At Minimum Wage
- ☹  Housing Affordability
- ☹  Income Equity: Gap Between
        Rich and Poor
- ☺  Unemployment Rate

**Education Indicators**
- 😐  Adult Literacy
- ☹  Daycare Workers Salaries and
        Turnover
- ☺  Grade Three Achievement Scores
- ☺  Lifelong Learning – Library Use
- ☹  Pupil/Teacher Ratios

**Natural Environment Indicators**
- 😐  Air Quality
- 😐  Bird Population Surveys
- ☺  Food Grown Locally
- ☹  Pesticide Use
- ☺  Surface Water Quality
- ☺  Water Consumption

**Resources Use Indicators**
- ☺  Domestic Waste
- ☹  Ecological Footprint
- ☹  Energy Use
- ☹  Population Density
- 😐  Transit Usage for Work Trips
- 😐  Transportation Infrastructure
        Spending

**Wellness Indicators**
- ☹  Access to Primary and
        Alternative Health Resources
- ☹  Childhood Asthma
        Hospitalization Rates
- 😐  Healthy Birth Weight Babies
- ☹  Self Rated Health
- ☹  Support for the Most Vulnerable
- 😐  Youth Wellness

might be appropriate, but if there is an interest in measuring real impacts, this technique will not do it.

The next level is an evaluation of the strategy's efficiency. This might engage the participants in a subjective evaluation of how well the implementation worked, from a cost-benefit point of view. It would give an anecdotal sense of whether the participants could observe real progress or improvement in the conditions that were being changed by the strategy. Was it their perception that the resources for effecting the change were used well, or was there a lot of inefficiency and waste? Another variation on this type of evaluation is what has been called the interpretivist/constructivist form, where the evaluation strategy focuses on "answering questions about process and implementation, and what the experiences have meant to those involved."[11]

Still another level of evaluation measures the strategy's effectiveness in achieving the desired state. To do this, clear cause and effect relationships have to be discerned and described. There also needs to be a qualitative and/or a quantitative analysis of the current, evaluated conditions compared to the baseline data collected at the outset. For this type of evaluation, the project would have had to define specific outcomes at the beginning, so that there is a clear measure of effectiveness. Defining cause and effect relationships requires a level of system analysis that fits with a strategy based on systems understanding, so this type of evaluation would be easier to achieve with the types of projects developed with the methodology described here. One form of evaluation that accomplishes this has been called "theory-based evaluation,"[12] which relies on the development of a project logic model to clearly articulate the theory behind the way the strategy was implemented and defines the expected outcomes from a particular course of action.

The most difficult and in-depth evaluation technique goes even one step further and tries to identify the factors that contributed to, or that inhibited, the success of a strategy. What were the system conditions in place that worked to make a project or strategy either succeed or fail? This evaluation has the potential to be very useful in the development of strategies that draw from the information collected, although without clear baseline data and a plan for ongoing data collection and analysis, it might be difficult to achieve.

In their wonderful book, *Assessment in the Learning Organization: Shifting the Paradigm*, Arthur Costa and Bena Kallick discuss a collective paradigm shift as follows: The future is not a result of choice among alternative paths offered by the present, but a place that is created — created first in mind and will, created next in activity. The future is not some place we are going to, but one we are creating. The paths are not to be found, but made, and the activity of making them changes both the maker and the destination.[13]

## SUSTAINABLE COMMUNITIES

Ultimately, the success of efforts to improve sustainability in communities will be evaluated based on whether or not all the human needs are being satisfied in the community. It is important to recognize that the satisfaction of needs must be considered as a whole package. While it may be possible on a temporary basis to substitute one satisfier for another, over the long run, unmet needs will lead to impoverishment, and this in turn can lead to both individual and social pathologies. So, if Americans go shopping to satisfy their unmet needs for self-expression and creativity, or for spiritual connections, or for meaning, this might work up to a point, but over time it will lead to serious social problems. Indeed, it already has.

By beginning the process of sustainability planning with a comprehensive needs assessment, a community can lay the groundwork for ongoing monitoring and evaluation of all the ways human needs are being satisfied locally. As strategies are found to meet needs more effectively, the gaps that were identified in the needs assessment will be closed, and the overall levels of happiness and personal satisfaction will increase.

Happiness, personal satisfaction, peace, beauty, wisdom, compassion, a sense of belonging, strong relationships, nice neighborhoods, all of these things are difficult to quantify, difficult to reduce to data points that can be gathered methodically over time, analyzed, dissected, and reported. Yet, these are the hallmarks of a sustainable community, the reasons that we want to go on living. A community that works to satisfy people's needs and that evaluates its success based on the degree to which all of its systems work together to produce these emergent characteristics of the human endeavor will be evaluated as successful, even by those who have never heard of sustainability, or indicators, or projects and strategies.

CHAPTER 12

# The Living, Learning, Caring Community

A T THE ROOT OF ANY COMMUNITY is the sense of common destiny, the idea that people share their dreams and hopes and troubles and challenges. The collective action of the members of a community, whether it is a local village, or a global network of people with shared interests, is what creates and defines the community system. As soon as people are working together for a common goal, a shared vision, then the collective entity is already greater than the sum of its parts. The goal can be safe water services for all residents, or quality education for the children, or defense from attack. Whenever people work together to meet their common needs, the things they are able to do together are more than the things they could do as isolated individuals. The collective action, taken as a whole, makes a system.

Communities are whole systems, complex systems, and are open to global forces and trends that can influence how they use resources to grow, adapt, and change. Understanding communities as whole systems leads to an integrated understanding of how the collective physical processes at work within a city exhibit emergent properties that are comparable to metabolism and health on a biological level. On the political and social levels, the emergent properties of community systems also can imitate the ways in which human beings learn, and grow, and change. Creating a community that is resilient and adaptable, that learns effectively, and that cares for its members should be one of the goals of any sustainable development project.

If cities were human beings, the analysis of their metabolism and the health might be analogous to a regular medical check-up. If people were taking in more energy than they needed, they would get fat. If they had to look far and wide for the resources to support their lifestyles, they would be overextended and broke. Our cities take in 75 percent of the resources used on the planet, and the outflow of resources from cities is much less, but what does flow out is often harmful — wastes, pollution, hazards. Cities accumulate mass over time as a result. One aspect of the fat of our cities is the pollution that compromises the quality of life. The fat of the planet is the slow warming of the atmosphere caused by the emissions from the transportation of all those goods and services. Diets are no fun, but health does improve when people eat less and exercise more. Our cities, our planet, can do the same thing.

Already, all over the world, cities are learning how they can reduce resource use and minimize waste. They are learning how to be more efficient, how to innovate different ways to meet human needs. Food is being grown within the city limits, on rooftop gardens and vacant lots. New public transit services are being established, to move people around without using fossil fuels. Manufacturing facilities are redirecting the heat they generate into energy production, heating nearby buildings, producing electricity, or making hot water. The emergent metabolism of a city reflects the interaction of the economic and environmental systems at work. Cities need to redesign the degenerative linear flow of resources into, and waste products out of, their borders, so that they create cyclical processes that more closely reflect the processes of natural ecosystems.

The capacity for a city to learn, to adapt, to care for its residents, is an important emergent property of the social and governance structures in place. Like individuals, cities that learn, cities that care, are going to be more resilient over time. What are the ways in which cities learn? How can a community become a more caring place to live?

## THE LEARNING COMMUNITY

It is a challenge to create a learning organization in a small non-profit where people all share the same mission and values. It can feel like an enormous task to convert large organizations, especially governmental organizations, due to the power that entrenched bureaucratic practices exert over the structure and operations of government. But to make a whole city a learning community? Impossible ... right?

Wrong. At least one community, Greenwood South Carolina, has already made substantial progress towards this goal, which is described in a case study by Charlotte Roberts in *The Fifth Discipline Fieldbook* by Peter Senge, et al. What started as an effort by a group of local businessmen and the Chamber of Commerce to improve the workforce has grown to be a dynamic project encompassing the whole community, extending even to the maternity ward in the local hospital, where new babies are greeted with the "Born to Read" program.[1]

How does this happen? It starts with a systems understanding, committed leadership, a shared vision, an effective working team, and a strong basis for measuring progress — all of these elements are what makes a learning community. Even with these in place, however, we need a new mindset. We need to understand our own ignorance. Communities are extremely complex systems, and even with the best guidance about how systems work, perfect data, and an effective working group, we can't begin to know what is required to create sustainable community systems. The process of change in communities is a journey, not a destination, and so it's important to understand that the learning process is how we move forward. This means accepting uncertainty and making room for mistakes. It's impossible to learn without these two factors causing problems — we don't like to make mistakes, and we get nervous when we have to make decisions without all the data about a given situation. Yet the openmindedness that uncertainty demands and the adaptability that mistakes can foster are critical to growth and change, however uncomfortable they might be.

Another key way to create a learning community is to invest in and support new kinds of training and educational activities — for everyone from the top CEOs and the Mayor to the citizens who volunteer at the local food shelf. If learning is valued by everyone, then people can create a field of possibilities and will have the open minds needed to embrace the change that's required.

This new paradigm of learning as the way forward can be seen in several initiatives for urban development, including a framework for urban planning and management known as CASE — Cities as Sustainable Ecosystems, that has been developed by the UNEP International Environmental Technology Center in Osaka, Japan. CASE offers municipal leaders several excellent tools to begin the process of creating sustainable cities, including training modules on urban environmental management, risk assessment, and technology assessment. Yet even with their expertise and the vast database of information they provide urban leaders, the IETC acknowledges that the learning community/city is an essential condition to develop the behaviors, policies, strategies that will bring about the paradigm shift that is needed to implement CASE successfully.

> ... there are few more pressing public policy issues than the integration of environmental considerations into all urban activity with the ultimate goal of achieving a sustainable society. At the present time, however, our understanding of what this entails is preliminary and limited, in part due to the significant limitations of the existing intellectual framework within which environmental issues are defined.

To promote the kind of learning that is required for sustainable cities, CASE calls for city leaders to investigate the interdependency of legal, economic, cultural, scientific and technological activities and policies as they affect environmental protection and the evolution of environmentally sustainable technology, and to study the different regulatory tools and approaches to determine how cities' and citizens' behavior change.[2]

## THE CARING COMMUNITY

Some of the same mindsets and skills that are required to be a learning community are also important if cities want to be a caring community. We need to care about our neighbors and our city to be open to the diversity of individuals, ideas, and cultures that public involvement will generate. The listening skills and conflict management strategies needed to develop a strong team are also facilitated by a genuine concern for others and a generosity of spirit that allows for difference while remaining committed to a shared vision.

A caring community is made up of individuals who care, in addition to being an emergent property of a collective effort to pay attention to the needs of the people who live there. Individuals are born with a predisposition to care for each other, yet there are systems that support the development of this capacity, and those that undermine it. It is not a given. A culture that idolizes violence — where some of the most popular pastimes are watching people wrestle with each other in a dramatic show of brutality — does not teach people how to care.

Looking at the faith and wisdom traditions that support a culture of peace and compassion, it is possible to identify certain common practices that might be very important in terms of helping people learn to care for each other. Many of these traditions have meetings where their shared values are reinforced through ritual and dialogue. They get together regularly, outside of their families, outside of their workplaces, and form a community that transcends boundaries like clan, corporation, state, and nation. They have smaller groups that work to extend a hand of friendship to people who are sick, or alone, or in crisis. They have other committees that raise money to support projects that assist people who are poor, homeless, war-torn, and who need healthcare, transportation, education, and other services. There are education programs for their own members — for everyone from young children to adults. This is not to say that every religious practice works to make the world more sustainable — there are certainly many that promote hatred and divisiveness as much as the dominant secular culture does. But there are lessons to be drawn from the traditions that have made an impact in the area of growing people who are not desensitized to the suffering and poverty of the world.

The foundation of sustainability is based on the premise that we care about the world we are leaving to our children. Paying attention to the sustainability orientation required for each of our needs to be met without denying future generations the ability to meet their needs is itself an act of caring. Below, each need is discussed with some of the thinking that can be used to help meet the need sustainably.

On an aggregate level, cities are the largest governments on earth. They are the closest level of government to the people they serve, and they have more of a direct impact on the everyday lives of their populations than national governments ever will. Our cities operate on a level where they have to care about the well-being of the people. They are on the front lines of the work that needs to be done to create an alternative future for the Earth. It's time that the support of cities became the main priority of state and national governments, as it has in South Africa, where the role that the national government has to serve local governments is actually embedded in the constitution.

## HEALTH CARE

Health — whether it is individual health or community health — is a critical dimension of sustainability. A sustainable society is a healthy society. Improving and maintaining community health is one of the goals of any sustainability planning process. Individuals in a system can't be healthy if the system itself isn't healthy. Health and sustainability are almost synonymous, in fact, because the determinants of sustainability also predict the long-term health of any given community. Health can be defined as having two main elements:

1. being in good physical condition; and
2. the absence of disease.

The U.S. healthcare system has been struggling over the past 25 to 30 years with several serious problems: how to lower costs, how to reduce the need for medical intervention, how to provide healthcare equitably, and how to maintain the highest quality of service. Risk reduction, prevention, well-baby care — all of these initiatives have grown out of the system's struggle with these sometimes contradictory goals.

How to strengthen the healthcare system so that it is sustainable is a challenge for the entire country today and is not something that is easily addressed at the local level. By using the core definition of sustainability — providing for today's needs without eroding our ability to meet needs tomorrow — it becomes possible to look at the whole system and identify its elements that may be eroding its capacity to deliver good health to the community as a whole.

One of the critical tensions in the managed care paradigm that is regulating the delivery of healthcare today in the United States is found in two conflicting goals: reducing the cost of healthcare and maintaining a high quality system that provides the level of care people have grown to expect. The practices that have been implemented to achieve these goals have reduced the access people have to healthcare through managed-care rationing and capitation. A systems analysis of the vicious cycle that has been the result of these practices can be illustrated with the simple reinforcing loop in Figure 12.1.

Figure 12.1 A Vicious Cycle in Healthcare

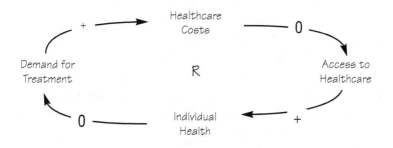

The fact that all of these variables serve to reinforce one another (reinforcing cycles are illustrated by the R in the center of the diagram) is indicative of an unsustainable cycle in our current healthcare system. Points of strategic intervention can also be identified — increased access, lower-cost services, lower cost insurance, etc. The sustainability orientation for the healthcare system needs to recapture the care part of the equation, and put patients on the priority list before the profits of the companies that have control of the system now.

## SPIRITUALITY

Spirituality means many things to many people. The roles that spiritual and/or religious leaders play in our society are often controversial. Wars are still being fought in many parts of the world because of, or related to, religious differences. The relationship that spirituality plays for sustainability must therefore be carefully articulated, so as not to appear sectarian, parochial, or offensive to people who do not participate in any spiritual or faith-based communities.

Many people experience spirituality as an intensely personal and private element of their lives. They are not inclined to discuss it with other people and do not see their individual spiritual practices as being part of a larger community. Other people participate in different faith communities or service organizations, regularly practicing a kind of social spirituality that comes with regular worship services and service projects.

Whatever their form, doctrines, or organizations, there are common threads woven among the various spiritual practices. One of these common threads is an emphasis on relationship — to self, to Earth, to other people, to a higher power. There are other common threads: an interest in excellence and wisdom; an understanding that spiritual gifts include courage and creativity; a desire for purity; and a mandate for forgiveness, mercy, justice, loving kindness, sacrifice, and service to others.

The question of sustainability rests on whether or not we are enhancing or eroding our ability to provide for the world's needs in the future. The cyclical renewal processes that can be found in so many different parts of our lives can also be perceived in the role that spirituality plays for individuals and for communities. Spirituality, and an adherence to the positive and life-enhancing principles that most faith communities espouse, taps into nothing less than the creative and regenerative energy of the universe.

No spirituality policies have been developed or passed recently in most cities around the world, for obvious reasons. Nor would it be appropriate to suggest that cities start to enact this type of policy. For the purposes of sustainability planning, however, it is important to recognize the spiritual needs of the community, and to support all the organizations that meet those needs, without regard to particular spiritual practices.

## A Best Practice for Spiritual Development

*Vermont Ecumenical Council: Interdenominational Activities*

The Vermont Ecumenical Council reaches out to all faith communities, and supports several committees that focus on different subjects of concern to the community. There are nine member denominations, all of whom are Christian, but since there is no real interfaith organization in Vermont, to some extent, the council serves this purpose.

The member denominations include the American Baptists, Episcopalian, Evangelical Lutheran, Presbyterian, Roman Catholic, Friends, United Church of Christ, United Methodist Church, and the Greek Orthodox.

The newsletter that they send out goes out to clergy and other contacts all over the state, including those in non-Christian faiths, even though they are not official members of the organization.

The Faith and Order committee of the Council deals with issues like baptism and marriage. They will be publishing a booklet on marriage for all the clergy in the state. The committee is working to reach consensus on what the different denominations share as common ground regarding marriage. The other committee is called Peace, Justice, and the Integrity of Creation (PJIC), which is more of an advocacy committee – they support the Livable Wage campaign, children's poverty issues, and relieving debt in Third World countries. A subcommittee of the PJIC is called Peaceful Communities, which brings together faith community members, people from the Department of Corrections and victim advocates, to raise awareness about how clergy can better help victims of crime.[3]

Best practices for spirituality are those that people and their religious or spiritual organizations use to promote dialogue among the different faiths, to increase mutual understanding and acceptance of divergent beliefs. They are also found in counseling and education efforts that help people recognize their spiritual gifts such as talents or skills they can offer to the world, and that support their further spiritual development.

## LIFELONG EDUCATION AND TRAINING

Education and training are more important today, in the information age, than ever before. As people grow and develop, their personal and professional opportunities and the creativity of the community as a whole is inextricably linked to the education that individuals are able to obtain. Yet perhaps because of its importance, public education is facing several serious challenges to its long-term viability. School funding has been a critical issue in the United States, where the property tax base has been primarily responsible for the majority of school budgets. Making educational opportunities available to all students in a way that does not reflect the relative wealth or poverty of their individual towns or families is a goal of current educational policy.

The school calendar, developed at the beginning of the 20$^{th}$ century when over 70 percent of the American public lived on farms, is becoming less and less viable in a country where the vast majority of adults work in full-time jobs outside the home. This mismatch has left millions of children around the country with very few structured activities between 3 p.m. and the time when parents arrive home after work. The FBI statistics show that 60 percent of juvenile crime occurs between the hours of 3 p.m. and 6 p.m. Youth risk behaviors such as premarital sex, drug abuse, alcohol consumption, and other unhealthy choices have all been increasing.

Meanwhile, a growing movement to improve the social assets that youth have — a feeling of being connected to the community, adult role models, service learning that teaches students the value of community service, and positive reinforcement of healthy choices has shown us through studies and surveys that these assets are currently very low. Increasing the quality and quantity of positive activities that help youth choose career paths and personal commitments that enhance their ability to have a happy and fulfilling life is a critical community need.

Today's job market is also a challenging place, where people need to upgrade their skills and educational levels continually to stay employed. Educational opportunities throughout people's lives are needed, so that human resources and skills are continually maintained.

The question of sustainability relates to education in a variety of different ways. How are educational systems enhanced and improved over time? Are there political and economic factors that can erode their quality and their health? How do we train youth and adults to behave in ways that promote sustainability in all aspects of their lives? How do educational institutions support the unique cultural and educational needs of their community, and how does the community have a voice and a role in the educational process?

Education should expand and not limit the choices available to future generations. Learning should take place in safe, attractive, well-equipped schools. It should also occur in a wide range of community-based settings, where youths learn firsthand the value and importance of community service. Learning should encourage young people to respect and appreciate cultural differences and provide them with a strong commitment to lifelong learning. Finally, all students should be able to succeed in some type of learning, regardless of their backgrounds or learning styles.

Community surveys and discussions with local youth have consistently spotlighted the dearth of organized recreational, social, and community service opportunities for young people. There is a need to strengthen existing programs and develop new facilities and efforts aimed at providing young people with supervised, secure, and healthful gathering places and more opportunities to get involved with their community in constructive ways. Stronger linkages between schools, social service agencies, and community-based programs are especially needed for youths at risk.

Education should be a lifelong process, available to people of all ages to provide them with the skills they need to be successful and responsible members of their community. Preschoolers through senior citizens should benefit from a wealth of opportunities to build the social and job skills critical to being successful members of any community.

## ART, MUSIC, AND CULTURAL HERITAGE

Art, music, and cultural heritage activities in a community meet our needs for self-expression, for beauty, and connection to our cultural and historical traditions. Self-expression has long been recognized as a fundamental human right; it is the subject of the First Amendment to the U.S. Constitution. Aesthetic considerations have a growing influence on the ways in which new developments are permitted, as does the preservation and redevelopment of historical and cultural attributes of the architecture involved.

How do these activities relate to sustainability? Unfortunately, the debate about sustainability has been largely limited to issues associated with economic development and environmental protection. When projects have been implemented around the world, often a one-size-fits-all approach is taken, using methods and understandings that are culturally embedded in the West, and ignoring local traditions and culture.

Placing culture, art, and music at the center of the sustainability debate asks practitioners to acknowledge the importance of local culture. Without a local understanding of how to apply sustainability concepts with respect for local customs, art, and traditions, the innovations introduced will be inherently unsustainable. In addition, if these needs go unmet, the results can be harmful. How much rampant consumerism can be attributed to unmet needs for self-expression? All of the advertising for unnecessary products plays off this need — express yourself by buying this car, this pair of shoes, this painting. Make your mark on the world by owning this meaningless product.

A sustainable art, music, and cultural heritage sector in a community provides a wide variety of opportunities for people of all ages. Art, music, drama, and other creative forms of self-expression are important parts of every school curriculum. Participating in cultural activities is not expensive, not seen as something that's only possible for the wealthy. Historic treasures are respected and protected. The capacity for future cultural activities is enhanced through active education programs and ongoing public support for the arts.

Community initiatives incorporate the arts, music, and culture of a community into the efforts it makes. Development projects support this sector by incorporating public art and architectural design. Artists, playwrights, musicians, dancers, writers, architects, poets, sculptors, jewelry makers, potters, furniture makers, all of the creative members of the community are recognized for their contributions.

Art, music, poetry, beauty, all of these activities are such an essential part of our humanity. The fact that they have been virtually absent from sustainability discussions points to a serious flaw. Communities need to see their arts and culture as something more than a frill whose budget can be cut in a pinch. They need to understand that integrating arts and culture into their planning and activities is a way to make all of their efforts more effective.

## RECREATION

The word recreation means refreshing oneself and restoring health through activities that are enjoyable and entertaining — re-creating yourself by having fun. The idea of recreation is linked to the root idea of sustainability because it contains the idea of renewal, or rebirth. When we think about recreation, we think about fun. Fun, in turn, contains the idea of enjoyment, or something that can produce joy, laughter, or amusement. Joy is perhaps an elusive state of being, but unlike many of the other subjects of sustainability planning, our pursuit of it is guaranteed to Americans by the Constitution of the United States: life, liberty, and the pursuit of happiness.

Our needs for joy, refreshment, renewal, and the restoration of health, are very important. Communities meet these needs by creating space for recreational activities, by running recreational programs, and by integrating these facilities and programs into the neighborhoods, so that people have easy access to them. Employers and educational institutions can also support our need for recreation by providing programs and activities that enhance people's skills and awareness of opportunities that are available.

Yet some forms of recreation have negative environmental impacts. Motorboats with two-stroke engines produce greenhouse gasses at ten times the rate of cars and discharge oil and gas into the water. Other motorized recreational vehicles also consume fuel, produce air pollution and greenhouse gasses, and erode trails. Sustainable recreation alternatives are needed to help reduce the attraction of these types of pastimes.

## SAFE NEIGHBORHOODS

The need for personal and community safety is fundamental. Without safety, it is impossible to advance other initiatives that might improve the quality of life in a neighborhood or community. Safety is peace, with no fear of violence. Safety is comfort, knowing that you are supported in your living environment. Safety is directly linked to the quantity and quality of our interactions and relationships with those who live around us. Studies show a direct correlation between the level of crime in a neighborhood and the frequency of social contacts between people in the neighborhoods.

Crime in neighborhoods happens within households — domestic violence, child abuse and neglect; between individuals — noise, vandalism, burglary, assault, rape, trespassing, and other crimes; between the economic classes within a community — poor quality housing, health violations, rental disputes; and between individuals and the government — traffic violations, drug abuse, and other illegal activity that does not necessarily involve a victim.

There are many roots of criminal behavior, and volumes of research and writing on the subject. Understanding some of the causes of crime makes it possible to better understand the ways in which sustainability planning can help reduce crime and increase safety in neighborhoods. Juvenile justice experts have been working for several years on the asset-based approach to reducing crime among youth, for example. The theoretical basis for this approach is that by increasing the resiliency of youth through the development of their personal assets, it is possible to reduce the likelihood that they will engage in criminal behavior. A list of 40 assets developed by the Search Institute,[4] includes a feeling of connection to the community and having other adults play a meaningful role in the lives of youth. See Figure 12.2.

Unresolved disputes can erode relationships to the point that criminal behavior may result. If there is not an effective way for neighbors and individuals to resolve disputes quickly and economically, tensions can build and increase the likelihood of a problem. If people feel that they have to call the police, the city zoning administrator, or some other authority figure before they can take steps to resolve a dispute, then this is an indicator that perhaps more informal networks are needed where a dispute can be addressed before it becomes a problem.

Many types of crime have an intergenerational link. Abused children are likely to become abusers when they become parents. Children of drug abusers or alcoholics are more at risk than their counterparts. If a man's father beat his mother, he is more likely to become an abusive husband. We understand these things, but as of yet we do not have effective ways of breaking the links between generations. Domestic violence and abuse is sustainable already — we need to think of ways to eliminate its reproductive capacity.

## FIGURE 12.2 DEVELOPMENTAL ASSETS

Extensive research led the US-based Search Institute to identify 40
essential building blocks of adolescent development. The more of these
assets that are present for children and youth, the lower is the likelihood of problem behaviors and the higher the probability of positive
outcomes. A survey is now available that allows communities to measure
these assets in their youth. More information on the developmental
assets approach is available from www.search-institute.org.

### EXTERNAL ASSETS

| Asset Type | Asset Name | Definition |
|---|---|---|
| SUPPORT | Family support | Family life provides high levels of love and support. |
| | Positive family communication | Young person and her or his parent(s) communicate positively, and young person is willing to seek advice and counsel from parent(s). |
| | Other adult relationships | Young person receives support from three or more nonparent adults. |
| | Caring neighborhood | Young person experiences caring neighbors. |
| | Caring school climate | School provides a caring, encouraging environment. |
| | Parent involvement intek schooling | Parent(s) are actively involved in helping young person succeed in school. |

| EMPOWERMENT | Community values youth | Young person perceives that adults in the community value youth. |
|---|---|---|
| | Youth as resources | Young people are given useful roles in the community. |
| | Service to others | Young person serves in the community one hour or more per week. |
| | Safety | Young person feels safe at home, at school, and in the neighborhood. |
| BOUNDARIES AND EXPECTATIONS | Family boundaries | Family has clear rules and consequences, and monitors the young person's whereabouts. |
| | School boundaries | School provides clear rules and consequences. |
| | Neighborhood boundaries | Neighbors take responsibility for monitoring young people's behavior. |
| | Adult role models | Parent(s) and other adults model positive, responsible behavior. |
| | Positive peer influence | Young person's best friends model responsible behavior. |

| | High expectations | Both parent(s) and teachers encourage the young person to do well. |
|---|---|---|
| CONSTRUCTIVE USE OF TIME | Creative activities | Young person spends three or more hours per week in lessons or practice in music, theater, or other arts. |
| | Youth programs | Young person spends three or more hours per week in sports, clubs, or organizations at school and/or in community organizations. |
| | Religious community | Young person spends one hour or more per week in activities in a religious institution. |
| | Time at home | Young person is out with friends "with nothing special to do" two or fewer nights per week. |
| **INTERNAL ASSETS** | | |
| COMMITMENT TO LEARNING | Achievement motivation | Young person is motivated to do well in school. |
| | School engagement | Young person is actively engaged in learning. |
| | Homework | Young person reports doing at least one hour of homework every school day. |

|  | Bonding to school | Young person cares about her or his school. |
|---|---|---|
|  | Reading for pleasure | Young person reads for pleasure three or more hours per week. |
| POSITIVE VALUES | Caring | Young person places high value on helping other people. |
|  | Equality and social justice | Young person places high value on promoting equality and reducing hunger and poverty. |
|  | Integrity | Young person acts on convictions and stands up for her or his beliefs. |
|  | Honesty | Young person "tells the truth even when it is not easy." |
|  | Responsibility | Young person accepts and takes personal responsibility. |
|  | Restraint | Young person believes it is important not to be sexually active or to use alcohol or other drugs. |
| SOCIAL COMPETENCIES | Planning and decision-making | Young person knows how to plan ahead and make choices. |
|  | Interpersonal competence | Young person has empathy, sensitivity, and friendship skills. |

| | Cultural competence | Young person has knowledge of and comfort with people of different cultural/racial/ethnic backgrounds. |
|---|---|---|
| | Resistance skills | Young person can resist negative peer pressure and danger-ous situations. |
| | Peaceful conflict reso-lution | Young person seeks to resolve conflict nonviolently. |
| POSITIVE IDENTITY | Personal power | Young person feels he or she has control over "things that happen to me." |
| | Self-esteem | Young person reports having a high self-esteem. |
| | Sense of purpose | Young person reports that "my life has a purpose." |
| | Positive view of personal future | Young person is optimistic about her or his personal future. |

## CIVIC PARTICIPATION

Civic participation encompasses a wide variety of ways that we exercise our personal and collective power in a community. By participating in decision making, or simply by having the personal freedom to pursue our own interests and objectives, we enhance the community's ability to exercise power. When power is shared equitably in a community, the community itself is more resilient in the long run, because more people have the skills, the courage, and the wisdom to help guide the community in a positive direction.

## Access

The need for access is related to the degree to which we are all empowered to obtain information, to influence decisions, to participate in community activities, and to secure specific rights. Access can be defined as both a way in, a means of entering, and as a right or opportunity to use or obtain something. In both senses, access has a relationship to power, and so it is a need that falls within the governance system in communities.

In the United States, access is addressed in several different ways. The Americans with Disabilities Act (ADA) has created a fairly comprehensive system that guarantees many forms of access to people with disabilities — access to public and private buildings, access to job opportunities, access to decision making. The people who drafted the U.S. Constitution considered access as one of the human needs that was worth protecting with specific constitutional rights. Equal access to jobs, education, and other community benefits is spelled out in the Fourteenth and Fifteenth Amendments. Access to justice is also addressed in the Fifth, Sixth, and Seventh Amendments.

The degree to which a community meets its citizens' need for access in a sustainable way can be evaluated by the proactive steps that it takes to provide information, to provide opportunities, and to open the decision making and conflict resolution processes to the community for input and oversight. Public access television allows community members to broadcast their events or to see public meetings at home. Handicapped access to public buildings helps insure that everyone can participate. Voter registration drives and absentee ballots help insure that people have access to the democratic process.

## Equity

The need for equity is expressed in some of the fundamental documents of the United States. "We hold these truths to be self-evident, that all men are created equal ...." Equality is an ideal to which democracies strive, but they often fall far short. The sense of justice, of fairness, is expressed strongly in the idea of equity. Two people doing the same work should be paid the same amount of money, regardless of their race or sex or age. Children should have the same educational opportunities, regardless of whether they are from a poor town or a rich town. Everyone should have the right to healthcare, to job opportunities, and to pursuing their own form of happiness.

Even though inequity is often expressed in the starkest terms on the economic level — people do not have equal access to financial resources in this country — the distribution of resources and responsibilities in an equitable manner is still fundamentally an expression of power, which is why it is a function of the governance system rather than the economic system. World history has certainly many cases of wars and revolutions that have been fought to gain power over economic resources and to equalize the distribution of resources and responsibilities.

Equity also relates to issues that go beyond purely economic considerations. Equal rights, equal responsibilities, equality under the law, all of these are ways in which the relative equity of a system is expressed. Equity is also a fundamental principle of sustainability, relating directly to the idea of enhancing the capacity of community systems to provide for future needs. Any system that relies on only a few of its members to carry out important functions is inherently less stable than one where there is widespread knowledge and ability to fulfill the requirements of the system. This principle applies to a small group of people controlling anything — the money, the power, the benefits; all of these are functions that are more stable if they are widely shared by community members.

History shows that established democracies are less likely to go to war against each other. Recent research has discovered that overall health in a particular country can be predicted by the level of equity in the system. The poorest people in a country with a relatively high level of equity can in fact be healthier on average than the richest people in a country with sharp inequities.

The sustainability of a community can be enhanced by increasing the relative level of equity in all areas — economic, social, environmental, and in government. Sustainable strategies in this area are, therefore, those that work to increase overall opportunities and decrease inequity.

## Self-Determination

Freedom requires access and equity, and it expresses itself in people's level of self-determination. People need to be able to make decisions to regulate their own lives. They need to choose their professions, their housing, their hobbies, and their friends. If they are denied this fundamental human right, then they rebel, and if even this is denied them, they often do not survive.

How does a community work to either enhance or erode people's self-determination? There are many things that the community can do to make people more, or less, free. The human need for self-determination relates to the power and choices people have over decisions that affect their lives. A community enhances its capacity for self-determination by building decision-making institutions that are designed to involve all of the stakeholders in making community decisions.

The need for self-determination can be seen in practices that are unsustainable as well. Since it is such a powerful human need, it must be taken into consideration when strategies are being designed to address problematic practices that are driven by this need. For example, the American reliance on the automobile can be traced directly to the freedom that it provides its owners. People can go where they want, when they want. Attempts to change this pattern of behavior frequently fail precisely because the alternatives offered don't provide the same level of freedom and convenience as the car.

## Conflict Resolution

Communities have a variety of ways to resolve conflict, most commonly through institutions and mechanisms that protect human and property rights. Stable, impartial, and fair conflict resolution systems are critical elements of any governance structure. Laws, judiciary systems, permitting agencies, and other measures which provide quick and low-cost resolution to conflict are critical to the creation of a sense of trust and a willingness on the part of new investors, businesses, families, and individuals to locate in a community.

Two important trends in the area of conflict resolution that speak to the sustainability of the system are alternative dispute resolution strategies and conflict prevention techniques. Both of these practices help to build social well-being in a community, while at the same time improving efficiency of all systems by reducing the time and money that needs to be invested in the conflict resolution process.

Preventing conflict in the first place is the most effective strategy, but like a lot of development work, it involves a commitment of resources to an area that is not yet in crisis. Conflict prevention strategies include supporting community events and facilities that bring people from different ethnic and socioeconomic groups together, providing healthy and safe after-school activities for children, including marginalized groups in local governance structures, providing safe parks, transportation systems, and sports facilities that are used by all of the groups in a community. These are all ways to build ties between people that can reduce the potential for conflict. On a family level, the social safety net and the education system are important institutions to involve in strategies that reduce the stress leading to domestic conflict and violence.

Alternative conflict resolution strategies go beyond the more traditional judicial model and involve the community and the stakeholders in the resolution of the conflict. They provide more support to the victims of conflict or crime. Their focus is to reintegrate the parties of the conflict into the community, in order to repair the broken community bonds resulting from conflict. Two important skills that are taught and reinforced through alternative conflict resolution are open communication and attentive and respectful listening.

Conflict resolution relates to sustainability insofar as it evolves into a system that cares for people, that distributes rights and responsibilities equitably, that involves the stakeholders in the decision-making process, that increases the skills of the participants, and that increases the vitality of natural resources by providing healthy strategies to resolve environmental conflict, and that conserves valuable resources, which might be expended on conflict without an adequate system in place.

## ECONOMIC DEVELOPMENT

The human needs for meaningful work and money are met through economic development initiatives. This is why efforts in economic development are predominantly about creating new jobs for people.

Business development strategies by the government are oriented toward employment. Increasingly, the education system is being pushed to accommodate the labor market, as employers are demanding that the education system produce skilled workers who will function effectively in the available jobs. The community as a whole recognizes the need for new job creation; many rural communities struggle with the fact that for their children to find work, they need to go to larger metropolitan areas that are far away.

The multiplier effect is one of the central elements of our economic understanding. The financing systems we have, where people place their money on deposit at a bank, or in stocks, or in insurance policies, make capital available for business development, while at the same time it is theoretically available to the people who put it on deposit. Money is always working double-time. If the sources of investment are local banks and local businesses, then this money can be more readily available locally to help the economy grow. Economists measure the local multiplier of specific economic development initiatives by using complex formulas to calculate how much recirculation through the system occurs with any given initiative. What they are really trying to determine is how much additional growth will be generated as the money is circulated in the local economy.

Sustainable economic development is fundamentally concerned with creating jobs and opportunities that are meaningful for people and that minimize the impact on the environment. Economic entities that harm the environment invariably also harm the individual workers, so it's important to both the human and the natural systems that we develop enterprises that meet our current needs in ways that enhance our ability to meet future needs. Another important feature of sustainable economic development strategies is that they reach out to people at all socioeconomic levels, to insure that economic opportunity is available to everyone. In Burlington, Vermont, the STEP-UP for Women program described on page 239 is one such strategy.

## CLEAN AND SAFE ENVIRONMENT

People need a clean and safe environment. This means clean air, clean water, uncontaminated soils, and healthy buildings. Wildlife and natural systems also need a clean and safe environment; the emphasis on human needs does not mean to ignore the interconnected ecosystems

## STEP UP for Women

## Northern New England Tradeswomen

STEP UP for Women is a program of Northern New England Tradeswomen (NNETW), a Vermont non-profit organization founded in 1987 to help Vermont women enter, advance, and remain in the skilled trades or other non-traditional activities through a comprehensive program of recruitment, training, referrals, placements, networking, advocacy, and retention activities.

STEP-UP was piloted in 1985 to train women for non-traditional employment opportunities that offer a true path to economic self-sufficiency. In over fifteen years of continuous programming, more than 700 Vermont women have completed the program. Of that number, over 85 percent have found employment – primarily in the skilled trades.

The STEP UP program offers training and support to help women move into non-traditional and higher paying jobs such as carpentry, electrical, plumbing, and automotive jobs. This can be a life-changing experience as it not only offers hands-on skills but also prepares women for all aspects of employment including physical conditioning, communication skills, and recognizing and dealing with sexual harassment. The program also fills a need for employers who are looking for workers at a time when there is a shortage of good employees.

NNETW's other programs include:

Employment Diversity in Highway Construction (EDHC) – An assessment, referral, and placement program in highway construction occupations and on-the-job training for all women and men of color.

WOMENBUILD – A work experience program in housing construction and rehabilitation. Women in Apprenticeship and Non Traditional Occupations Technical Assistance Project (WANTO) – A technical assistance project for employers.

Rosie's Girls – A summer trades exploration program for girls ages 11 to 13 to learn trade and technical skills.[5]

involved. Recognizing a healthy environment as a fundamental human right has not yet been institutionalized on the national or the international levels, however. This is the next frontier for sustainable development advocates.

Sustainable development has long been associated with environmental protection. It's time to ask what the sustainability orientation is toward a clean and safe environment? Does it mean that all other human needs should be sacrificed for this goal? When is some environmental degradation or impact justified because of other needs being met?

The working definition of a sustainability strategy is that it does not erode the capacity for future generations to meet their needs, and it doesn't prevent current needs from being met. So the orientation toward a sustainable clean and safe environment would be one where there is a balance with the other economic, social, and governance needs being met. If a community is experiencing a housing crisis, for example, where families are being evicted from their homes and being forced to live in motels because of the high housing prices, the need for affordable housing must be balanced with the ongoing pressure to preserve open space.

Strategies that minimize environmental impact, that reduce the emissions, effluent, and the waste stream from homes and businesses by trying to identify how the pollution can be prevented in the first place are practices that work to promote a sustainable safe environment. Treating waste that is already being produced, recycling materials whenever possible, and finding markets for by-products of manufacturing processes are ways in which current problems can be mitigated.

The Natural Step first broached sustainable development's relationship to human needs, saying that in a sustainable society "resources are used fairly and efficiently in order to meet basic human needs globally."[6] It calls for an equitable distribution system for resources that meet human needs. The Natural Step states that in order for a society to be sustainable, nature's functions and diversity cannot continue to be systematically impoverished by:

1. Increasing concentrations of substances extracted from the Earth's crust, including fossil fuels, mining of metals and minerals, greenhouse gasses, metal toxicity, and the contamination of surface and groundwater.

2. Increasing concentrations of substances produced by society, including synthetic organic compounds like DDT and PCBs, freon, and ozone-depleting compounds.

3. Physical displacement, over-harvesting, or other forms of ecosystem manipulation by taking more from the biosphere than can be replenished by natural systems, and by destroying the habitat of other species.[7]

## ENERGY

Energy is one of several secondary human needs, because we value the things that energy provides to us more than the energy itself. We require energy because we need heat, or light, or cooked food. Yet without energy, we would also have a hard time meeting these primary needs, so for the purposes of sustainability planning, energy should be considered.

The provision and use of nonrenewable energy is one of the most problematic processes underway on the planet, so the ways in which we meet our needs for energy have very important consequences for sustainability. The increased use of fossil fuels is leading to global climate change. Fossil fuels are responsible for oil spills worldwide and for air, water, and soil contamination everywhere they are produced. Nuclear energy is responsible for disasters like Chernobyl, for radioactive contamination everywhere uranium is mined and enriched for fuel use, and, for the long-term, a seemingly insoluble waste problem.

To meet our needs for energy without denying future generations the energy they need, or a clean and safe environment, or drinking water, there are three orientations for energy production and use. The first is that energy use should be minimized wherever possible. Energy efficiency is regarded by smart utilities today as an energy source, rather than the more traditional way of viewing it as a reduction in revenues.

The second sustainability orientation for energy is to meet needs for energy with renewable sources — solar power, wind energy, hydroelectricity, forests, and other sources of biomass. Renewable energy production meets a variety of environmental and economic objectives. These include:

• Reducing dependence on fossil fuels and nuclear energy, with corresponding reductions in emissions of sulfur, nitrogen, carbon, and radioactive waste.

- Reducing dependence on energy imports, which are a net drain on any region's economic vitality.

- Stimulating the local economy by relying on local resources for energy production, such as the generation of electricity biomass and other alternative fuels.

- Providing new opportunities for economic development through the innovation and development of new products that utilize renewable energy.

The third sustainability orientation for energy is that its sources should be cost-effective and as inexpensive as possible. Energy is a critical element of economic development. Therefore, an emphasis should be made on renewable energy development, on sources and production facilities that can provide energy in a cost-effective manner.

## HOUSING

Housing is a critical component of sustainability planning because the cycle of poverty is exacerbated by a lack of affordable housing. People who are negotiating their way between homeless shelters and soup kitchens don't have time to look for jobs — their focus is meeting their most basic needs. So increased homelessness is often occurring at the same time as jobs are going unfilled for a lack of workers.

The City of Burlington, Vermont, has adopted a policy toward housing that makes use of well-established non-profit housing organizations to support what it calls the Housing Tenure Ladder. The Housing Tenure Ladder is a model that acknowledges all the incremental steps in the process of securing affordable and high quality housing, beginning with homeless shelters and working up to fee simple ownership.

Citizens and organizations in Burlington are supported at every rung of housing tenure, through the programs funded by the city and through the various businesses and non-profits that work to provide housing. People who find themselves in shelters are gradually encouraged to move into transitional housing. People in transitional housing move up to rental housing with support services. People who take advantage of the support services offered are better equipped to find regular employment that would allow them to move into housing provided by several of the local non-profit rental organizations. In turn, these organizations are actively organizing the people who rent

Figure 12.4 HOUSING TENURE LADDER

Fee Simple Ownership
Community Land Trust
Limited Equity Ownership
Condominium
Limited Equity
Condo Cooperative
Limited Equity Cooperative
For-Profit Rental
Resident Controlled Non-Profit Rental
Non-Profit Rental
Rental with Support Services
Transitional Housing
Shelter Housing

from them to take more control over their living spaces, creating resident-controlled rental housing. Of course, there also are rental units available by owners who are more traditional, for-profit investors. As people move up the tenure ladder, they are better able to pay market-rate rents.

Owning a home is an important value in our culture, and this is made possible in Burlington through a variety of ownership structures. Limiting equity in housing ownership makes it less possible for owners to profit from the fluctuations in the real estate market and more possible for people to afford housing ownership for the first time. Land Trust housing ownership helps keep housing permanently affordable by controlling the ownership of the land and through limiting equity. All of these steps on the housing tenure ladder are supported in some way by the collective actions taken in Burlington.

## TRANSPORTATION

Transportation has quickly eclipsed manufacturing as the main source of air pollution in the United States and elsewhere. Over 50 percent of the harmful air emissions nationwide are a direct result of automobiles. The combustion of fossil fuels is also an important source of greenhouse gasses, which in turn contribute to global warming. It is not an exaggeration to say that transportation is a key sustainability issue for the 21$^{st}$ century.

The sustainability orientation for transportation requires that we move from high-impact forms of transportation (like individual cars) to lower impact forms (like pedestrian travel, bicycles, and mass transit). The problem is that the individual automobile is such an important part of our culture, is so convenient, and offers the greatest amount of personal mobility that it is a hard task to wean people from its use. The strategies required to reduce dependence on the automobile, and to reduce the emissions, traffic congestion, and other negative impacts, have to be multifaceted.

## WASTE PROCESSING

As human beings, we will always generate waste. Food waste, waste water, air emissions, manufacturing waste, agricultural waste, business waste; the pile just keeps getting higher. The amount of solid waste that each American generates every year has doubled over the last 50 years, in fact. We are throwing more away per capita than ever before. The cost of disposal every year has topped $8 billion dollars — our third largest domestic expenditure.

Nationally, 90 percent of our solid waste is deposited in landfills around the country. Even with improved safety and environmental features, landfills remain an inefficient and potentially harmful waste management strategy. One of the most pressing issues for waste managers is that, in many areas, we have run out of space to site landfills. More than half the cities in the United States will fill their landfills in the next several years.

The waste management orientation for sustainability goes beyond the reduce, reuse, recycle policies of the past. Recreating and redesigning products so that they generate little to no waste and rethinking how we meet material needs so that we can achieve zero waste is the challenge for waste planning today. Life cycle planning, industrial ecology, and systems thinking are all contributing to this trend. The groundbreaking work of the Interface Corporation closes the manufacturing loop by manufacturing new carpet out of old carpet, rather than dumping old carpet in a landfill.[8] They provide customers with carpet leases, conceptualizing floor covering as a service, rather than as a product. They save an enormous amount of resources by using removable tiles of carpeting, so that the areas of the floor that get all the wear can be maintained without throwing away the carpet that is still in good condition.

Of course, the reduce, reuse, and recycle efforts are no less necessary. In the past ten years, people have far exceeded the projections for recycling in the United States, which has substantially reduced the amount of new landfill space required. While very few states have passed a source reduction law, many states are working outside of the regulatory environment to reuse containers and have made some laws to eliminate unnecessary packaging through tax credits, extra taxes, and product bans.

## WATER

Water is the foundation of life. We can't live without it for more than a few days. Whatever cities do to make themselves more sustainable, the water cycles at work within their boundaries need to be near the top of the list of issues to be addressed. To this end, the International Council for Local Environmental Initiatives (ICLEI) announced in 2001 a Global Water Campaign designed to help cities redesign their freshwater management systems to change them from systems that are net consumers of freshwater to systems that work within natural cycles and limitations. The Council has established five milestones for municipalities that are interested in joining the campaign:

1. Inventory and forecast direct and indirect impact on local water resources.
2. Establish targets for water quality and water quantity.
3. Develop and obtain approval for a Local Water Action Plan.
4. Implement policies and measures.
5. Monitor and report results. [9]

One key emerging issue for cities and water is that, as the resource gets more scarce in relation to the demand for it, privatization and pricing structures are being put in place to regulate its distribution, making it impossible in many parts of the world for the poorest people to have access to safe water.

## CONCLUSION

There is always plenty of work to do when considering how to meet individual needs more effectively and sustainably, and for better or for worse, we spend a lot of our time focused on solving isolated problems for safe water, or waste disposal, or affordable housing. While this work can often be very important, we tend to lose sight of the whole system, to the detriment of the individual solutions we design. Similar to Maslow's hierarchy of needs in his theories on human development, there is also a hierarchy of needs in community development. The sustainable development movement has emerged largely from the environmental movement, and so many of its efforts and strategies relate to how to solve environmental problems. But, the environment is the end of the pipe; it is the level where all the dysfunctional practices in our social, governance, and economic systems express themselves.

The social values we share and the ways in which we care for each other in communities are where the most leverage exists for real change in our systems. This is why the visioning process has been so important in recent efforts to pursue sustainable development —through the visioning process the community collectively articulates what it cares about. When agreement is reached on this core issue, then it is much easier to get the governance and economic systems to respond.

Yet, vision and shared values aren't the only elements of what could be described as the caring sector of a community that are critical for the success of sustainable development plans. We have other gifts that come from the same source, spiritual gifts that we need to call on in all of our community work. We need wisdom to make the right choices in order to meet the needs of everyone on the planet more equitably. Wisdom to understand the root causes of what might appear to be a problem on the surface, but we know is just a symptom of something deeper. Wisdom to find ways of resolving conflict peacefully, instead of resorting to violence. Wisdom to pass on our important spiritual traditions to our children, so that they will have reservoirs of strength to draw from when they are faced with the same questions and issues.

We need courage, another spiritual gift. We need courage to stand up to the sacred cows of Western society — to challenge the idea that everyone has a right to a big car with an internal combustion engine so they can drive whenever or wherever they want, regardless of the environmental consequences. We need to challenge the idea that the best way to live is in a large, isolated home built on one-half an acre of good agricultural soil that we proceed to fill with grass that in turn is maintained with heavy applications of pesticides, herbicides, and a lawnmower with a two-stroke engine that puts more greenhouse gasses into the atmosphere in an afternoon than a car does in a month. We need to find ways to incorporate our wisdom traditions in the educational system and look for ways to transmit the kind of values and practices that all of the various traditions share without imposing any one of them on people.

We need to find creative ways to inspire people and design new strategies. Artistic expression is a profound way of bringing the caring we have for each other and for our planet to life. Art and music touches people in ways that other forms of communication do not. Integrating the artistic community and the arts into any effort that is made to envision a better future for the community is a critical way to speak to the people who need to get involved. The arts transcend political and economic divisions and have the power to inspire people to do things they might not have considered doing before. Communities must be creative when they are designing strategies to change their systems. It is no accident that corporations engage hundreds of artistic consultants when they are trying to introduce new products to the general public. We must mobilize this creativity to introduce new practices that aren't depleting the environment and reducing our capacity to continue to survive on the planet.

Another spiritual gift that will help us insure that human beings can continue to live on Earth is perhaps the most important one of all: compassion. Compassion for the millions of people who barely survive while we consume the lion's share of the world's resources. Compassion for all the creatures that are sacrificed to human voraciousness every day, so that many of them are wiped off the face of the Earth forever. Compassion for our children and grandchildren who are going to have a horrific mess to clean up if we don't get our act together. Compassion for other cultures and even for people who have harmed us — driven by desperation and poverty to acts of senseless destruction. Forgiveness, which is rooted in compassion, is one of the most powerful leverage points there is.

We have to inspire people on their deepest levels to change their behavior and their collective actions to respond to our inherent and persistent human needs. This takes more than individual efforts; it takes the emergent and transcendent forces that we can marshal through spiritual practices and collective endeavors. To succeed, we must involve all sectors of society, and draw from both ancient traditions and new technologies, from our hearts, our minds, and our spirits.

# *Endnotes*

## Introduction

1. Enrique Penalosa, former Mayor of Bogota, Columbia. *Keynote Speech at University of Virginia Symposium on World Summit on Sustainable Development*, November 15, 2002.

2. PONTIFICIUM CONSILIUM AD CHRISTIANORUM UNITATEM FOVENDAM: DIRECTORY FOR THE APPLICATION OF PRINCIPLES AND NORMS ON ECUMENISM, #215 [online] [cited Tuesday, May 6, 2003] Published by the Vatican. <www.internetica.it/directory.htm>.

3. The Earth Charter [online] [cited Wednesday, May 7, 2003] <www.earthcharter.org>.

4. The Melbourne Principles [online] [cited Wednesday, May 7, 2003] <http://epanote2.epa.vic.gov.au/EPA/Publications.nsf/515bc2fde7bf9 3f44a2565b6001ee896/0e0f3f532b 811f3eca256c1c00021ceb/$FILE/Melbourne%20Principles.pdf>.

## Chapter One

1. Charles Dickens. *A Tale of Two Cities*. Signet Classics, 1999, p. 1.

2. Daniel Sershen. "Independent NGOs Criticize Kyrgyz Local Elections." *Kyrgyzstan Daily Digest* [online] [cited Tuesday, December 18, 2001]. Published by Eurasianet.org. <www.eurasianet.org/resource/kyrgyzstan/hyper-mail/200112/0037.shtml>.

3. Herbert Girardet. *The Gaia Atlas of Cities: New Directions for Sustainable Urban Living*. Gaia Books, 1992, p. 68.

4. Martin Buber. *On Intersubjectivity and Cultural Creativity*. University of Chicago Press, 1992, pp. 97-98.

## Chapter Two

1. Terry Gips. *The Natural Step's Fourth Condition for Sustainability and Manfred Max-Neef's Basic Needs Analysis.* [online] (Copyright June 16, 1999) [cited July 25, 2002] <www.mtn.org/iasa/tgmaxneef.html>.

2. Abraham Maslow. *Motivation and Personality*, 2nd ed. Harper & Row, 1970.

3. Jurgen Habermas. *Knowledge and Human Interests*. Blackwell Publishers, 1986.

4. World Commission on the Environment. *Our Common Future, From One Earth to One World, An Overview by the World Commission on Environment and Development*. Oxford University Press, 1987.

5. *The Natural Step's Four System Conditions* [online]. The Natural Step US, The Presidio, Thoreau Center for Sustainability. [cited July 25, 2002] <www.naturalstep.org/what/index _what.html>.

6. IBID.

7. The National Center for Self-Esteem. *Organizational Mission Statement*. [cited December 22, 2002] <www.self-esteem-nase.org/>.

8. The World Bank Group. *Social*

*Capital for Development*. [cited May 8, 2003] <www.worldbank.org/poverty/scapital/>.

## Chapter Three

1. Elizabeth Kline. *Northern New England Sustainable Communities Implementation Project: Lessons Learned.* Tufts University: Global Development and Environment Institute, 1997, p. 8.
2. IBID, p. 11.
3. North Plains Groundwater Conser-vation District. *Ogallala Aquifer: General Geology, Stratigraphy, and Hydrology.* [cited September 22, 2002] <www.npwd.org/Ogallala.htm>.
4. Mathis Wackernagel, Chad Monfreda and Diana Deumling. *Ecological Footprint of Nations, November 2002 Update.* [online] Redefining Progress, 2002. [cited October 5, 2002] <www.rprogress.org/publications/ef1999.pdf>.
5. United Nations Development Programme (UNDP). "Overview," *Human Development Report 1998.* UNDP, 1998. [cited October 20, 2002] <www.undp.org/hdro/e98over.htm>.
6. Wackernagel et al.
7. IBID.
8. Anti-Slavery International. *United Nations Meets on Global Slavery.* [online] May 24, 2002. Thomas Clarkson House, The Stableyard. [cited June 15, 2002] <www.antislavery.org/index.htm>.
9. Robert Putnam. *Bowling Alone: The Collapse and Revival of American Community.* Simon & Schuster, 2000.

## Chapter Four

1. Sir Isaac Newton. *The Principia.* 1687.
2. Carl G. Jung. *The Archetypes and The Collective Unconscious: Collected Works of C. G. Jung Vol. 9 Part 1.* Princeton University Press, 1981.
3. David X. Swenson, Ph.D. *The Ouroboros Effect: The Revenge Effects of Unintended Consequences.* [online] [cited December 22, 2002] <www.css.edu/users/dswenson/web/revenge.htm>.

## Chapter Five

1. City of Burlington, Vermont. *Legacy Action Plan 2000.* [online] [cited December 22, 2002] <www.iscvt.org /burlington legacy.pdf>.
2. Paul Markowitz. *April 2002 Trip Report to Balaclava.* Institute for Sustainable Communities, 2002, p. 3.
3. City of Geneva, New York. *Vision Statement.* [online] [cited December 2, 2002] <www.geneva.ny.us/city manager/vision_statement.asp>.
4. City of Flagler Beach, Florida. *Vision Statement.* [online] [cited December 2, 2002] <www.cityofflaglerbeach.com/VisionStatement.htm>.
5. City of Independence, Missouri. *Vision Statement.* [online] [cited December 2, 2002] <www.ci.independence.mo.us/vision_statement.stm>.
6. The Earth Charter. [online] [cited Wednesday, May 7, 2003] <www.earthcharter.org>.

## Chapter Six

1. The Earth Charter. [online] [cited Wednesday, May 7, 2003]

<www.earthcharter.org>.

2. The Melbourne Principles. [online] [cited Wednesday, May 7, 2003] <http://epanote2.epa.vic.gov.au/EPA/Publications.nsf/515bc2fde7bf93f44a2565b6001ee896/0e0f3f532b811f3eca256c1c00021ceb/$FILE/Melbourne%20Principles.pdf>.

3. The Earth Charter. [online] [cited Wednesday, May 7, 2003] <www.earthcharter.org>.

4. More information about the Temenos Project can be found at <www.arkofhope.org>.

5. More information about the Americans with Disabilities Act can be found at <www.usdoj.gov/crt/ ada/ adahom1.htm>.

6. Ruth Leger, Sivard. *World Military and Social Expenditures 1993.* World Priorities Inc., Washington, DC, 1993, p. 42.

7. "Special Report: Executive Pay." *Business Week.* (April 16, 2001).

8. World Resources Institute. [online] [cited May 9, 2003] <www.wri.org>.

9. More information about the Institute for Sustainable Communities can be found at <www.iscvt.org>.

10. More information about the UNEP International Environmental Technology Center can be found at <www.unep.or.jp>.

11. The Melbourne Principles. [online] [cited Wednesday, May 7, 2003] <http://epanote2.epa.vic.gov.au/EPA/Publications.nsf/515bc2fde7bf93f44a2565b6001ee896/0e0f3f532b811f3eca256c1c00021ceb/$FILE/Melbourne%20Principles.pdf>.

12. *Press Conference by the International Council of Local Environmental Initiatives.* World Summit on Sustainable Development. September, 2002. [online] [cited October 20, 2002] <www.un.org/events/wssd/summaries/020826conf1.htm>.

## Chapter Seven

1. Joyce Wycoff. *Transformation Thinking.* Berkley Books, 1995.

2. Greenleaf, Robert K. *The Servant as Leader.* The Robert Greenleaf Center, 1970.

3. Larry C. Spears. "Servant Leadership: Quest for Caring Leadership," *Inner Quest* #2, 1994.

4. Lao Tse. *Tao Te Ching.*

5. Alan AtKisson. *Believing Cassanrdra.* Chelsea Green Publishing, 1999, pp. 178-187. Also, please check his web site at <www.AtKisson.com> for more information about the Innovation Diffusion Game and other exercises to get people thinking about sustainability.

6. California Legislative Analyst's Office. *Analysis of Propositions for Election, March 5, 2002.* [online] [cited May 9, 2003] <www.lao.ca.gov/initiatives/qryPropositions_by_election_3-2002.asp>.

7. Michael Doyle and David Strauss. *How To Make Meetings Work: The New Interaction Method.* Berkley Publishing Group, 1976.

## Chapter Eight

1. Donella Meadows et. al. *The Limits to Growth.* Universe Books, 1972.

2. Donella Meadows. *Leverage Points: Places to Intervene in a System.* Sustainability Institute, 1999, p. 2.

3. IBID.

4. United States Department of Justice. *Operation TIPS: Terrorism Information and Prevention System.* [online] [cited July 15, 2002] <www.citizencorps.gov/>.

5. Thomas Kuhn. *The Structure of Scientific Revolutions.* University of Chicago Press, 1962.

6. The information about the structure of land ownership in the Danelaw was uncovered in research I did at the Institute for Heraldic and Genealogical Studies in Canterbury, England.

7. Donella Meadows. *Leverage Points: Places to Intervene in a System.* Sustainability Institute, 1999, p. 5.

**Chapter Nine**

1. Donella Meadows. *Leverage Points: Places to Intervene in a System.* Sustainability Institute, 1999.

2. IBID.

3. Jacqueline Ottman. *Green Marketing, Opportunities for Innovation.* NTC/Contemporary Books, 1998.

4. Center for Media Education. *Children & Television: Frequently Asked Questions.* [online] [cited February 5, 2003] <www.cme.org/children/kids_ tv/c_and_t.html>.

5. Alternatives for Youth, Inc. *Helping Kids Succeed.* [online] [cited November 20, 2002] <www. alternativesforyouth.org>.

6. More information about the Public Safety Project can be found on the Legacy Project website, [online May 9, 2003] <www.cedo.ci.burlington.vt. us/legacy/strategies/ 11-org-publicsafety-main.html>.

7. Quoted in "Quotes: So they said, and they said, and they said again"

in *The Earth Times.* September 4, 2002. Johannesburg, South Africa, p. 8.

8. More information about the Burlington Electric Department's programs can be found on the Legacy Project website, [online] [cited May 9, 2003] <www.cedo.ci.burlington.vt. us/legacy/strategies/ 06-org-efficiency-main.html>.

9. Amory B. Lovins and L. Hunter Lovins. "Energy Forever." *The American Prospect*, February 11, 2002.

10. Sustainable Communities Network. *Case Studies.* [online] [cited September 25, 2002] <www.sustainable.org/casestudies/ studiesindex.html>. Revised January 26, 2002.

11. More information about the Neighborhood Action Project can be found on the Legacy Project website [online May 9, 2003], <www. cedo.ci.burlington.vt.us/ legacy/strategies/04-org-commjustice-main.html>.

12. *The Holy Bible*, Revised Standard Version.

13. Walter Wink. "Jesus' Third Way," in Robert Herr and Judy Zimmerman Herr, *Transforming Violence: Linking Local and Global Peacemaking.* Herald Press, 1998, p. 37.

14. IBID, p. 38.

**Chapter Ten**

1. Margaret Wheatley. *Leadership and the New Science.* Berrett-Koehler Publishers, 2001, p. 92.

2. Paul Hawken, Amory and Hunter Lovins. *Natural Capitalism.* Little Brown Publishers, 1999.

3. International Council for Local Environmental Initiatives. *Creating a*

*Framework for Integrated Resource Management in Heidelberg, Germany.* [online] [cited December 17, 2002] <www3.iclei.org/localstrategies/ summary/heidelberg.html>.

4. United Nations Environmental Programme. *Sustainable Consumption Initiative.* [online] [cited December 17, 2002] <www.uneptie.org/pc/sustain/ design/green-proc.htm>.

5. More information about ISO 14001 can be found on the website [online May 9, 2003], <www.iso14000.com/>.

6. More information about Manitoba's Sustainable Development Act can be found on the website [online May 9, 2003], <http://web2. gov.mb.ca/laws /statutes/ccsm/s270e.php>.

7. More information about the City of Santa Monica's sustainable procurement program can be found on the website [on line May 17, 2003], <www.santa-monica.org/ environment/policy/purchasing/ policies.htm>.

## Chapter Eleven

1. Renner, Michael. Vital Signs. Worldwatch Institute, 2002. [online] [cited November 20, 2002] <www.worldwatch.org/pubs/vs/ 2002/overview.html>.

2. IBID.

3. IBID.

4. Cosgrove, William J., and Rijsberman, Frank R., for the World Water Council. *Making Water Everybody's Business.* Earthscan Publications, 2002. [online] [cited September 20, 2002] <http://watervision.cdinet.com/ chpt3.pdf>.

5. Mathis Wackernagel, Chad Monfreda, and Diana Deumling. *Ecological Footprint of Nations,* November 2002 Update. [online] Redefining Progress, 2002. [cited October 5, 2002]. <www.rprogress.org/publications/ ef1999.pdf>.

6. United Nations Environment Programme Regional Initiative on Information and Communication Technologies and the Environment.  ITC e-Choupal, India. [online] [cited October 22, 2002] <www.un.org/esa/ sustdev/success.htm>.

7. IBID.

8. Common Ground of Monterey County. *Success Stories.* [online] [cited August 15, 2002] <www.commongroundmc.com/>.

9. United Nations. *Sustainable Development Success Stories.* [online] [cited December 4, 2002] <www.un.org/esa/sustdev/ success/nyc_wsfp.htm>.

10. Sustainable Calgary Indicators. *State of the City 2001.* [online] [cited December 22, 2002] <www.telusplanet.net/public/ sustcalg/sooc2001.htm>.

11. W.K. Kellogg Foundation. *Evaluation Handbook.* January 1998, p. 10.

12. IBID, p. 11.

13. Arthur Costa and Bena Kallick. *Assessment in the Learning Organization.* Association for Supervision and Curriculum Development, 1995.

## Chapter Twelve

1. Peter Senge, Richard Ross, Bryan Smith, Charlotte Roberts, Art Kleiner. *The Fifth Discipline Fieldbook:*

*Strategies and Tools for Building a Learning Organization.* Doubleday, 1994, pp. 502-504.

2.  Steve Halls, Director, UNEP International Environmental Technology Center, Osaka, Japan. [online] [cited August 9, 2003] <www.unep.or.jp/ietc/ NewApproach/CASE/ CASEcontent3.asp>.

3.  More information about the Vermont Ecumenical Council can be found on the Legacy Project website [online] [cited May 9, 2003] <www.cedo.ci. burlington.vt.us/legacy/strategies/ 12-org-ecumenical-main.html>.

4.  Search Institute. *Assets.* [online] [cited December 4, 2002] <www. search-institute.org/ assets/>.

5.  More information about STEP UP for Women can be found on the Legacy Project website

[online] [cited May 9, 2003] <www.cedo.ci. burlington.vt.us/ legacy/strategies/ 05-org-stepup-main.html>.

6.  *The Natural Step's Four System Conditions.* [online] The Natural Step US, The Presidio, Thoreau Center for Sustainability. [cited May 9, 2003] <www.naturalstep.org/what/index_ what.html>.

7.  IBID.

8.  More information about the Interface Corporation can be found on their web site [online] [cited May 9, 2003] <www.interfaceinc.com/flash/flash _C.html>.

9.  The International Council for Local Environmental Initiatives. *Water: Local Level Management — a valuable tool for municipalities.* [online] [cited December 15, 2002] <www.iclei.org/water/idrc_local_ level_management.htm>.

# Index

## T
The Natural Step, 34-35, 240-241
Temenos Project, 106-107
Town Meeting, 18, 19, 20-21

## U
United Nations, 34, 53, 206, 208, 218
United States Environmental
　　Protection Agency, 152, 197

## V
Vermont Ecumenical Council, 223
vicious cycles, 44-46, 60-61, 75, 221
virtuous cycles, 75, 79, 206
visioning process, 93-98, 121-122, 169,
　　206, 246

## W
Wackernagel, Mathis, 53, 205
Wheatley, Margaret, 193
Wink, Walter, 180-181
World Bank, 46

# About the Author

GWENDOLYN HALLSMITH has worked on sustainable development in many different capacities, including positions such as Deputy Secretary of the Vermont Agency of Natural Resources, the Town Manager of Randolph, Vermont, as the Regional Planning Director in Franklin County, Massachusetts, and as a Senior Planner for the Massachusetts Office of Energy Resources. Hallsmith has also worked with the U.S Environmental Protection Agency to establish Environmental Management Training Centers throughout Central and Eastern Europe. She has a Master's degree in Public Policy from Brown University, and has had over twenty years of experience working on environmental issues. She is currently Campaign Coordinator for the Vermont Earth Charter and a Pastor with the United Federated Church in Williamstown.

If you have enjoyed *The Key to Sustainable Cities*
you might also enjoy other

# BOOKS TO BUILD A NEW SOCIETY

Our books provide positive solutions for people who want to
make a difference. We specialize in:

**Environment and Justice • Conscientious Commerce
Sustainable Living • Ecological Design and Planning
Natural Building & Appropriate Technology • New Forestry
Educational and Parenting Resources • Nonviolence
Progressive Leadership • Resistance and Community**

*For a full list of NSP's titles, please call* **1-800-567-6772** *or check out our website at:*

**www.newsociety.com**

## NEW SOCIETY PUBLISHERS

"There is a widespread belief that the global environmental challenge is overwhelming, with the five largest cities having a combined population of about 200 million. As more people decide to live in cities, both small and large, they create considerable ecological footprints. While solutions may exist, they won't happen without the support and involvement of people. Taking this as her starting point, Gwendolyn Hallsmith, in *The Key to Sustainable Cities*, shares her considerable experience in harnessing the energy and enthusiasm of communities to achieve sustainable solutions. She sees the city as a living breathing organism, and she shows how communities and cities can use systems thinking to make the way they work, live, and play more sustainable through focusing on their needs. She provides insights and practical skills that practitioners can apply to the towns and cities in which they live. While the task ahead may be daunting, with this book it will at least be a little easier."

— Harry Blutstein, Director of Integrating Sustainability in Melbourne, and the former Director of Sustainable Development for EPA, Victoria, Australia